WITHDRAWN

HARVARD LIBRARY

WITHDRAWN

Christ Among Them

Christ Among Them:
Incarnation and Renaissance in Medieval Italian Culture

By

Edoardo Mungiello

Cambridge Scholars Publishing

Christ Among Them: Incarnation and Renaissance in Medieval Italian Culture, by Edoardo Mungiello

This book first published 2008 by

Cambridge Scholars Publishing

15 Angerton Gardens, Newcastle, NE5 2JA, UK

British Library Cataloguing in Publication Data
A catalogue record for this book is available from the British Library

Copyright © 2008 by Edoardo Mungiello

All rights for this book reserved. No part of this book may be reproduced, stored in a retrieval system, or transmitted, in any form or by any means, electronic, mechanical, photocopying, recording or otherwise, without the prior permission of the copyright owner.

ISBN (10): 1-84718-541-X, ISBN (13): 9781847185419

BT
220
.M87
2008

Wer sagt, daß alle verschwinden müssen? Weir weiß, möglicherweise
der Flug des Vogels verwunden Sie des Remains und möglicherweise
überleben Blumen Liebskosungen in uns, In ihrem Boden.

Es is nicht die Geste, die dauert, aber es kleidet Sie wieder in der
Goldrüstung - von Brust zu knie- Und die Schacht war – ein Engel
trägt ihn nach Ihnen so rein.

—*Was Überlebt,* Rainer Maria Rilke.

"S'a voi piace
Montare in su, qui si convien dar volta,
Quince si va chi vuole andar per pace."

—*Purgatorio, XXIV, 139-141.*

Per la mia famiglia; defunti, vivi, e futuri.

Non enim, secundum positionem huiusmodi, Deus carnem assumpsissetut fieret homo, sed magis homo carnalis Deus factus fuisset; et sic non verum esset quod Ioannes dicit: Verbum caro factum est (Ioann. I, 14), sed magis e converso caro Verbum facta fuisset. Similiter etiam non convenirent Dei Filio exinanitio aut descensio (kenosis) sed magis homini glorification et ascension; et sic non verum esset quod Apostolus dicit: Qui, quum in forma Dei esset...exinanivit semetipsum, formam servi accipiens (Philipp. II, 6, 7), sed sola exaltation hominis in divinam gloriam, de qua postmodum subditur: Propter quod et Deus exaltavit illum (Philipp. II, 9). Neque verum esset quod Dominus dicit: Descendi de coelo (Ioann. VI, 38) sed solum quod ait: Ascendo ad Patrem meum. (Ioann. XX, 17), quum tamen ultrumque Scriptura coniungat; dicit enim Dominus: Nemo ascendit in coelum nisiqui descendit de coelo, Filius hominis, qui est in coelo (Ioann. III, 150, et: Qui descendit, ipse est et qui in ascendit super omnes coelos (Ephes. IV, 10). Sic etiam non conveniret Filio quod missus esset a Patre, neque quod a Patre exiverit ut veniret in mundum, sed solum quod ad Patrem iret, quum tamen ipse utrumque coniungat, dicens: Vado ad eum qui missit me (Ioann. XVI, 5); et iterum: Exivi a Patre, et veni in mundum: iterum relinquo mundum et vado ad Patrem (Ioann. XVI, 28); in quorum utroque et humanitas at divinitas comprobatur.

This position destroys the whole mystery of the Incarnation. Instead of teaching that God assumed a human nature, it teaches that a mere man became God. This contradicts John who said that the Word became flesh and not that the flesh became the Word.
Similarly, such a position disallows the Son of God from extinction and descent to emphasize the glorification and ascension of man. And here it contradicts the Apostle Paul who says: In this way He took shape, by emptying (*exinanivit*) Himself, and accepting the nature of a slave" (*Phil.* 2, 6), considering only the exaltation of man to the level of God's glory, of which Paul later says "that is why God exalted him to such a height."
Nor can the Lord's statement be true in this, namely that "I have come down from heaven (*John*, 6. 38) but only his later statement, "I am going up to him who is my Father" (*John* 20, 17). Scripture, though, combines these things: "No man has ever gone up to heaven; but there is one who has come down from heaven, the Son of Man who is in heaven' (*John* 3, 13)...
Again "it was from the Father I came out, when I entered the world and now I am leaving the world and going on my way to my Father" (*John* 16, 28): in these two movements of descent and ascent both the divinity and the humanity of Christ are made manifest."[1]

---

[1] Thomas Aquinas, *Summa Contra Gentiles* Bk. IV, Chap. 28, 1024. (Paris: Migne, 1863).

TABLE OF CONTENTS

ACKNOWLEDGEMENTS viii

A BRIEF NOTE x

PREFACE xi

INTRODUCTION xiv
REASONS FOR RENAISSANCE

CHAPTER ONE 1
JERUSALEM LOST AND CHRIST DELIVERED

CHAPTER TWO 19
EUROPE IN THE PRESENCE OF CHRIST

CHAPTER THREE 33
FRANCESCO: CENTER AND CIRCUMFERENCE

CHAPTER FOUR 55
THE CATHARS AND INCARNATIONAL DENIAL

CHAPTER FIVE 69
OCKHAM, GIOTTO, AND THE WEIGHT OF THE WORLD

CHAPTER SIX 87
THE FIRE NEXT TIME: DANTE, TRANSFORMATION,
AND INCARNATIONAL CODA

EPILOGUE 117
UNDER GOD, IN THE FLESH

BIBLIOGRAPHY 133

INDEX 153

ACKNOWLEDGEMENTS

This work was first conceived after a Cross examination. Dr. Richard Cross, to be exact, who heard my nebulous ideas about "Christ the neighbor." He nodded and added that what I had hastily sketched was a good idea, despite what I had written. A few days on, Dr. Nicholas Crowe and Dr. Mark Philpott offered the curious looks the Oxford don has cultivated to imply that something wasn't as bad as all that. To these men and Dr. John Fenelay at the Centre for Medieval and Renaissance Studies at Oxford, I am grateful. A special thanks to Father William Davidge of the Pusey Library for leaving me alone with the books, and also to the choirs of New College and Magdalen for the spiritual bath every Evensong, and the incense at the Oratory every Sunday. For that matter, thanks to St. Mary the Virgin for the tower, the Bodleian for the books, and the Trout for the fire.

My deep thanks to Father Gabriel Coless and Dean James Pain of Drew University for encouraging the quest for Incarnation, and spending time reading drafts of my meanderings. Both men embody all that I admire about the gentleman-scholar, an ideal so glaringly absent from the present crop of academics, who fret over expertise, leaving genteel wisdom a-begging. I hope to continue in the tradition of the Christian humanist, an ideal that these two men represent in their work and in their lives. A thanks also to that sylvan university, Drew, which let the birds and leaves replenish what the frenetic world insisted on withdrawing, if only for a time.

For my mother and mother-in-law, who, with the wisdom of the Italian matriarch, realized a man like me needs two mothers, and for my extraordinary family, both given and adopted, for the truly extraordinary sacrifices they continuously make for me. Especially for my nieces and nephews: Michael, Christopher, Antonella, Stephanie, Claire, and Joseph, who will probably never read this, but will always know that dedications are not confined to ink. They are the hope of my heart, and the love of my blood. I wish God's great smile to shine on them, as their faces have lovingly assuaged the passing of my youth. I love you all.

A song of gratitude goes out to the constellation of strength I call my friends. Much of what the wise call success is measured in the draughts drunk and meals shared among them.

For Florence, Rome, Assisi, Venice, Padova, Oxford, London, Chartres, Paris, Vienna, New York City, and many others. Thank you Western Civilization. Yes *this* civilization, *this* culture, warts and all, is worth saving. It is worth celebrating, and for all the right reasons.

Of course, without the extraordinary grace, guidance, and love of my wife, Diane, I would not have the courage or the wherewithal to do what I need to do within this brief vigil of the senses. If you ever met her, you'd realize why I became an optimist, and why my hope of love is colored by the brown of her eyes, and composed by the sound of her voice. She carries our child. Could I say more without sullying those four words? I am the luckiest of men. Thank you, my love.

Finally, and I know my wife will not begrudge me this, for the extraordinary man who spent half of his life being my father. His final days burnished the faith he held since childhood into the looking glass of Incarnational Christianity. How happy he must be to know face to face that darkly grasped God in whom he trusted. In that vision, for that vision, are my hopes and prayers.

A Brief Note

This little essay does not attempt to account for every cultural and political event that happened (or may have happened) during the Italian century under discussion. There are some brow raising omissions that may seem unforgivable at first glance; Frederick II, Jacopone da Todi, the Humiliati, and the Waldensians are peripheral if present at all. This admission is more in the way of stemming any critique based solely on comprehensive inclusion. The book in short is an essay defending the notion that a particular brand of Christianity was principally responsible for what became the individualism of the Western World, specifically the so-called resurgence of cultural identity called the Renaissance. It is not, nor cannot be, a history of Europe or Italy, during the thirteenth century. That said it is not confined to a particular discipline that would limp following threads to their appropriate ends. As the Age (here termed the Incarnational) was one of speculum, the reflection best suited to explain the culture is one of metaphor and symbol. There is a methodology here, but it adheres to the cadences of the Age and not its statistics. It may be that this essay is in itself a betrayal of the principles of the Incarnational Age; another dull scalpel wrought of words, words, words to set in motion a pageant and conjure the stilled flames which once burned and danced for Christ. Perhaps. Or perhaps beneath it all, this too can reflect the sincerity of a time when men attempted to act like Christ because they didn't know what was 'good' for them. It was the hope of Francis and Bernard. It has become the hope of many since who see gain and success in an ethos of charity, service, love and sacrifice. It is a noble tradition, and one which I seek to join in the fullness of faith for its expectations. Essays are easy compared to that.

Preface

A sustained query into the origin and nature of the individual in Western Society will come upon many presumptions laid down firmly by previous scholars. The literature on the development of the Western personality through historical influences in the Middle Ages may be immense but a diligent sifting will show the same nuggets of gold still in the tray after the waters have receded.

The nature of Christ himself, or the perceptions concerning his cultural place, within the sphere of the centuries under discussion is unavoidable in Western historical studies. Two books served to steer the shoals. Of course Jaroslav Pelikan's magisterial book, *Jesus Through The Centuries,* remains a touchstone. The nature of Christ within the Middle Ages was succinctly and admirably laid about by the scholar who concisely telescoped the achievement of centuries into an hourglass. Especially moving are Pelikan's thoughts on Bernard's contribution to Christian mysticism beginning to take hold of the Age. Many observations in the present discussion serve as no more than a Baedeker through some chapters in Pelikan.

The other book, Graham Ward's *Christ and Culture* is more a repository of the current debates on Christology referencing the past as counter levers for much of the arguments raised. Although the dissertation deals with a specified historical period and its understanding of Christ in the world, Ward's incarnational theology makes use of von Balthasar and Moltmann to a degree that greatly aided and supplemented my view of these theologians, who play a strong role in my own understanding of Christ as *fons et origo* in culture.

Arno Borst's insistence on the advent of the *persona* preoccupied me as much as Walter Ullmann's codification of a theory of legalism and its comprehension in assessing the reflection on entity in the Medieval mind. As far as the theories concerning separatism in orthodoxy, I can make no strides that have not been covered over and over by the careful and exuberant pens of Malcolm Lambert, Gordon Leff, and Raoul Manselli. When at Oxford on the High, I bought an exorbitantly priced volume on the Albigensian Crusade (of which I came across later in Paris-much more moderately priced) just for Lambert's signature.

The major influence in the actual writing was the work of Miri Rubin on the role of the Corpus Christi processions in Medieval Europe. Although the development of the feast is outside the scope of this investigation, there was a wake in which I could trawl for the pertinent discussions.

Jacques Le Goff and Beryl Smalley's identification of Pauline doctrine as rehabilitating the novelty of the *imitatio Christi* to the new Mendicant Orders, as well as the Frenchman's tireless advocacy of new studies in medievalism led to a comprehensive outlook only fortified by Colin Morris' magisterial view of the cultural shifts both responsible for and initiated by a new type of psychology.

Aaron Gurevich and Gerhardt Ladner developing theories of self-examination through solitude influenced my thinking immensely. Ladner especially in his essays on *homo viator* and the Life of the Mind in the Twelfth Century became Ur-texts for many of my suppositions. Such thoroughness in a scholar coupled with a concomitant *vrai geste* in rhetorical flourish gave me reason to pause at pursuing any ideas so enticingly hinted at.

Caroline Walker Bynum's view of the interior landscape as helpful but not decisive in producing the modern equivalent of the individual was a good barometer to keep exuberance in check, as well as her pioneering in 'body' theories of the Middle Ages. Von Balthasar and Moltmann have already been mentioned, although this study is naturally interdisciplinary and makes no claim to originality in theological discourse. Among theologians, and after Bernard and Abelard, their thinking on Christ was paramount in my Christology, with the single ineffable exception of the *poverello* from Assisi.

Lizette Andrews Fisher's Columbia dissertation *The Mystic Vision in the Grail Legend and in the Divine Comedy* (1917) was as decisive in my thinking as Ladner's essays into the period under discussion. It was (along with Curtius and Lewis' *Allegory of Love*) a work that sent me into a particular direction in considering the literature of the period as reflective of greater themes in the historical and theological arenas.

These interpretations of the period in question are more than sufficient to allow for a framework to be reared needing precious little addition. Yet it is not in hopes to overthrow but in desire to connect that the present endeavor is taken. It is neither comprehensive nor universal. It will investigate the nature of the individual within the Italian peninsula between (roughly) 1180 and 1300. It shall by necessity look both forward and backwards from the dates given for purposes of illumination.

It shall hold a meandering route that at times touches and at other times runs through the *zeitgeist*. It always maintains a parallel course and attempts no further exercise than this; to follow the historical events and the cultural products that define the ethos with the question "and where is Christ?" Not in any metaphorical sense and not with the cadence of the dispossessed anthropologist, but the actual Christ as perceived by the careful chronicler of the Age. For it is the time when Jesus was known to be in the Eucharist, lurking among the individuals of the Age, perhaps causing individualism itself.

It, perhaps, may not be overstatement to say that the Renaissance that was to come was as much a specific reaction to a particular understanding of Christology within the cultural sphere as it was a reawakening of Classical ideals through a new paradigm of European selfhood outside of Christianity. Understood in this way of the Incarnation helped to produce an action based Christianity amenable to the needs of the Roman Church.

The *kenosis,* which is precedent in Incarnation, leeched the culture of the impurities of selfishness in understanding and activating personality. The fulfillment of a communion with God by the act of penance, begun by Innocent in the Fourth Lateran Council led to investigating conscience with the caveat of *kenosis* as an understood penumbra.

After the Plague and within the new fabric of Italian culture of the Fifteenth Century, insistence upon text and exegetical delimitation, coupled with the same impulse in the North led to notions of personal conscience that identifies the Reformation. This can now be seen as a true break, and hence end to the pursuit of a Christian praxis that produced the cultural explosion of the Italian peninsula in the *Duecento* and early *Trecento.*

It may be that this by itself is no revelation and perhaps by the end of the discussion much that will be said will have little effect on an understanding of the period already firmly in place. If this is true, then I exercise the right to be redundant, without, I hope, the risk of repetition.

Perforce my discussion will be interdisciplinary and range through the theology, history, art, and literature of the times. It cannot be exhaustive and yet my hope is that it will not be perfunctory. By tracing possible interpretative reactions of both intellectuals and the rising Mendicant Orders to the figure of Christ, a new tool will be offered to the historian to properly assess achievement in the cultural products of the time. Taking themes and motifs prevalent in the Middle Ages, I range cross disciplines to demonstrate how such motifs may have been understood in the time and how we, as inheritors of the tradition of Western culture, may be rightfully or wrongfully understanding them.

INTRODUCTION

REASONS FOR RENAISSANCE

> There is indeed some light in men: but let them walk fast; walk fast, lest the shadows come.
> —Augustine, *Confessions X, xxiii, 33.*

Human nature is such that the call for a personal relationship with God is predicated upon the assumption that we understand ways to communicate with Him. Consequently we fall upon a reliance of codes forged in the crucible of interpersonal human experience. To speak of a personal savior is a reductivist method of implicating the Godhead as a personality, that is, as a friend. This is more particular to the act of speaking and writing, where language can be the experiential mode by which friends agree or disagree.

Since language is by nature parochial, it cannot be universal. And since it cannot be immediately universal, needing translation, it is impure. Should we think of God only with these baser tools? Can we think of him in any other way? Human nature needs to communicate with a divinity so it assumes a language able to comprehend him. A deity not prone to the vicissitudes of mortal fortunes begets the necessity of understanding the human within the divine.

When it becomes increasingly clear that the Deity is aggressively *sui generis,* theology erects a bridge over the chasm of the unknown, and the rubrics of language become rarified. Bad theology begins to limp under the weight of a leaden tongue in a clouded head. Sometimes, if the theology is any good, the bridge springs from, and ends in the human heart. When it does, it finds that the arts have beaten the path there long before. Rhetoric and philosophy rest their weary abstractions at the door of instinct and can only claim wearily when they arrive at the long conquered truth, *et in arcadia ego.*

The Judaeo-Christian God began as a Maker, and makes what he can communicate to us. His is not the way of the abstract, but of the real. The humanity he informs begins a selfsame quest for permanence in the emptying of talent, and sees such a resolution as necessary. With time and hindsight, those of us made in that image by those imaginations, see clearly that that resolution was revolution.

For those able to distinguish honest craftsmanship from an exploitation of faith, it is a duty to trace what can be essentially convincing to the mind when explanations concerning God rear themselves above the calm Elysian pitch of logic. The arguments, convincing or otherwise, leave a wake in their path, like pulling a fishermen's net on drying sand. One can realize that the catch was negligible if the imprint is ephemeral. But if the furrows go deep, the sea has done its share in giving to the fisherman his fill. Indeed his catch can be shared when the fish betrays affinities with fowl. When the catch is like yet unlike, when it says more about those left, then those caught, then understanding can be laid out, like a table for a feast.

The overwhelming evidence from the Middle Ages has led some to call it an Age of Faith. This is a half-truth that does disservice to the practical potentialities of the Medieval mind. The term Age of Faith is oft mistook to mean that there was a docile and debilitating acceptance of the spiritual status quo that was the legacy of the earliest Latin Fathers. Instead, the men of those times (and some very influential women) began to fabricate a spiritual world resonant with the world of tangibles, perhaps even (to an extent) inhabited by the Real, rather than the Numinous. Consequently this insistence on *speculum*, or reflection, tended to embolden rather than enervate, the quest for identity.

Since Burckhardt, the Renaissance has held the distinction of vanquishing the ogre of "fatalism" which seemed to be the Middle Ages. Even after Curtius' sympathies for the literature of the Middle Ages, the common view remained of an Age of Faith as a dim anteroom to the triumphant Age of Man. A closer look will prove that like so many prejudices, it is kernel not the corn of fact that supplies the meal, and as such, leaves us all a little hungry. There are grounds for divorce, here. For it is the understanding of the contradistinction of the Trinity that has, superficially at first, but lastingly, caused Medieval Man to see himself anew. And such vision demands separation from the tired formulas that leave the Middle Ages in the Middle Ground.

Like many revolutions throughout history, The Incarnational Age was ushered into existence through the crucible of war. Others were the result of the influence of new institutions that sprang up throughout Europe almost hand in hand: Mendicancy and Universities. A new breed of man was forming: one beginning to be concerned with his civic functions as well as his spiritual duties and one prone to influence outside of the acceptable hierarchy of Church and State.

The purpose of this essay is to follow lines of cultural thought within Europe and specifically Italy between 1180-1300 that gave rise to a particular conception of the individual. This conception, I shall prove, had as much to do with negation as affirmation and as such, sustained a tension partly responsible for the explosion of creativity that was to follow on the peninsula following the Black Death. It was a concept at first broached by the *raison d'etre* of the Franciscans and was inaugurated by a sense of loss, the very real loss of Jerusalem to Saladin in the late twelfth century. It became a subconscious reflection of Medieval Man's continuum within the historical canvas on God's easel and activated by the aesthetic of Incarnation. God and man had begun a dialogue at long last, and the language, the vernacular of salvation, was Jesus Christ.[2] The Incarnational Age had begun.

The Crusades were a watershed in European history, and not more so than in the concept of the historical self. For the Crusades became an opportunity for the European Christian to see himself as part of history and not subject to it. He became a lever of God in history, rather than a pawn of time immemorial.

They were finally worthy to enter history; Godfrey and Tancred joined the worthies of antique memory and the men who had dreamed of a united Latin Christian kingdom that spread to, and contained therein, the Holy City of Christ's earthly trajectory became the midwives of God's purpose. It became an empirical fact that the men engaged in taking up the cross were helping to reengage the divinity in history. Such men were bound to see themselves in a new light, but it should not be assumed that this new dispensation was one of privilege. Indeed, the greatest impetus toward selfhood began in the Crusades but took its final, definitive form

---

[2] A succinct definition of the Incarnational relationship most suited to this study is given by Michael Robson, "Bonaventure" in *The Medieval Theologians: An Introduction to the Theology in the Medieval Period,* G. R. Evans., ed. (Oxford: Blackwell, 2001), 191. "The Deus-homo becomes humanity's neighbor, brother, friend, and teacher and gives himself in the passion as the price of redemption, thereby manifesting his charity and benevolence. The perfection of creation is matched by that of the redeemed order...The Incarnation demonstrates the closeness of the bond between the Creator and fallen humanity and this is reflected in the lexicon of friendship which is restored by the most amicable mediator capable of uniting Creator and creature."

from the Mendicant Orders that predicated their vocation upon loss, not gain.

The Crusades had by this time become problematic as far as permanent conquest was concerned. The defeat at the hands of Saladin had many psychological ramifications as well as cultural implications. Those that concern us have to do with how the Crusaders and then Europeans in general began to understand Christ and his Incarnation. The loss to Saladin allowed for a particularly geographical notion of a Christ outside of Europe to be replaced by a Christ within Europe. The actuality of presence went from place to being.

The new crusade, not military but intellectual, began to seek the Christ among us rather than the places he walked. This does two things for identification with Christ: It understands Christ himself as now a *homo viator*, a fellow pilgrim upon this Earth and it quickens a sense of eschatology, because of a sense of defeatism. Both these ideas played prominent roles in the period's cultural residue, and both are reflexes inherent *par excellence* within the Franciscan Order. In this new dispensation the Christ found would be actual, and salubrious to idea of the self. The individual would no longer see himself as adjudicated by authorities outside of his understanding and therefore bereft of hope and action, but as a potentiality; as a guest of the Bridegroom, as a neighbor, perhaps even as a friend of Jesus himself.

As Francis would teach, the idea was to copy virtue by an aggressive mimicry of Christ. This is a radically new idea and as such comes with radically new cultural manifestations. Indeed it is the purpose of this book to justify certain acts of peculiar originality that led to the explosion of cultural production known as Renaissance as being understood as ornamental to the citizenship of a terrestrial, corporal Christ. What Christianity gained by eventually losing the Holy Land during the Crusades was a new sense of self.

By 1215 the Franciscans and Dominicans had been given official status and their Rules codified (or atrophied) by Innocent III unwilling to risk more with a potent heresy rampant in the Languedoc. To marshal the resources of such sons as Dominic and Francis and to codify an understanding, an orthodox understanding, of the Eucharist was a simultaneous thrust to the Cathars and a bolstering of the faith throughout a Christendom now threatened with the loss of Palestine. The decrees of the Fourth Lateran Council attempted in this understanding to renew Christian understanding through bold and untried measures, and to level the field of infidels, placing stable and resolute markers of orthodoxy where there might spring doubt.

One of these markers was Innocent's imprimatur on the theory of transubstantiation which mirrored his understanding of the True Presence hitherto explicated in the Fourth Lateran Council and in his *de Sacramento Altaris Mysterio*. Another was the binding of intentional Penance to a necessary Communion, leaving the Christian free to make an honest assessment of the self before seeking absolution to enter into a deeper communion with his brethren. A third, as mentioned previously, was the official recognition of the new Mendicant Orders, which would later become the instruments of dissemination, by the improved uniformity of the *ars Praedicandi*. They would become the hounds of conscience and the explicators of doctrine, by both their intellectual achievements in the nascent Universities of Bologna, Padua, Oxford, and Paris, and by their insinuation within the urban life of North Italy.

Such a situation within the times of a concurrent rise of the merchant class began to germinate new theories of what it meant to be a Christian and indeed the theological concerns of the early thirteenth century had raised a deeper and more troublesome question; what did it mean to be Christ?

If such a question were raised, the theory of the Incarnation within the Eucharist began to be a referential point of the utmost significance and indeed the proliferation of the *cultus* surrounding the host and its worship attest to the fascination for Christ in the world. More than this the adumbrated theories of the theologians worked their way down to a populous eager to know Jesus through sense, not argument. These theories, although sent through orthodox channels and through the Orders' hierarchy to the crowds became remarkably protean by a benign misapprehension within the greater societal sphere. A Christian was being encouraged to meditate upon a dualism hitherto left to the theologians, and the result was a new dialogue amenable to commoner minds.

Now the Dominicans and the Franciscans were offering them *exempla*, at times living (Francis himself) of the attainability of Christ himself within the realm of the senses. The concentration upon actual witness was a result of the intense interest upon the Eucharist itself as a *locus latreia*. Things reserved to divine speculation and within the limited purview of ecclesiastical hierarchy had come down to earth. Christ was here, now, there and everywhere. The relationship between believer and his worship became personal, and as such could be personalized. This was prepared through long years by the ordeal of the Crusades, which promised to return the sepulcher of Christ to his people and a Christology of extraordinary and intense psychology, such as that of Abelard or

Bernard. It also manifested a new and radical understanding of art within the function of liturgy and as a reflection of urban consciousness.

The result was that the understood and tried Augustinian lines of division between the Sacred City and the Secular City had become nebulous and hence the frontiers could be breached by intrepid believers now asked, nay, compelled to investigate their motives. This would entangle a psychology of introspection with one of worship. It was also a fresh look at the humanity of a Savior long outside of the ken of observation. The obvious eye of any theological storm concerning Christological identity in the time under scrutiny would be the Incarnation.

The Incarnation, as understood by the theologians and the spiritualists of the Age, was the central tenet in Medieval perceptions of a soteriological Christology. Why God came into history was an ongoing debate in the Western theology. But the ramifications of theology were far removed from the dour realities facing the proponents of the cultural life, the rising class of burghers. And the foot soldiers of preachers that emanated from the Mendicant Orders were invested with making sense of a reality that were bound to live in, for their own sake and the sake of their flock. It is only with distance that the historian can apply words that would have had resonance to only the cultured few in describing the potentialities and purposes of many. *Kenosis* may not have seemed familiar as a word to the Medieval man, but as a concept it was his distinction.

The new theory of atonement took into account by way of reference (but not word) the theory of kenotic salvation. *Kenosis*, the Greek word for emptying, is a contention in modern christological soteriology, but did not cause a great stir in the Middle Ages. Paul's hymn-like Philippians 2: 5-11, has exercised a profound effect on the contemporary dialogue concerning the Incarnation, and on myself, through the writings of Moltmann and von Balthasar, as well as the synthesis of Graham Ward in his *Christ and Culture*.

The passage reads that Christ "emptied himself" to accept the death of a slave "even death on the cross." Abelard's concept of Atonement spoke to the compassion this activates within the worshipper. As such, it had a persuasive power over cruder conceptions of the Incarnation for the very simple reason that it was more palatable to the reality of what Medieval man was, rather than aggressively exploiting his fear.

Kenosis, an emptying, was an accurate reflection of the instincts of a defeated psyche which wished to exorcise the more dubious aspects of its heritage by assuming the novel and precious vocations thrust upon it by the will of an active and newly historical God. The Mendicant Orders, the

Eucharistic Controversy, the Cathar heresy and the Troubadours all arrayed themselves in a reality at once imminent and passing. A spirituality that invoked the spirit through the distinguishing marks of flesh, both positive and negative, became the hallmarks of the Age, and was infinitely more responsible for the explosion of creativity on the Italian peninsula than the recovery of classicism. Identity was not an outgrowth of having, but a result of losing.

The later Franciscan controversy, the withering away of the troubadour ideal, and Giotto's solidity and painterly corporality sought to make room for the weight of the world that was descending upon the mercantile and intellectual classes by the mid-fourteenth century. Ownership, coinage, double entry bookkeeping, civic guilds, and political maneuvering, all dull and necessary workhorses of the magnificent cart of capitalism, pulled the European into an age of predictable seasons outside of the realm of nature, where the colors of the Fall would not surprise but be proscribed by a diligently up to date *Mater Ecclesia*. Society was closing in on Christ and man was caught in the conspiracy. It was good that Francis had not lived to see this.

And yet Franciscan extremists insisted not upon ownership through contemplation, but on the negation of possession that forms the very basis of a specified identity. Perhaps it is much to say that the notion of the individual as a right bearing legal entity emerged from the conflict over Franciscan poverty, but the notion, lived by Francis, that Medieval man can attempt to imitate the life of Christ Himself without post-lapsarian guilt impeding the attempt, and in the full light of the ecclesiastical authority which hitherto had codified behavior towards Christ is significant and indisputable. Francis was *kenosis* personified without the concomitant responsibility of emptying divinity for humanity. Instead, and ironically Francis emptied his humanity for his sanctity and earned the respect of a world he tried so hard to escape.

The issue of the influence of a particular notion of the Incarnation within the Franciscan Order in its early years became a troubled one. Their view of the Christ-like life was predicated upon a renunciation of significant, if not extreme, proportion. The lengths to which the Friars Minor would renounce possession were not a matter of moderation or of degree. The Franciscan depended upon a total abnegation to begin his life as a Friar. The ineluctable right for renunciation was a duty for the Franciscan but the attempt to give it a Rule based on the temporal life of Christ supposed that Christ was poor and that second that his poverty was an intrinsic and crucial aspect to the messianic purpose of the Incarnation. Christ being was not enough in this sense: Christ denying was the sticking point and since identity could be viewed as the capacity to live either having or wanting, the focus on denial constitutes a radicalization of the Christian life, as the fascination with Francis in his own time and ours can attest.

Poverty therefore to the Franciscans is not an end to itself but it is as a lifestyle an exercise for ultimate and final sacrifice. The *imitatio Christi* is a wiping away of identity by proclaiming identity. The potential heresy that lies within this attempt is that the acolyte sees himself as Christ. This was certainly the case for Francis, who although aware he himself was not Christ, took to taking on his suffering. This can be seen as a negative reflex, couched as it is, in the sorrowful Jesus, and adumbrating any possible alter interpretations of the Christian life. Against the Medieval propensity to see the Christian life as a vale of tears as inherently negative, it set itself a goal to mimic the Incarnation, by which the concept of the speculum of the Medieval imagination is satisfied.

The attempt to bridle legalistic notions of the individual to the Franciscan life can be done, but as Pope John XXII testified, it will be arrived at in an attempt to dispute the notion of their vocation. The debate over the competing notions of dominion and use as exemplified within the life of Christ Himself resulted in a dualistic rendering of the Christian life, and specifically the implied legitimacy of either one in the context of the Medieval world. Poor or possessive the Jesus of the Gospels had become a temporal concern as a temporal entity and concomitantly the emphasis was now, in the legal wranglings over the poverty debate and in the primary impetus of Francis' vocation, on Jesus within the world and not Jesus without.

For the rest of the rising mercantile class that began to understand the notion of the personal Savior, the *imitatio Christie* was outside of their temporal possibilities. Now did the necessity of Penance before Communion to eradicate the obvious guilt of possession become a catalyst for charity. Still, this giving was personal and possessive, which identified the giver as generous patron rather than anonymous donor. Guilt could only have so many inroads to vanity. This would be, as has been noted, a real *fons et origo* for cultural production in the century to follow.

The waning scholasticism of the Universities, the personal interpretative power of parish priests upon penance, the uniformity of homiletic subjects as manuals became more widespread, the rise of an increasingly urban elite and the pacification of the West under the impetus of Crusade all contributed to the rapid dissemination of key ideas that concurrently became digested in particular, even provincial ways because of the concurrent rise of cities, and the increasing use of the vulgar tongue in poetry and prose, personal interpretation in artistic endeavor, and the rise of nominalism as a challenge to absolutes. Within all this heaving metamorphoses the still point of reference remained the Christian faith, centered on Jesus Christ. As Christ as person became a consistent idea, the relationship towards that idea would become one of identification; and just as much as Christ could be us, we indeed could be Christ.

Incarnation and its precedent sacrifice, *kenosis*, were grounds by which the Medieval man could divorce himself not from reality, but the pre-conditions for existence. He, by accepting the Christian understanding of relinquishing, could imitate Christ, and by such an emptying, fulfill his emptiness by whatever he deemed necessary to sustain the personal in a rapidly changing world. And what this was, in effect was a fabrication of identity by a curious denial of what we would call personality. The Augustinian good within men was possible only by activity, a positive activity within the Incarnational dispensation, saddled as it was by the grief of the world. For the heroes of this Age the shadows were kept at bay because they believed themselves capable of perfection. The books and words of the Ancients would have fallen on fallow soil had not Christ come first. This I believe had much to do not only with engendering a new sense of identity in the West, but also gave rise to an individualism that would quicken the later Renaissance into its fullest expression.

CHAPTER ONE

JERUSALEM AND CHRIST DELIVERED

It is here we are compelled to say with the prophet, "Who will change my eyes into a fountain of tears, that I may weep night and day the massacre of my people?" Nevertheless, far from allowing ourselves to be cast down or be divided, we ought to be persuaded that these reverses are only to be attributed to the anger of God, against the multitude of our sins; that the most efficacious manner of obtaining the remission of them is by tears and groans, and that at last, appeased by our repentance, the mercy of the Lord will raise us up again, more glorious for the abasement into which he has plunged us...We ought not then to attribute our disasters to the injustice of the judge who chastises, but rather to the iniquity of the people who have sinned.[1]

A dream fulfilled becomes a reality destined to mortality. Gregory the VIII's lament is a justly famous *de profundis*, which, although it spoke to the wound delivered, it betrayed the novel approaches to an emancipation of spirit that had begun to unravel in the Middle East among the transferred Crusaders of the Latin West. By the time of the fall of Jerusalem, things had begun to germinate in the European mind that would eventually slough off the *Christus Pantokrator* implied in Gregory's desperate jeremiad, and don the mantle of a new Christianity. This new paradigm would begin to see Christ as fellow rather than judge.

The dream of a Christendom emanating from Jerusalem and binding the West in a politicized theology had to be exploded after Saladin's victory in 1187, but there was a fruit to be plucked from the defeat: A new idea, a new dream, not subject to the whims of political change and the shifts of strategic supremacy in war. Jerusalem lost became the genesis of a renaissance of personal identity tied almost exclusively to the body, the actual corporeal body, of Christ. Medieval man was to be justified by approaching God on equal terms in the body of His son.

---

[1] Gregory VIII, "Audita tremendi" in *The Crusadse: A Reader*, S. J. Allen and Emilie Amiet, eds. (Peterborough: Broadview Press, 2003), 164.

The initial success of the first Crusader knights in conquering the object of their most fervent desire gave way to the necessity of organizing and governing what is at once a desert city and a spiritual oasis. By the time of the First Crusade in 1098, Latin Christianity had codified a system of parallel hierarchies of papacy and empire, the clerical and the lay, within the larger framework of the Church. After the conquest of Jerusalem, things needed reconsideration, because, although led by knights and feudal barons of varying degrees of nobility, a common people in their multitudes had gained the victory.[2] The tenuous nature of the victory, the introduction of a lay power hitherto neglected, the beautiful and strange Orient now passing before their eyes as a reality, and the shining and hallowed city of the golden stone which passed roughly beneath their bloody hands: How can we properly gauge the effect these were to have on the warrior who already had his purpose sanctified as "taking up his cross?"[3]

Between the years of 1099-1189, the span of its Christian kingdom, Jerusalem was the shining central jewel of *Outremer* although it's significance was more symbolic than economic. The deserted city after the Frankish siege needed repopulation after the eventual conquest in 1099, and moreover, once populated begged the skills of a certain class of craftsmen to cater to the pilgrims who would eventually throng the city.[4]

---

[2] See Yael Katzir, "The Second Crusade and the Redefinition of Ecclesia, Christianitas, and Papal Coercive Power" in Michael Gervers, ed. *The Second Crusade and the Cistercians* (New York: St. Martin's Press: New York, 1997), 1 -13, 4.

[3] "In connection with the question of individuality it is very important to stress the following: people find themselves in a situation in which their stories are interwoven with the universal historical process, which they experience in a symbolic way as the history of human salvation. Through the mediation of the Church and the liturgy of the individual becomes aware of his or her personal involvement in that history. . At that point... the overlapping of the 'small' and 'great' eschatologies becomes possible, even inevitable...this overlapping accentuates the importance of the individual in the current of historical time. " Aaron Gurevich, *The Origins of European Individualism.* Translated from the Russian by Katherine Judelson. (Oxford: Blackwell, 1995), 109.

[4] William of Tyre wrote that Baldwin's request was greeted with satisfaction by these new Syrian pilgrims who "...were attracted thither not only by reverence for the place but also by affection for our people and the love of liberty. Many, even without being invited cast off the harsh yoke of servitude and came that they might dwell in the city worthy of God. " It seems that a contemporary document such as this states the connection between the weakening of feudal propensities in the newly formed state and a diversified demographic. The shift to an exchange

The poor Franks, in need of food and slow to grasp the significance of the problem, could not rely on the industry of the many peasants who had taken up the cross. King Baldwin I (1110-1118) remedied this by importing the Syrian Christians from the countryside and allotting them parcels of the city for habitation (Syrian Christian Quarter), hoping such an influx of native talent would massage the industry of the destitute city.[5]

Yet, at this fragile beginning of the Latin Kingdom the preconditions of the economic disaster that was the conquered city led the European social infrastructure of the Crusaders to fray and become mutable. Feudalism as it was understood in the Latin West, became untenable, although the exertions and pressures of the jurists of the Latin monarchy attempted to stitch the gaping wounds left by continental displacement. The influx of Syrian Christians lent the cast of demography a somewhat Eastern face, reflected in some of the art and the liturgies to be newly sung in the Church of the Holy Sepulcher. The new Jerusalem was just that; new.

At first this fact was evident through the harsh economic realities, but it was certain subtle social factors that led to a development of a unique hothouse of political ideas in the European population of Jerusalem. Although never flourishing into an overt revolt in the new desert society, the classes engendered by the conquest would have a profound influence once these new ideas took wing to the old shores of Europe, and lead to a paradigm-changing epoch in the High Middle Ages.[6]

Even before the loss of the Jerusalem, the idea of crusading had been given a strong theological framework and was invested with a mystical import by the inheritors of a particularly monastic frame of reference.[7] Within this context, the adamantine ties to the actual body of Christ which the Holy Land enjoyed was connected to the idea that the Savior needed salvation by those *made* worthy of the act. The danger, which had befallen the West in the form of Islamic expansion, was a threat to the unity of the Body of Christ, and as such, the God of History was once more activating a response as He had done in Scripture. In turn, the celestial could become temporal by this theological and intellectual

---

based economy was necessary to provide a homogeneous understanding to retain a stable population. For the above quote, see *The Crusades: A Reader*, 85.
[5] Mustafa A Hiyari, "Crusader Jerusalem, 1099-1187," in K. J. Asali, ed. *Jerusalem in History*. (New York: Olive Branch Press, 1990), 130-177 p. 142.
[6] See Adrian Boas, *Jerusalem in the Time of Crusades Society: Landscape and Art in the Holy City under Frankish Rule* (Routledge: New York, 2001), 36-38.
[7] See Jonathan Riley-Smith, *The First Crusade and the Idea of Crusading* (Philadelphia: University of Pennsylvania Press, 1986), 137-152.

blurring. The interface between god and man was once again being implemented by the effusion of blood, a new martyrdom to a new *patria*; not for any duke or lord, but for Christ himself.[8]

These were glorious times to be alive and Bernard of Clairvaux, for one, trembled with the fulfillment of the Age:

> This age is like no other that has gone before: a new abundance of divine mercy comes down from heaven; blessed are those who are alive in this year pleasing to the Lord, this year of remission, this year of veritable jubilee. I tell you, the Lord has not done this for any other generation before, nor has he lavished on our fathers a gift of grace so copious. Look at the skill he is using to save you. Consider the depth of his love and be astonished sinners. He creates a need – he either creates it or pretends to have it – while he desires to help you in your necessity. This is a plan not made by man, but coming from heaven and proceeding from the heart of divine love.[9]

Along with the apocalyptic undertone of a temporal fulfillment, the Lord himself began to be approached as either complicit with the ideals of the contemporary man or by the zealous interpreter as a paradigm capable of real emulation. Christ, or the reference to him, began to be couched in the social terms of a knight, whose honor had been besmirched, or an aggrieved landowner, distressed at the loss of his rightful patrimony.[10]

---

[8] "From the outset, therefore, one should at least consider the possibility whether-before the full impact of legal and humanistic doctrines became effective-the new territorial concept of *patria* did not develop as a re-secularized offshoot of the Christian tradition and whether the new patriotism did not thrive also on ethical values transferred back from *patria* in heaven to the polities on earth. " Ernst H. Kantorowicz, *The King's Two Bodies: A Study in Mediaeval Political Theology* (Princeton: Princeton University Press, 1957), 235.

[9] From Jonathan Riley-Smith, *The Crusades: A History* (New Haven and London: Yale University Press, 2005), 122.

Bernard, as could be expected, placed a premium on the polysemous significance of Jerusalem itself, as maternal land: "In via estis, fratres, quae ducit ad vitam, in via recta et impolluta, quae ducit ad civitatem sanctam Jerusalem illam, quae libera est, quae sursum est, quae est mater nostra. " From "De Diversis Sermo XXII: De quadruplici debito" in *Patrologiae Latina* (henceforward *PL*) 183 (Paris: Migne, 1862), 595.

[10] Examples abound beginning with Baldric of Dol and Urban II himself at Clermont. The *Chronicle* of Villehardouin's underlines a Compact with the Venetians to take up arms "on behalf of the noble barons of France who have taken the cross in order to avenge the shame of Jesus Christ and to reconquer Jerusalem".

Christ himself can, in the Western imagination prevalent at the time, become as vindictive as his Christian soldiers, blurring the nature of mercy inherent in him, and perhaps justifying vengeance in his servants. In the famous *Chanson d'Antioche,* part of a late twelfth century song cycle, the dishonored Christ speaks from the cross to Dismas, the thief on his right, about his beleaguered city, and the rightful inheritance to be restored by his faithful Crusaders:

> "Friend" he said, "the people who will avenge me are not yet born or baptized but they will come with their sharpened swords to kill these fiendish pagans who would not listen to me. Then my land will be delivered and reconquered. Holy Christendom will be exalted. But it will be a thousand years before the Holy Sepulchre becomes a place of pilgrimage and an object of veneration. Men of those times will come to serve me as if they were my sons, and I shall treat them as such: I shall be their safeguard and they will enter into possession of their inheritance in paradise...Friend you may be sure that a people will come from beyond the sea to avenge the death of their father. There won't be a pagan left from here to the Orient. The Franks will be the undisputed masters of the land and the soul of anyone who perishes on the journey will be saved."[11]

The duty bound Christian then was enjoined to participate in an elaborate ritual of vendetta for a de-sacralized Savior. Not only that, but the unenviable familial standing of the second son in a noble house was mitigated by the fact that inheritance in this understanding was not based upon birth order. Christ retained a significant rite of *auctoritas* beneath the veneer of a man despised and rejected. This paradox could only be resolved in the spiritual and temporal sphere by the suffering king, who could both bestow blessings and accept personal indignation. The deliverance sought after cut two ways, for the Crusader and for Christ, and only those willing to leave everything were privy to this marvelous and unique opportunity.

The Crusade then became a methodical way of Medieval man to understand the world, and his role in it, which, despite the distances involved, claimed Jerusalem as it's goal. The pilgrimage became a way to emulate the itinerant nature of Christ in his ministry and served to disassociate the European from the ties that bound him too fondly to his

---

In Edward Peters, ed., *Christian Society and the Crusades 1198-1229* (Philadelphia: University of Pennsylvania Press, 1971), 3.
[11] Translated in Susan Edgington, "Holy Land, Holy Lance: Religious Ideas in the Chanson d'Antioche" in *The Holy Land, Holy Lands, and Christian History,* R. N. Swanson, ed. (Woodbridge: Boydell Press, 2000), 146-147.

familiar earth. He became what his God was, and strove to reestablish what his Savior had conquered; all this under the guise of the wandering man, the dispossessed in search of possession, a *homo viator*.[12]

Man as wayfarer in this phase of medieval thought, combined modes of alienation with order, as the influence of monasticism and a burgeoning spirituality combined to offer the sincere Christian a dilemma: What was the best way to order the world when the ultimate purpose was to remove yourself from it? Alienation became a pre-requisite of order and Christ's sojourn an exemplum of how to best engage the times by withdrawing from them. This accorded the serious pilgrim a deep respect from his contemporaries, as the goal (in a quite literal sense), was the ultimate sacrifice of a martyr's death if the example were to be followed to the bitter end. A pilgrim strove to be a sort of speculum of his worship, a Christ in the flesh.[13]

This was nothing new as it was a ripening of the conceptual fruit first reared by Augustine in the *City Of God*; namely that the rightful Christian was a pilgrim so long as he remained tied to the terrestrial and hence fallible nature of the worldly city. Salvation depended upon a flight from the world- a *fuga mundi*. Perhaps the most far ranging among the chief ideas that developed through crusade, the *fuga mundi* was the acorn that grew the oak of a renewed spiritualized laity on the European continent.[14]

The merchant class of privilege had bifurcated and spawned the *homo viator as* pauper, mendicant, beggar, and at times,(negatively) leper or

---

[12] For the most complete treatment of this phenomenon, see Gerhardt Ladner "Homo Viator: Medieval Ideas on Alienation and Order," in his *Images and Ideas in the Middle Ages: Selected Studies in History and Art* (Roma: Edizioni di Storia e Letteratura, 1983), 937-974.

[13] Brenda Bolton's conclusion on this is that the "Church in western society had not yet found a solution to the problem of individual rebirth in a renewed society," (103). This, to my mind, was not the purpose of the Church in its political pose upon the age. Monolithic treatments deny the exuberance and evolutionary processes of the Body of Christ within the laity. The Church was, in this time, western society in toto, and it's political responses at times did not reflect the cultural reactions to the age which jolted it forward into novel understandings of the self.
See Brenda Bolton, "Paupertas Christi: Old Wealth and New Poverty in the Twelfth Century," in *Studies in Church History: Vol. 14. Renaissance and Renewal in Christian History,* Derek Baker, ed. (Oxford: Basil Blackwell, 1977), 95-103.

[14] See Andre Vauchez "The Church and the Laity," in *The New Cambridge Medieval History. Vol. V: c. 1198-c. 1300,* David Abulafia, ed. (Cambridge: Cambridge University Press, 1999), 182-203, esp. 197-199

criminal. Absence by either denial or want was to be the new medium to establish identity in positive rather than in negative terms, an epiphenomenon that would ripen and bear fruit in the Franciscan model.[15] It was a paradigm perhaps only possible with the rise of cities, so that the excluded could view themselves as an apposite of the agreed upon nexus of society.

This being so, Jerusalem had a privileged rank in the paradigm, as it was both a city and The City, both terrestrial and spiritual, idea and reality. The idea of Jerusalem (tying in nicely with the nature of the new urbanized social systems)[16] became directly connected to the figure, the physical figure of Christ: In that these new social identities based themselves around the witness of the land wherein the Savior walked, spoke, and died. Such an idea became a social as well as a spiritual hope. Jerusalem had become, by the Crusades, a literal as well as a spiritual goal, which corresponded chronologically with the rise of urban centers in Southern Europe and the slow decline of feudalism in the North.

The loss of the city made immediate pilgrimage impossible until much later and hammered home the reality of withdrawal from the sands that once dusted Jesus' feet. The common Crusader, be he knight or no, was severed from the experience of his God, the actual, tangible experience for which he took up his own cross in the first place. The swell of support for Urban's appeal was unprecedented and the First Crusade a seeming historical exercise in bellicose serendipity. This being so, the spiritual aspects of the quest, although misapprehended by the conquering armies of the Latins, could be said to have been a real motivational force outside of overt clerical influence. Later it became evident that theologians had wished to perpetuate the crusading effort into a certain "monastery on the move".[17]

---

[15] See Brenda Bolton, " Paupertas Christi: Old Wealth and New Poverty in the Twelfth Century" 95-103. Bolton's conclusion is that the "Church in western society had not yet found a solution to the problem of individual rebirth in a renewed society", (103) which wasn't it's function in any age to my mind. Say rather that the conflicts arising later in the poverty of the Mendicants widened a gulf between the hierarchical political sphere and the spiritual laypeople. The Church itself was both. The monolith of the Church as political presence is justified if the concentration is upon the strengthening of the Papal powers, especially under Innocent III, but the Church was and is the people who make it up, especially in a cultural sense, which is how is should be seen in the present discourse.

[16] See Bronislaw Geremak, *Poverty: A History*. Translated by Agnieszka Kolakowska. (Oxford: Blackwell, 1994), 21-23.

[17] Jonathan Riley Smith, *The Crusades: A History*, 47.

Culturally, this was conceived as a *renovatio* rather than a colonization, wherein the conquerors sought not so much to supplant as to renew.[18] Economically and socially, this can be deduced by the telling debilitation of previously held beliefs of fiefdom and service. The novelty of the situation in the captured city engendered a concretized method of exchange, making the parameters of this economy the walls of Jerusalem themselves.[19] The new dispensation did not readily take to the old ideas of servitude of Frankish feudalism, although the status of Jerusalem was unique in the *Outremer*.[20]

Dangerously for a church and state dependant upon hierarchical structure and duty, the *fuga mundi* could be wed to the *imitatio paradiso*; that is that the act of renunciation which is concomitant with the pilgrimage to Jerusalem became an act of selfhood disguised. And such an act became eschatological in the sense that the liberation of the Holy City was tied to a divine purpose incumbent upon the Crusaders to fulfill. So, for an unlettered warrior, battle scarred and knowing little well besides the call of war, what better way to attain paradise than by storming it? For Jerusalem, like Rome, is and was a city at once in Heaven and on Earth,

---

[18] Riley-Smith's preface in the above mentioned text, (p. xxv), mentions that historians of the period have "lost interest in the question whether the Latin settlements in the East were colonies or not. . (although)...the conviction that the settlements were examples of earlier colonialism is stll axiomatic in Arab and in some Israeli circles. " It is difficult to assert that the paramount concern for the exodus of warriors into the East was for colonization as it is well known that following the conquest of Jerusalem, a sizable proportion of the warriors returned to Europe, their quest fulfilled, which left the early demography of the city at sixes and sevens. Rather, colonization, or a form of it, was a social outgrowth of the necessity of conquest: *Post hoc*, not *propter hoc*.

[19] "The fief holders in the Latin Kingdom in the first quarter of the twelfth century are all homini novi ...(and)... the use of money became ubiquitous and was introduced clumsily into a sort of feudalism set up ad hoc for the terms of conquest," in Joshua Prawer, *The Latin Kingdom of Jerusalem: European Colonialism in the Middle Ages*, (London: Weidenfeld and Nicolson, 1972), 65-67.

[20] Hans Eberhard Mayer's work contends that the dispersal of fiefdoms became ubiquitous save for "most church lands, the properties of the military orders and the autonomous quarters of the Italian communes. " This would leave Jerusalem in a position of solitude as it was all three at once, with Baldwin IV, (at the time immediately preceding the loss) as the titular head of a state that extended beyond its walls. See Mayer's "The Latin East, 1098-1205" in *The New Cambridge Medieval History, v. IV., c. 1024-c. 1198. Part II*, David Luscombe and Jonathan Riley Smith, eds. (Cambridge: Cambridge University Press, 2004), 644-674, esp. 668.

and now the theologians were not only hinting that the ramparts could be breached, they were encouraging it.[21]

The new vocation, and it was a novelty introduced by crusade, exercised temporal and spiritual levers that had been newly forged by the tangible Jerusalem and played upon the nascent forms of individualism within the Medieval man. Jerusalem made real reinforced the Word made Flesh, heightened the relief of Christ as man, as neighbor, as suffering servant, as leper, as pauper, as knight, as king.[22]

Space itself was of interest to the new conquerors, and the reluctance of the Crusaders to raze and rebuild became evident soon. As far as sacred architecture went, the Crusaders were content to restore churches rather than rebuild them. After the conquest of Jerusalem by Saladin in 1187, the triumphant Muslims, who had much to criticize, remarked upon the extent to which the Crusaders had revivified the existing places of worship. Cadi el-Fadel was quick to note on returning to Jerusalem, that "Islam received back a place which it had left almost uninhabited, but which the care of the unbelievers had transformed into a Paradise garden."[23]

However much the Muslims appreciated the garden of Jerusalem, they were (and remain) bewildered at what they consider Christian idolatry. A real sticking point (pardon the pun) was the reality of the True Cross to the Christians and idea of it to the Muslims. The centrality of the cross in Christian worship was hard for them to comprehend.

---

[21]Baldric of Dol: "Certainly we must be filled with anxiety, lest the heavenly city be locked away and taken from us if, owing to our own weakness, malevolent foreigners keep us away from our house. ' Here the mystical connection between the two cities is more than mystical – it's magical. The loss of the real earthly Jerusalem may revoke Christian rights to the heavenly city. A similar attitude was expressed with great devotion by the ignorant masses who set out on the First Crusade, not quite sure if they were marching to an earthly or a heavenly city. Under God's command (Deo duce) they marched towards heaven's edge, which their church's also faced-the direction of the rising sun.... what was taking place in the city fulfilled prophecies of Jerusalem's renewal in preparation for the eschaton. " Page 345 in Joshua Prawer, "Christian Attitudes Towards Jerusalem in the Early Middle Ages" in Prawer, Joshua and Haggai Ben-Shammai, eds. *The History of Jerusalem: The Early Muslim Period, 638-1099* (New York and Jerusalem: New York University Press and Yad Izhak Ben-Zvi, 1996), 311-348.

[22] Jacques Le Goff, "Introduction" in *Medieval Callings*, Jacques Le Goff, ed. Translated by Lydia G. Cochrane (Chicago and London: University of Chicago Press, 1987), 5-7.

[23] Page 116 in Bernard Hamilton, "Rebuilding Zion: The Holy Places of Jerusalem in the Twelfth Century," in *Renaissance and Renewal in Christian History,* Derek Baker, ed. (Oxford: Blackwell, 1977), 105-116.

The Muslims historical self was tied to the Koran, so that recitation and memorization of it became commonplace early in the rise of Islam. Such a mooring gave the Muslims a strong sense of center and unity, incumbent upon a textual understanding, mirroring the tradition of the Jews.[24]

The Christians, in their view (and with good reason) were viewed as idolatrous. The Greek influence on the Christianity gave the Christian a bent to objectify the natural world, creating an intellectual arena where theological and spiritual ideas are concretized into image-making. The central image of Christianity is, of course, the cross. It serves as a *locus latreia*, a place to focus worship, and as a piece of evidence for the historicity of Christ's sacrifice. Also the symbol of the cross is iconographic paradox *par excellence*; the natural world twisted as an instrument of corporal death to prop up the regeneration of the supernatural. Of course such sanctification requires the conduit of the human toward the divine. How better than to put the natural mythic dimensions between man and earth to use at the service of the Cross? But here was another arena wherein Christian and Muslim parted ways: On the historicity of the crucifixion.

For in the Koran, we read that the crucifixion was an apparition of God, and that Jesus was translated to Heaven, a form of christological understanding that had been fought over earlier in the Church's history and would reappear again with the rise of Catharism in the Languedoc:

> They denied the truth and uttered a monstrous falsehood against Mary. They declared: We have put to death the Messiah, Jesus the son of Mary, the apostle of God.' They did not kill him or crucify him, but they thought they did, (or more literally, 'he was made to resemble another for them.)[25]

The cross then was an affront as to Islamic perceptions of Jesus as well as a distasteful reminder of the barbarous Franks who held Jerusalem in thrall. The Latin Christians had taken to bringing a relic of the True Cross into battle, a practice that had a disastrous epilogue when Saladin retook Jerusalem. Eyewitness accounts by the Muslims give a hint at the absolute centrality of the relic and the idea after the Horns of Hattin:

---

[24] See Albert Hourani, *A History of the Arab Peoples* (New York: Warner Books, 1991), 14-21.
[25] From the "al-Nisa" sura of *The Koran*. Translated by N. J. Dawood (London: Viking, 1956), 102.

The cross was a prize without equal for it was the supreme object of their faith. To venerate it was their prescribed duty, for it was their God, before whom they would bow their foreheads to the ground, and to which their mouths sang hymns. They fainted at its appearance, they raised their eyes to contemplate it, they were consumed with passion when it was exhibited and boasted of nothing else when they had seen it. They went into ecstasies at its reappearance, they offered up their lives for it and sought comfort from it, so much that they had copies made of it which they worshipped, before which they prostrated themselves in their houses and on which they called when they gave evidence. So when the great cross was taken great was the calamity that befell them, and the strength drained from their loins.[26]

The mentioning of the copying of the cross for individual purposes of worship re-emphasizes a common phenomenon in early Medieval man, which was the necessity of relics in localizing their ideas of the Numinous. Of course, the Muslims and the Jews for that matter, considered such things blasphemous and could point to strong Scriptural precedent to support them, but the Latins had brought into Jerusalem a carnal reality to their salvation.

Christ's iconographic aspects were not confined to the Christ of the crucifixion and the ministry. A telling anecdote reinforces the gulf between Muslim and Christian concerning the nature of Christ and his carnal reality:

> I was present myself when one of them (the Franks) came up to the amir Mu'in ad-Din-God have mercy on him-in the Dome of the Rock, and said to him: Would you like to see God as a baby?' The amir said he would, and the fellow proceeded to show us a picture of Mary with the infant Messiah on her lap. 'This,' he said, 'is God as a baby.' Almighty God is greater than the infidels' concept of him![27]

Could God be greater than that to one who risked life, limb, and fortune to storm a backwater in the desert hundreds of miles from his home? What Imad ad–Din did not understand is that the Christian faith itself was predicated upon the Atonement, the sacrifice of God as man to Peter Abelard, bridge the chasm between man and God. Indicatively, an influential shift in emphasis on the theology of the Atonement had

---

[26] Imad ad-Din (1125-1201), quoted in *Arab Historians of the Crusades* selected and translated by Francesco Gabrieli. Translated from the Italian by E. J. Costello (New York: Dorset Press, 1969), 137.
[27] Usama ibn Munqidh, Amir of Shaizar (1095-1188), quoted in *Arab Historians of the Crusades*, 80.

occurred with the writings of a Christian philosopher dead forty years before the victory of Saladin at Hattin.[28]

Abelard's theory, in contrast to the prevailing notions of the time best exemplified by Anselm of Canterbury was that the crucifixion was not a ransom paid for supreme justice but a merciful act of love to compel the Christian redemption. Anselm, writing a year before the First Crusade in *Cur Deus Homo*, said that by sinning, man needed to offer God endless penitence: Such satisfaction can only be accomplished by God himself. "The answer to this difficulty, according to Anselm, is found in the God-Man Jesus Christ. For in Jesus, humanity is represented, infinite satisfaction is rendered; obedience is still owed to God alone."[29]

Abelard's is a doctrine that depends upon an active Christianity, to see the crucifixion as *exemplum*, rather than seeing the redemption in "purely objective, political or forensic terms."[30]

> As a result our hearts should be set on fire by such a gift of divine grace, and true love should not hold back from suffering anything....Therefore our redemption through the suffering of Christ is that deeper love within us which not only frees us from slavery to sin, but also secures for us the true liberty of the children of God, in order that we may do all things out of love rather than out of fear-love for him who has shown us such grace that no greater can be found.[31]

Indeed Abelard's treatment of grace and redemption, which is found primarily on his *Commentary of Paul's Epistle to the Romans*, concentrates on the suffering Christ, in the flesh, and the willingness of the Incarnation to partake fully in His humanity.[32]

---

[28] See 'Atonement' in *The Oxford Dictionary of the Christian Church* F. L. Cross and E. A. Livingstone, eds. (Oxford: Oxford University Press, 1997), 122-124.
[29] David Hogg, 'Anselm' in *The Dictionary of Historical Theology* Trevor Hart, ed. (Grand Rapids: Eerdmans, 2000), 18.
[30] Marcia Colish, *Medieval Foundations of the Western Intellectual Tradition: 400-1400* (New Haven and London: Yale University Press, 1997), 279.
[31] Peter Abelard, "Commentary on the Letter of Paul to the Romans*,*" in *The Christian Theology Reader* Alister McGrath, ed. (Oxford: Blackwell, 2001), 343.
[32] "Nihil quippe affligendo gravat aliquem, nisi quod contra ejus genitur voluntatem. Et in nullo quis patitur, nisi quod eus voluntati adversatur. Anima itaque Christi non tam afflictiones passionum velle quam tolerare dicenda est. Sed qui etiam Christus ipse alibi profitetur non se venisse voluntatem suam facere, sed voluntatem Patris. Unde et pro magni it merito et virtute reputandem est, cum amoris quis Dei suae penitus abrenuntiat voluntati, imo et, ut ipse alibi Christus ait, adhuc et animam suam oderit. Quodam itaque modo mors ipsa humanitati Christi dominata est, quando eam videlicet prae augustia sua reformidabat, et transire

Abelard's reflections on a binding reciprocation of compassion also had its impact on the conception of the city before Aristotle's *Politics* became the central text of urbanization in the West.[33] Abelard's emphasis upon intention of mind rather than the offending act in surveying the moral landscape of sin, galvanized a paradigm of thought based upon individual circumspection of conscience.[34] The harmony of interrelationships in the City depending upon this and then the fraternal *caritas* exemplified in the Gospels and the Acts of the Apostles made Abelard ahead of his time and a bit of a utopian. But this thinking was idealized as was Jerusalem before the Christian conquest, and reflective of a philosophical yearning to modify behavior within a personal moral compass that would, in practice, be a reflection of the Divine Love of Christ on the Cross.[35]

Abelard's concentration on a personal and physical response to suffering mirrored closely the views of one whom would later become his nemesis and who was at once the Papacy's most eloquent preacher of the Crusades: The afore-mentioned Bernard of Clairvaux. These forceful yet inimical personalities, who debated niceties of doctrine before the Fall of Jerusalem, seemed to have agreed surreptitiously on one thing only: a new conception of Christ as a kindler of compassion for the human condition, and as active participant within it.[36]

---

potius quam venire volebat, quasi nolens sustinuit propter injunctum sisbi a Patre obedientiam. " From Peter Abelard, "Expositio in Epistolam Pauli ad Romanos, l. II, c. VI l," *PL. 178* (Paris: Migne, 1864), 876.

For a full treatment of the Humanity of Christ in Abelard see Richard Weingart, *The Logic of Divine Love: A Critical Analysis of the Soteriology of Peter Abailard* (Oxford: Clarendon Press, 1970), 104-109.

[33]" Abelard brings together the classical and Judaeo-Christian elements and, in basing his concept of civitas on charity and fraternity, effectively, if implicitly repairs the Augustinian rupture between city and state. " Page 47 in David Luscombe, "City and Politics before the Coming of the Politics: Some Illustrations," in *Church and City 1000 – 1500: Essays in Honour of Christopher Brooke*, Abulafia, Franklin, and Rubin, eds. (Cambridge: Cambridge University Press, 1992), 41-55.

[34] See Thomas Gilbey, "Abelard, Peter" in *The Encyclopedia of Philosophy: Vol. I* Paul Edwards, ed. (New York: Macmillan, 1967), 3-6.

[35] ". . the most frequently cited example. . (in the discovery of the individual in the twelfth century). . Abelard . . (whose). . ethics locates the ethical value of an act in the actor's intention not in the outward deed. " Caroline Walker Bynum, "Did the Twelfth Century Discover the Individual?" In the *Journal of Ecclesiastical History* 31, no. 1 (1980): 1-17.

[36] "Abelard and Bernard, unlike Anselm a few decades earlier, no longer see the essential reason for the Incarnation and Christ's Passion in the offended majesty of God which demands satisfaction, but in the love of God which gives itself freely to

This brief excursus into the theology of atonement as it was being rendered concurrently at the time of the Crusades serves to present a real shift in emphasis in the nature of God's relationship to Man. It would only be logical that actual exposure to the site of salvation would incur a deeper bond between the European and his God.

Even the places of Christian worship became stages of re-enactment with an image of Christ available. This was nothing new in Europe, but the effect in the Lord's tomb must have been overwhelming. A Christian from the Slavic East describes his pilgrimage to the Church of the Holy Sepulcher:

> And the Lord's tomb is like a little cave cut into the rock, with small doors so that men can enter stooping on their knees for it is low and round....And as you enter the cave by the small door, on the right hand there is a kind of shelf cut into the rock of the cave and on this shelf lay the body of our Lord Jesus Christ. This sacred shelf is now covered with slabs of marble... This holy cave is faced with beautiful marble like a pulpit and there are 12 pillars around it also of beautiful marble. And above the cave is a beautiful chamber on pillars, round at the top and covered with gilded silver cups. And on top of this chamber stands Christ made in silver and larger than a man, and this was made by the Franks.[37]

The witness to the imaging of Christ in Jerusalem itself while new social ideals were beginning to take root in the Holy Land becomes a reference of particular poignancy: Christ was present where he had been present. Places of pilgrimage not only became populated by the wayfarers of Europe but by the reflection of the Incarnation itself, and the insistence on this carnal aspect of the historical Jesus. The image of Christ, the icon, must have had a different effect within Jerusalem than in Autun, or Paris, or Rome, and indeed the True Image which later was transferred to Rome from Jerusalem, was thought to had a particular efficacy above and beyond the thousand of "copies" that existed in other churches.[38]

---

humankind. The experience of this divine love fires the human heart to a reciprocal love." Berndt Hamm, *The Reformation of Faith in the Context of Late Medieval Theology and Piety,* Robert J. Bast, ed. (Boston: Brill, 2004), 133.

[37] Abbot Daniel of Chernigov (c. 1107), quoted in Jaroslav Folda, "Jerusalem and the Holy Sepulchre in the Eyes of Crusader Pilgrims," in *The Real and Ideal Jerusalem: Jewish, Christian, and Islamic Art: Studies in Honor of Bezalel Narkiss,* Bianca Kuhnel, ed. (Jerusalem: Journal of the Center for Jewish Art, 1998), 158-164, esp. 159.

[38] See Gerhard Wolf, "Laetere Filia Sion. Ecce Ego Venio et Habitado in Medio Tui: Images of Christ Transferred from Rome to Jerusalem" in *The Real and Ideal*

Pilgrimages to the Holy Land would later become like an attraction at a modern theme park, and the masters of ceremonies would be the Franciscans. The *ordo peregrinationis* was pure theater; a ritualized excursion through the principal sites of Jerusalem with a friar present at all times to underline the efficacy of a certain place, or to give anecdotal evidence on the history of another.[39] Jerusalem, after becoming a tactile reality had been ordered and the landmarks were set up to remind the Christian that the pilgrimage was the nature of it's rubric, an attempt at *renovatio* for the body and the mind.

The attempts at fabricating a pilgrimage based upon a decisively idealized conception of Jerusalem reinforced the absolute necessity of maintaining ties to this Holiest of Holies. The well-being of Europe depended upon a stabilized and peaceful state in the East, and as this was so, the pilgrim's self conception was tied to the Land. The pervasiveness of this penetrated society in Europe with a concentration of thought bordering on obsession.[40]

Such an obsession was evident in the reaction of the liturgy to the defeat at Hattin. Europe responded by recycling prayers and psalms of mourning, reserved for critical times, to lament and pray for the Crusader dead.[41] Indeed Masses for the Dead became ubiquitous as news of the disaster became more well known, which prompted the Cistercians to say these Masses daily throughout their communities after 1190. The tendency to see the Crusaders as heirs to Vespasian and Titus, Jerusalem's Roman conquerors, gave way to seeing them as culpable for their losses.

Liturgy, began using the texts of lament that described the Old Testament Jews after 1187, a people unworthy to settle in God's Holy

---

Jerusalem: Jewish, Christian, and Islamic Art: Studies in Honor of Bezalel Narkiss, 419-429.

[39] "Visiting the Holy Places was not left to individual whim and was by no means a random, free exploration. " In Nicole Chareyron, *Pilgrims to Jerusalem in the Middle Ages.* Translated by Donald Wilson (New York: Columbia University Press, 2005), 84-86.

[40] "The conviction that the Christian lands in Syria and Palestine were of the utmost importance to Europeans and that their loss was a sure sign of God's manifest displeasure pervaded nearly all levels of thought in the period 1198-1229. Visionaries, lawyers, calculating and idealistic rulers. . and popes expressed again and again the view that only by regaining the Vision of Peace-the allegorical meaning of Jerusalem-could Christian society be certain of divine favor. " From Edward Peters' introduction to *Christian Society and the Crusades 1198-1229,* xi.

[41] I owe the following insights to Amnon Linder, "The Loss of Christian Jerusalem in Late Medieval Liturgy," in *The Real and Ideal Jerusalem: Jewish, Christian, and Islamic Art: Studies in Honor of Bezalel Narkiss,* 165-172.

Place of Peace.[42] Innocent III himself composed a prayer to remedy the catastrophe that befell the mind and body and spirit of the Christians after the loss of Jerusalem:

> O God, who disposes all with admirable providence, we supplicate and pray you who extricate from the hands of the enemies of the Cross the land that your only begotten Son consecrated with its own blood, and restore it o the Christian cult (cultui Christiano), thus guiding mercifully the vows of the faithful-longing for its liberation-to the way of eternal salvation.[43]

Innocent calls on God who seems devoid of Trinitarian qualities, as the pope distinguishes the spilling of the Son's blood (and the sacrificial aspect of the Incarnation) from the providence of a removed Deity. For the most powerful pope in history, this was a new note of resignation, accepting a will of a juridical God over the strength of men to release Jerusalem and deliver it into the hands of the faithful. Innocent would later do all he could to make sure that the faithful were one.

Perhaps the greatest historian of the Crusades in the English-speaking world opened his third volume with the memorable phrase, "Bad news travels fast,"[44] in describing the loss of Jerusalem and the Horns of Hattin. But the news was incomplete, as the transference of the psychological gains had not yet occurred. The modes of identity tethered to the Incarnation would flourish on the European mainland when attached to a new rendering of the idea in the Eucharist. To underline this, by 1215, almost thirty years after the initial catastrophe at Hattin, Innocent III made auricular confession a necessity before communion. In the same document at the Fourth Lateran Council, the call to Crusade was renewed and the Holy Land evoked. The same document concluded the debate over Eucharistic properties and substance by making the ancient idea of transubstantiation an article of faith. All this, beginning with the profound pathology of contrition was tied, however obliquely, with the capitulation of the City of Peace to Saladin.

---

[42] "New practices evolved early on, and as early as 1188, new texts were composed somewhat later, yet not later than the first two decades after the Fall of Jerusalem. This new creativity is significant. It suggests that the generation of 1187 found traditional liturgy to be not entirely satisfactory, and that it demanded new practices as well as new texts through which it could express its attitudes towards Jerusalem and the Holy Land," Linder, "The Loss of Christian Jerusalem in Late Medieval Liturgy," 167.
[43] Quoted in Linder, 169.
[44] Steven Runciman, *A History of the Crusades: Volume III. The Kingdom of Acre* (Cambridge: Cambridge University Press, 1954), 3.

But these were all in the future. What exposure to the Holy Land did was prepare the psyche of Medieval Man to consider himself worthy. The Christ of History was now to be considered *in situ* rather than as an abstraction and thus, tantalizingly close to the experience of the Crusader. The fabled Jerusalem of their collective imagination had been met, and engendered within them a sense of the boundless within its walls. A veritable paradise on Earth, Jerusalem was responsible for the quickening of a longed for refinement within the fire of experience. And its capitulation after almost a century of rule was crucial to a nascent idea: Medieval identity began as the reality of a Christian Jerusalem was lost to history. Christ Himself was now, psychologically to the retreating Franks, among the exiled. The slings and arrows of fortune had seen defeat in the Holy Land transform into a metaphoric dispensation of a radical new grace, as wonderful as it was unexpected. Christ was bound for the European mainland and would settle into the collective psychology of Western Christianity with the full force of Presence. From that moment on, Christ would be among them.[45]

---

[45] "In connection with the question of individuality, it is very important to stress the following: People find themselves in a situation in which their life stories are interwoven with the universal historical process, which they experience in a symbolic way as the history of human salvation. Through the mediation of the Church and the liturgy the individual becomes aware of his or her own personal involvement of that history...at that point...the overlapping of the 'small' and 'great' eschatologies becomes possible, even inevitable...this overlapping accentuates the importance of the individual in the current historical time." In Aaron Gurevich, *The Origins of European Individualism* Katherine Judelson, trans. (Oxford: Blackwell, 1995), 109.

Chapter Two

Europe in the Presence of Christ

"...so the Word became flesh and dwelling among us. We know that He is also the means whereby the soul is united with God in ecstasy during this life, and the theologian can very readily show that He is the means of eternal beatification..... . To have chosen once and for all such a center of reference and never to admit any other center-this cannot fail to have a profound influence not only upon the general economy of such a doctrine, but also on its smallest details; to forget this central fact is to lose comprehension of the whole system."[1]

    The central contemporary in the mediation of Christ with his people of the new European world into which he had been metaphorically placed, would of course be Francis of Assisi; but the orthodox hierarchy contained within it another figure who shared with the friar the abnegation of the wide world in the service of Christ. Whereas Francis wanted to change the world for Christianity by changing men into Christ, Innocent III (lawyer that he was) wanted to change men into Christians by changing Christendom.

    The presence of Christ is a phrase most commonly associated with the Eucharist in liturgical practices of the Latin Church. In the Early Church and in the later Patristic period there had been a remarkable unanimity in belief of the Real Presence based upon Scriptural precedent[2] and long tradition. By the time of the Crusades and the apogee of papal power under Innocent III, there had been some major intellectual challenges to the doctrine.[3] The settling played a major role in the life of the European

---

[1] Etienne Gilson, *A Gilson Reader: Selections from the Writings of Etienne Gilson*, Anton C. Pegis, ed. (New York: Hanover House, 1957), 107-108.
[2] Specifically John 6, 35-60 and I Corinthians 11, 23-29.
[3] Dating approximately from the mid-ninth century with the opening salvos between Florus of Lyons and Amalrius of Metz. Proceeding to the contentions of Paschasius Radbertus concerning Matthew 26 (*De Corpore et Sanguine Domini; Commentarium in Matth. 26; Epistula ad Frudegardum*) and the debate enjoined with *De Corpore et Sanguine Domini adversus Ratpertum* of Rabanus Maurus (c.

until the coming of modernity. It is the cultural ramifications of the doctrine, when coupled with other rising trends of the times, both social and cultural, that affected Medieval ideas of personality and place by inferring that Christ himself could be, indeed was, present among them.

How could this be, even metaphorically? It can be said that there was an exchange of vagabonds with the returning Crusaders. Jerusalem lost was lost by those marginalized by the societal infrastructures that had abandoned them to find their own way.[4] Such people were amenable to a creative solution to their displacement. The times were becoming theologically sympathetic with such subtle modifications in the psyche, and intellectuals, although outside the common milieu were not estranged from the hopes and desires of the meanest of the people. The bridge of intermediation between the ideas of theology and practical philosophy with the people was much greater than previously supposed.[5] This is not to say that complex ideas without modification were understood; but they

---

856), and it's anti Radbertian recapitulation with Ratramnus of Corbie. The intransigence of Peter Damian reaffirmed the centrality of the Real Presence in 1072 until the arrival of Berengar of Tours who began to countenance (in his *De Sacra Coena adversus Lanfrancum* of 1070) the orthodox arguments of the decretalist Lanfranc of Pavia who struck back (*Libellus de Sacramento Corporis et Sanguinis Christi contra Berengarium*). Berengar was later condemned as a heretic, (1078) although he believed in the Real Presence but denied the need to explain it away by any substantial reference to the material of the Host. The debate between Lanfranc and Berengar can be said to be the last stage of real development on the Eucharistic definition before the solidification of the doctrine by the Fourth Lateran Council. See the still indispensable Darwell Stone, *A History of the Doctrine of the Holy Eucharist* (London: Longmans, Green, and Co., 1909), 242-313; Frank Senn, *Christian Liturgy: Catholic and Evangelical* (Minneapolis: Fortress Press), 1997, 241-256; J.F. McCue, "The Doctrine of Transubstantiation from Berengar through Trent: The Point at Issue," in the *Harvard Theological Review* 61 (1968) 385-430.

[4] See Adriaan H. Bredero, *Christendom and Christianity in the Middle Ages: The Relations between Religion, Church, and Society*, translated by Reinder Bruinsma (Grand Rapids: William B. Eerdmans, 1994) , 80-90, especially " Jerusalem was regarded as the fitting destination for people with serious and insoluble problems," 88.

[5] "Sans doute serial – il anachronique de concevoir cette notion d'utilite sociale.... sous les especes de debouches professionnels précis, mais il est sur qu'on considerait alors que les connaissances maitrisees par les gens des savoir manaient tout naturellment al 'exercise de tache socialment legitimes d'autant mieux remplies que celui qui s'en acquittait possedait une meilleure competence intellectuelle. " Jacques Verger, *Les Gens de Savoir en Europe a la fin du Moyen Age* (Paris: Presse Universitaires de France, 1997), 38-40.

were indeed adumbrated almost immediately to ply their wares in the cultural marketplace of the thirteenth century.

The decision to go to Jerusalem required a change, a transformation required of the Crusader outside, at first, from the orthodoxy. The companies of knights would have formed, and did, societies that would ask for permission and benediction after the fact. In Italy, this was becoming more and more prevalent within the interactions between civic societies and ecclesiastical interests. After Hattin, Innocent himself became desperate to form consensus among the volatile and growing sub-societies growing up in the new Italian apostolic age and it's parallel of rising mercantilism.[6]

This nebulous relationship between the impulses of a rising middle class and previously rigid, feudal establishments, coupled with the return of a disenfranchised military minority began to have a grass roots effect that would result in what would become the primary avenue through which the Incarnational Age would move.[7] Innocent would be the legal mind of the presumptions of the Incarnational Age as much as Francis was its heart. The mind though spoke legally, and wound up being the first inadvertent Judas wearing the robes of the lawyer that would betray the sincerity of the movement: The first, but not the last, to mistake metaphor for message. Nonetheless by the end of Innocent's efforts and Francis' acts, Christ could be felt among men.

Innocent III, by the time of the Fourth Lateran Council did not exactly seek to differentiate between particulars in men, excepting in matters of their faith. Men and their personalities were not of interest to the totality of the faith. He was not interested in the neuroses of the individual, only their possibilities of faith through the collectivity of mutual love.[8] This

---

[6] See Brenda Bolton, "'Serpent in the Dust, Sparrow on the Housetop:' Attitudes to Jerusalem and the Holy Land in the Circle of Innocent III," in *The Holy Land, Holy Lands, and Christian History* R.N. Swanson, ed (Oxford: Boydell Press, 2000), 154-179. See also *Patrologia Latina* 207, 533.

[7] See Bredero, p. 99; and Peter D. Diehl, "Overcoming reluctance to prosecute heresy in thirteenth century Italy", in *Christendom and its Discontents: Exclusion, persecution, and rebellion, 100-1500,* Scott L. Waugh and Peter Diehl, eds. (Cambridge: Cambridge University Press, 1996, 47-66; and Robert Brentano's *Two Churches: England and Italy in the Thirteenth Century* (Berkeley: University of California Press, 1968), 340-352.

[8] See Arno Borst, *Medieval Worlds: Barbarians, Heretics, and Artists* (Chicago: University of Chicago Press, 1992), 58-59: "As Innocent disapprovingly quoted at the Lateran Council of 1215, the idea that their unity was merely collective and ostensible 'as we might call many men a nation or many faithful a church' did not apply to divine personae. Agroup of mortals certainly does not form one and the

could only be done by centering their attention away from themselves and towards Christ; as understood by the Church. But it must not be assumed that this was a totality of influence stemming from revenue as the later papacies of the late-fifteenth and early sixteenth could be said to have been. Even though this was an element, none could doubt that an effort at true ecumenicism was made when the Council was called.[9] Innocent's convocation was, if appearing megalomaniacal, nevertheless a sincere attempt to bring together the Christian faith under one tent.

The life and achievement of Lotario dei Segni, the future Innocent III are a rich haul better investigated in more complete terms.[10] For the purposes of the Incarnational Age we can better telescope his considerable achievements by recognizing a few consequences of his Herculean labors in attempting to pacify the Western world contained as they are in that seminal moment, the Fourth Lateran Council. In time, the results of Innocent's clarification of the Eucharistic Doctrine gave rise, in the middle of the thirteenth century, to the feast of Corpus Christi, which by itself, can seen to be a Latin acceptance on every sociological level of the Incarnational ideal.[11] The Mass of the thirteenth century represented the common site of universal bonding in the West, and the Christ as Presence was at the center of this worship.[12]

---

same thing, the same for each member; their unity comes from common faith or mutual love. Like the doctrine of the Trinity, the doctrine of transubstantiation, formulated at the same Council, insisted on strict differentiation between the *una persona* Christ and the *mysterium unitatis* of his church, between the true and mystical body as Innocent taught."

[9] See the introduction to the Fourth Lateran Council in *Decrees of the Ecumenical Councils Vol. I (Nicaea I-Lateran V)* Tanner and Alberigo. eds. (London and Washington: Sheed and Ward and Georgetown University Press, 1990), 228.

[10] See the bibliography at the end of Innocent's article in *The Oxford Dictionary of the Christian Church,* 834.

[11] Pope Urban IV commanded, in the 1264 bull of *Transiturus,* the worship of the consecrated host. The institution of the feast was compelled by the efforts of the Blessed Juliana during the early parts of the century. See "Corpus Christi, Feast of" in *The Oxford Dictionary of the Christian Church*, 420.

[12] "I have taken this to be a fact that the mass as a social institution during the later Middle Ages: that as a sacrifice it tended, like the original sacrifices of Cain and Abel, to represent its social universe as a concatenation of distinct parts while as a sacrament it represented and embodied unity and wholeness." In John Bossy, "The Mass as a Social Institution 1200-1700" in Past and Present 100 (1983), 29-61, 34-35.

With regards to the doctrine of transubstantiation the scholars save one, are unanimous in affirming the centrality of Lateran IV. Gary Macy argues that as far as philosophical speculation the doctrine was not exquisitely defined and led to

Innocent himself, although a man of the world, was cynical about its joys. Unlike Francis, Innocent saw the salvation through the Presence as a practical mystery, necessary to bring the wayward states of Christendom into an agreeable position on the soteriological act. It is of note that his two major pre-conciliar writings focus on the inefficacy of unaided humanity to reach salvation. This would seem like a natural expression of the Middle Ages, but the cynicism of *De Miseria Humanae Conditionis* and *De Contemptu Mundi* almost abrogates any participation with the world in the harshest of terms.

For both these reveal man not so much sinned against as sinning, a product of bile and dirt fit for worms and the grave.[13] They are sad, indeed lugubrious texts written by a Prometheus of the faith,[14] chained to the rock of the necessary bewailing his fate to a fetid world. They serve to illustrate that Innocent had no delusions about the realities of earthly existence, but also that such a world was the arena wherein the savior he truly believed in acted out his presumptions. Being a man of flesh and blood of his time, Innocent would accept the position of Pontiff by bringing his incredible talents to bear on the very real problem of how to save what he could only suppose was a forsaken race. He was a man of laws, and the law needed to be spoken through the brazen voice of Mother Church. It was the only hope of salvation.

The Fourth Lateran Council was as much an expression for the desire of solidarity as it was a clarification of doctrine. It is evident that Innocent saw it as a culminating point in his papacy, coming where it did, and presaging a fulfillment of sorts. In his opening address of the Council, the world-weary magistrate speaks to the gathered prelates in the words of Christ to his apostles before the consummation of the Passover Cedar.[15] This became curious, as his death followed hard after the calling of the Council. His yearning for the unity of the Christian world though, allowed for precious little debate, as within the constitutions of the Council he not only condemned heresy but the obstinancy of the Greek Church who had not sent full representation.[16]

---

many disputes among the scholastics concerning interpretation. See Gary Macy, "The Dogma of Transubstantiation in the Middle Ages" in *The Journal of Ecclesiastical History* 45, no. 1 (January 1994) 11-41.

[13] See Innocent III *De Contemptu Mundi* translated into Italian by Guido Battelli (Firenze: La Voce, 1924).
[14] Battelli, *De Contemptu Mundi*, 10.
[15] Luke 22:15. See Colin Morris, *The Papal Monarchy*, 447.
[16] See *Decrees of the Ecumenical Councils Vol. I (Nicaea I-Lateran V)*, 228.

There was no doubt that the doctrine to be expounded would follow a line of reasoning long adumbrated by the writings of Innocent himself, as mentioned, in the *De Sacro Altaris Mysterio*. This work gives an antecedent to the thinking that went behind the understanding of the Real Presence, and in a work meant as a personal reflection on the Eucharist.

> When Christ was ascending to the Father, because he promised his apostles and their followers to be with them until the ending of the world, he wished to stay not only by the grace of divinity, but by a real corporal presence. This is why he instituted this sacrament, wherein he is present with us here in another form, but within his true substance.[17]

It is evident that Innocent's concerns with the vicarage of the papacy was directly tied to his belief in the Eucharist, and his understanding of the Eucharist allowed no other interpretation than the transubstantiative.[18] As well as being a personal belief, the latter conciliar promulgation of the Real Presence of Christ was part of a multi-pronged attack to affirm an orthodox understanding based upon a rising trend of heterodoxy and fragmentation. As the Albigensians were becoming a threat and the Joachamites increasing frenzy for apocalyptic predilections were causing dissent even in the newly formed (and highly trusted) Franciscan Order, Innocent had to at once codify worship, accept differentiation in the Apostolic vocation, and anathematize dissent without alienating those sincere enough to be swayed by competitive doctrine.

Immediately in the first article of the Council's Constitutions (*De fide catholica*) Innocent leaves no room for doubt about the Presence of Christ in the Church and in the Sacrament:

> There is indeed one universal church of the faithful, outside of which nobody at all is saved, in which Jesus Christ is both priest and sacrifice. His body and blood are truly contained in the sacrament of the altar under the forms of bread and wine, the bread and wine having been changed in

---

[17] "Ascensus ergo Christus ad Patrem quia promisit apostolis eorumque sequacibus vobiscum ero cunctis diebus usque ad consumationem saeculi (Matt. 28) voluit remanere cum illis non solum per inhabitandem gratiam , nec per divinam tantum essentiam, verum etiam per corporalem praesentiam. Et ideo istud sacramentum instituit in quo praesens est nobiscum, sub alia quidem forma sed in propria vere substantia." "XLIV: De diversis causis institutionis"in *De Sacro Altaris Mysterio* Stanislao Fioramonti, ed (Citta del Vaticano: Libreria Editrice Vaticana, 2002), 336.

[18] See Giuseppe Barbaro, *La Dottrina Eucaristica negli scritti di Papa Inncenzo III* (Roma: Edizioni Paoline, 1953).

substance, by God's power, into his body and blood, so that in order to achieve this mystery of unity we receive from God what he received from us.[19]

This was a direct challenge to the Cathars, who saw such carnal necessities as ludicrous, as Christ (in their understanding) had no corporal presence, the Incarnation being the spiritual aid of Christ as a sort of angelic messenger sent from the Good God into the world of material evil. This being so, every heterodoxy was to be countenanced with ferocity even to the point of taking up a Crusade against them. The heterodox may revel in differentiation, but Innocent demonizes them by obliterating individuality in their sectarianism and wiping away their human identity by both metaphor and law:

> We condemn all heretics, whatever names they may go under. They have different faces indeed but their tails are tied together inasmuch as they are alike in their pride.... Catholics who take the cross and gird themselves up for the expulsion of heretics, shall enjoy the same indulgence, and be strengthened by the same holy privilege, as is granted to those who go to the aid of the Holy Land....He (the heretic) shall be intestable, that is he shall not have the freedom to make a will nor shall he succeed to an inheritance...Clerics should not, of course, give the sacraments of the church to such pestilent people nor give them a Christian burial nor accept alms or offerings from them.[20]

These were real legalistic ramifications especially for the moneyed classes, whose support Innocent would need in his dealings with the

---

[19] "Una vero est fidelium universalis eccelesia, extra quam nullus omnino salvatur, in qua idem ipse sacerdoset sacrificium Iesum Christus cuius corpus et sanguis in sacramento altaris sub speciebus panis et vini veraciter continentur, transsubstantiatis pane in corpus et vino in sanguinem potestate divina, ut ad perficiendum mysterium unitatis accipiamus ipse de suo, quod accepit ipse de nostro." *Decrees of the Ecumenical Councils Vol. I (Nicaea I-Lateran V)*, 230.

[20] "condemnantes universos haereticos quibuscumquenominibus censeantur, facies quidem habentes diversas, sed caudas adinvicem colligates, quia de vanitateconveniunt in idipsum....Catholici vero qui, cruces assumpto charactere, ad haereticorum exterminium se accinxerint, illa gaudeant indulgentia, illoque sancto privilegio sint muniti, quod accedentibus in Terrae sanctae subsidium conceditur...sit etiam intestabilis, ut nec testandi liberam habeat facultatem nec ad hereditatis successionem accedat....Sane clerici non exhibeant huiusmodi pestilentibus ecclesiastica sacramenta nec eos christianae praesumant sepulturae traderae, nec eleemosynas aut oblations eorum accipiant." "3.De haereticis" from the Fourth Lateran Council in *Decrees of the Ecumenical Councils*, 233-234.

contenders to the thrones of petty nobilities and the debate over the Emperor's seat. The success of this plan came after Innocent's death when his erstwhile charge, Frederick II recaptured Jerusalem for Christendom. It was Frederick, ironically, who led the fight against the dwindling heresies on the Italian peninsula, along with Gregory IX, yet more for his own benefit than that of a Church.[21] Although the relations between the Empire and the Church remained strained during the reign of Frederick II, Jerusalem had lost none of its importance. By this time the metaphoric importance of Incarnation had begun to take hold of the popular imagination. Frederick's triumph, and triumph it was, was both radical and anticlimactic.[22] The doctrine of the Real Presence had brought Christ into Christendom.

This doctrine had always been popular with the intelligentsia as a forum for debate in the universities. The theological debate over Eucharistic Presence had been going on since the ninth century and continues outside the jurisdictions of the Catholic Church today. The common people, largely left out of the scholastic cogitations, were helped along in accepting the startling doctrine by the Franciscans (of course) who tied the philosophy of the debate to an emotionalism absent in either Duns Scotus or Thomas Aquinas, the leading philosophers in the ongoing scholastic debates.[23]

The commoner, in turn, took heartily to the hyper-sensualism of the decree that God was among them in the Eucharist.[24] This in turn became a great repository of power within the clergy. As Innocent had insisted upon penitential rites before the taking of communion, the sacerdotalism of the West was given a great surge of influence. The popular understanding of the sacrament now drew closer and closer to a simplified understanding of real doctrine.

---

[21] See Peter Diehl, "Overcoming reluctance to prosecute heresy in thirteenth century Italy," in *Christendom and its Discontents: Exclusion, persecution, and rebellion, 1000-1500* S. Waugh and P. Diehl, eds. (Cambridge: Cambridge University Press, 1996), 47-66, 61;
[22] See Bjorn Weiler, "Gregory IX, Frederick II and the Liberation of the Holy Land" in *The Holy Land, Holy Lands, and Christian History* R.N. Swanson, ed. (Oxford: Boydell Press, 2000), 192-206.
[23] See David Burr, "Eucharistic Presence and Conversion in Late Thirteenth Century Franciscan Thought" Transactions of the American Philosophical Society (74) 3: Philadelphia, 1984; Richard Cross, *The Metaphysics of the Incarnation: Thomas Aquinas to Duns Scotus* (Oxford: Oxford University Press, 2002); W.B. Monahan *St. Thomas Aquinas on the Incarnation* (London: Trinity Press, 1946).
[24] See G. J. C. Snoek, *A Medieval Piety from Relics to the Eucharist: A Process of Mutual Interaction* (Leiden: Brill, 1995).

Christ Among Them: Incarnation and Renaissance in Medieval Italian Culture

The results of this were to draw the wool from the eyes of the laity who would have access to the strong center of their faith. The frenzy of processionals which were to dot the landscape in the mid fourteenth century have for their explanation the joy that attended the superlative feast of their present God. That such a god would deign to be among them and in such a manner, spoke to the real confluence of symbol and sign that predicated all the assumptions of the Incarnational Age. The Elevation of the Host into the Real Presence and that Presence being subjected to field tests of central communal significance charged the Incarnational Age as no previous Western epoch had been into a metaphorical reclamation of temporal fulfillment.[25]

These developments occurred outside true official sanctification of adoration; it was, by all means, a popular tradition rooted in the conviction of the truth of Christ's Presence.[26] Another consequence was that although the rites accompanying the partaking of the bread evolved from strict hierarchical codes forged to add to the mystery, the laity took it upon themselves to redouble the mystery by curbing their acceptance of the host, as the ingestion of the God must have played an enormous psychological role in the beginnings of the Incarnational Age.[27]

This reaction was arguably connected to the required practice of Penance preceding communion. Coupled with the ingestion of Christ, the free excursus on the self that comes from a sincere act of contrition fortified the confidence of Incarnational man in facing both Christ and his

---

[25] The preceding paragraph and a large portion of the thinking of this chapter is indebted to the work of Caroline Walker Bynum and Miri Rubin. Especially for this chapter (and the afore-mentioned paragraph) see Miri Rubin, *Corpus Christi: The Eucharist in Late Medieval Culture* (Cambridge: Cambridge University Press, 1991), 358-361, and her "Religious Culture in Town and Country" in *Church and City 1000-15000: Essays in Honour of Christopher Brooke* Abulafia, Franklin, and Rubin, eds. (Cambridge: Cambridge University Press, 1992), 3-22.

[26] See Josef Jungmann, *The Place of Christ in Liturgical Prayer* A. Peeler, trans. (Collegeville: The Liturgical Press, 1989), 262.

[27] See Rosalind and Christopher Brooke, *Popular Religion in the Middle Ages, Western Europe 1000-1300* (London: Thames and Hudson, 1984), 116-118. Also *Medieval Popular Religion 1000-1500 A Reader* John Shinners, ed. (Toronto: Broadview Press, 1997), 89: "As the theology of the Eucharist evolved…the emphasis on Christ's real presence in this sacrament had profound consequences for liturgical practices and popular belief…Perhaps most important for popular religion, lay people stopped receiving communion regularly for since Christ was really present in the host, receiving it became an event ot awesome importance, not to be trivialized by routine reception." See further Eric Palazzo, *Liturgie et societe au Moyen Age* (Paris: Auber, 2000), 39.

fellow. This introspection entered the dialogue of every Christian, not just the clergy, who had been privy to the notions of interior sight for some time.[28] Innocent was radical in his willingness to try to channel the fervor of personal spirituality into a common orthodoxy, making penitential books for confessors mandatory.[29] The mechanics of absolution remained constant, as these were laid out, but the extraordinary privilege of self-analysis only added to the notion that men themselves were worthy enough to be in the company of Christ even with the acquired knowledge of being all too human.[30] This, along with concomitant developments in liturgy, literature, and art among the educated classes began to fashion what would flourish in the Italian *quattrocento*; the interior man.[31]

Contrary to popular opinion, the requirements of Medieval society looked favorably upon being in the skin as the just or unjust were known

---

[28] Colin Morris, *The Discovery of the Individual 1050-1200* (Toronto: Toronto University Press, 1987), 70-75. See also L. Braeckmans, *Confession et communion au moyen age et au concile de Trente* (Gembloux: Duculot, 1971), 22.

[29] D.L. D'Avray, "The Transformation of the Medieval Sermon." Diss. Bailliol, Oxford, 1976, 7-10. See also Brenda Bolton, "Innocent III" in *Popular Belief and Practice* G.J. Cuming and D. Baker, eds. (Cambridge: Cambridge University Press, 1972), 73-82.

[30] "(Troeltsch posited)...that the individual soul receives eternal value from its filial relationship to God, in which the relationship is also grounded in the human fellowship. Christians meet in Christ, whose members they are. This tremendous affirmation takes place on a level that transcends the world of man and of social institutions, although these are from God. The infinite worth of the individual is at the same time a disparagement, the negation in terms of value of the world as it is; a dualism is posited, a tension is established that is constitutive of Christianity and will endure throughout history...Sociologically speaking, the emancipation of the individual through a personal transcendence, and the union of outworldly individuals in a community that treads on earth but has its heart in heaven, may constitute a passable formula for Christianity." In Louis Dumont, "The Christian Beginnings of Modern Individualism" in *The Category of the Person: Anthropology, Philosophy, History* M. Carrithers, S. Collins, S. Lukes, eds. (Cambridge: Cambridge University Press, 1985), 93-122, 98-99.

[31] "Medieval strategies for gaining knowledge of the interior world grew apace during the late Middle Ages: scholastic psychology, introspective devices in chivalric literature, metaphysical poetry, and the all the rest contributed. During the early *quattrocento*, the pull of the public world was so intense, and humanists so anxious to proffer support to the beleaguered ego, that a gulf between the cultivated civic person and the deepest recesses of interiority developed." Marvin Becker, "An Essay on the Quest for Identity in the Early Italian Renaissance" in *Florilegium Historiale: Essays Presented to Wallace Ferguson* J.G. Rowe and W.H. Stockdale, eds. (Toronto: University of Toronto Press, 1971), 295-312, 307.

as organic entities within the larger state, and expected to conform but within the parameters of their own bodies.[32] The body itself as a locus of the salvation process was a central concern to the Medieval mind, and eradicating stain from the soul devolved upon the possibilities of corporal resurrection.[33] Even corpses were attendant to the longings expressed by Innocent and evident in the Crusades, as the dead were all shod for the pilgrimage to Jerusalem.[34] The circle of existence did indeed imply a speculum of peregrinations based upon Christ and his life and promise.

This would become a salutary but threatening experience, as the relative post-penitential comfort with which the living saw them extended to the care of the dead. Little by little the encroachments of a purely secular character began to crowd the sacred spaces of burial in the churches of Europe. Soon recumbent figures graced the walls of Christ's House.[35] His neighbors in the terrestrial prison had come home to die. The integrated man, from cradle to grave was a product of the Incarnational Age, and the thirteenth century a rapturous return to naturalism by supernaturalism, as much a popular reform as an intellectual one.[36]

---

[32] See Antony Black, "The Individual and Society," in *The Cambridge History of Medieval Political Thought* J.H. Burns, ed. (Cambridge: Cambridge University Press, 1988), 588-606; "heology emphasized both the communion of divine love and the individual's personal relation with Christ. Since it is through their very act of being what they are by faith that individuals are incorporated, they would not be the same individuals if separated from the body..There was an intrinsic connection between medieval cosmology and he organic view of society...the visible Church, being the extension in time and space of the invisible, shared all its essential features...apparent division meant that some party was schismatic." 592.

[33] See Caroline Walker Bynum, *The Resurrection of the Body in Western Christianity, 200-1336* (New York: Columbia University Press, 1995), 341; 'Yet for all its incoherence and self-contradiction, the doctrine of the resurrection has been of enormous consequence in shaping assumptions we still hold concerning personhood and survival. Much about our current Western notions of the individual has taproots in medieval discussions of the ontological significance of the body."

[34] Ibid, 212.

[35] See Andrew Martindale, "Patrons and Minders: The Intrusion of the Secular into Sacred Spaces in the Late Middle Ages," in Studies in Church History 28: The Church and the Arts Diana Wood, ed (Oxford: Blackwell, 1992), 143-178, and Karl Bauch, "Das mittelateriche Grabbild Figurliche Grabmaler," *Jahrunderts in Europa* Berlin (1976), 134-155.

[36] See Walter Ullmann, *The Individual & Society in the Middle Ages* (London: Methuen 7 Co. ltd., 1967), 104-106.

The implications of transubstantiation did not end at the debates of Paris or Oxford. It also provided fodder for the rising concern among the laity of unintended magical consequences[37] that bordered on the macabre. This was inevitable if commoners were told that the Body of Christ was being eaten in front of their very eyes. This too raised questions that were to become the provenance of the laity rather than the clergy, as the sightings of Christ were popular tales as our present-day ghost stories.[38]

The official response was to codify the liturgical practices more strenuously and provide counter-*fabulae* based upon the Real Presence, underlining the efficacy of belief in the doctrine by implying doubt about it's truth was both heretical and dangerous. The role of Caesarius of Heisterbach in his *Dialogus Miraculorum* (1219-1223) relating the dangers of doubting the orthodoxy by popular tales, and William Durandus in his *Rationale Divinorum Officiorum* (1286-1291), explaining in detail the rites of the Mass and the appropriate interpretation, could be seen to be more relevant than either Aquinas or Scotus on the mysteries of the Eucharist for popular comprehension, as the former two were responsible for providing the amenable mysteries to be told and practiced.

In the case of Durandus, the constitutions of Lateran IV and Christ himself as Eucharistic Presence, provided the skeleton upon which he hung his rules of liturgical behavior.[39] Such care in the worship as Durandus exemplified in the decorations necessary for the altar, pointed the absolute necessity for men to be both textually and visually assured of the Mass as the reconciliation between themselves (sins and all) and

---

[37] Richard Kieckhefer, *Magic in the Middle Ages* (Cambridge: Cambridge University Press, 1989), 79-80.

[38] "Eucharistic devotion would also inspire sightings of Christ which were much closer to home. These appearances were, arguably, even more challenging than the inexplicable appearances of flesh on the altar since they featured an animated and often loquacious Lord…Christendom (was not) entirely surprised when its Lord strode into the lives of a select circle." 247, in Dylan Elliott, "True Presence/ False Christ: The Antinomies of Embodiment in Medieval Spirituality," in *Mediaeval Studies* (64), 2002, 241-265.

[39] See Gulielmo Durando *Rationale Divinorum Officiorum* (Naples: Joseph Dura, 1859):"Et secundum eos dum sacramentum a mure corroditur, ipse panis substantia comeditur, sub qua corpus Christi mox esse desinit, cum corrode incipit. Innocentius III dixit in Speculo Ecclesiae, quod forma panis frangitur et atteritur, sed corpus Christi sumitur et comeditur ea quae notant corruptionem referens ad formam panis, ea vero quae notant acceptionem ad corpus Christi." from "Liber IV. Caput Quadragesimun Primum de Sexta Parte Canonis," 260.

Christ.[40] This effort was also aimed to curb the enthusiasms of allegory that the cult of the Eucharist engendered, following Innocent's aim for a unified field theory of Eucharistic celebration.[41]

All these results of the Fourth Lateran Council had another side to them. Innocent's role in the temporal affairs of his day had an unintended consequence by application as much as by claim. His language in his decretals was the language of lawyers and begged inference with Canon Law. This gave the theologians and the decretalists ample opportunity to legalize the relationship of the Papacy to the super-terrestrial where Innocent had indeed made claims for the successors of Peter.[42] Perhaps unintentionally the language of Lateran IV had the effect of separating the Papacy from the dearest concerns of Incarnationalists, setting the Vicar of Christ in the juridical chair of God in a heavenly dispensation, forsaking (in the popular mind) the liturgical relationship that was made dogma at the Council, perhaps it's greatest triumph.

This would serve a much more tangible effort in Innocent's eyes, the combating and elimination of heresy. By marshaling the resources, both legal and popular available to him at the time, Innocent overshot his house by neglecting the greatest gains that could have been made by a Christendom tethered to the notion of Christ's Presence in the world. Instead, Innocent returned to the Innocent of *de contemptu mundi*, using the majestic gains of the Council politically, to strike at the growing heresy of the Cathars in the Languedoc.

He did not live to see the ramifications of his hopes, dying shortly after the Council in 1216. Ironically, the insistent legalism of Innocent served to distance his claims of the sacramentalized Christ as the central

---

[40] "Following Innocent III, William Durandus commented; 'Before the nativity of Christ, there were barriers of enmity in the world. The first was between God and men. The second was between men and angels. The third between man and man.' In at least one nativity painting in the early fourteenth century one may see one of the angels descending toward the shepherds carrying an olive branch (Bartolo di Fredi, Siena) Durandus continued: 'God ids born man because peace has been restored between God and man; he is born in the manger of an ox and an ass because peace has been repaired between man and man.'" In John Bossy, "The Mass as a Social Institution 1200-1700," 34. See also Durandus, *Rationale Divinorum Officiorum*, 172 and Innocent III, *De Saco Altaris Mystero*, 180.

[41] See G.J.C. Snoek, *A Medieval Piety from Relics to the Eucharist: A Process of Mutual Interaction* (Leiden: E.J. Brill, 1995), 35.

[42] "Inter Deum et hominem medius constitutus, citra Deum sed ultra hominem: minor Deo, sed major homine: qui de omnibus judicat, et a nemine judicatur: Apostoli voce pronuntians 'qui me judicat, Dominus est,' (I Cor. 4). "Sermo 2: In consecratione," *PL* 217, 657-658.

concern for the Christian.[43] It would be left to genius of Francis to bring Christ to the Christian. The example of evangelical poverty and the joy of God's troubadour retained Italy for the Church in the thirteenth-century, yet as the example of the Albigensian Crusade teaches those interested in *realpolitik*, cynicism has its darker purpose.

---

[43] See Ernst Kantorowicz, *The King's Two Bodies: a Study in Mediaeval Political Theology* (Princeton: Princeton University Press, 1957), 91-93.

CHAPTER THREE

FRANCESCO: CENTER AND CIRCUMFERENCE[1]

It is not in the will of God to save his people through dialectics.
—Saint Ambrose.[2]

Perhaps the single most important influence upon the new Incarnational culture outside of Jesus Christ himself was the small man from Assisi. Francis of Assisi (1181-1226) had, by the time of his death, come to literally embody the Christian ideal. By his anxious and fervent quest to quite fully approximate the life of Christ, he was in his own inimitable way, talking up the Cross. The accident of his birth, a merchant's son and not a *villein*, also established the interesting role class would play. The newly emergent middle class of whom Francis was an offshoot had become a harbinger not only of new powers related to the rise of trade, but new moral possibilities attached to the pursuit of gain.[3]

Guilt had played a large part of Francis' conversion to the Christian life and the vociferous nature of his casting off of the clothes of the world for the bare and coarse cloth of God speaks to the rise of a self fashioning

---

[1] The bibliography on Francis is enormous. Primary sources are drawn predominantly from the *Omnibus of Sources in English, St. Francis of Assisi: Writings and Early Biographies*, (henceforward *OSE*), Marion A. Habig, ed. (Chicago: Franciscan Herald Press, 1983), which contains the lives by Thomas of Celano and Bonaventure, along with the *Little Flowers* and *The Sacrum Commercium* as well as other important texts. Another primary source, *The Chronicle of the Franciscan Salimbene* has been translated and edited by the eminent G. G. Coulton, in his *From St. Francis to Dante* (Philadelphia: University of Pennsylvania Press, 1907, reprinted 1972). In Italian, *Gli Scritti di San Francesco d'Assisi e I Fioretti*, Augusto Vicinelli, ed. (Verona: Arnoldo Mondadori, 1955).
[2] " Sed non in dialecta complacuit Deo salvum facere populum suum." *Patrologiae Latinae* 16, "De fide" I, 5, 42, 537. See also I Corinthians 4, 20.
[3] See especially Richard Trexler, *Naked Before the Father: The Renunciation of Francis of Assisi. Humana Civilitas 9* (New York: Peter Lang, 1989), 107-108.

conscience,[4] bereft finally of allegiance, true attachment, to either the highest or the lowest of classes. God was somewhere in the middle in Francis' case and even though he famously distrusted learning,[5] the majority of his earliest followers were cut from the same social class; educated, newly moneyed, and urban. The call to poverty was not new, but in the hands of Francis it became a new weapon for dissecting sin, allowing a new man, conscious of his past and forward looking, to emerge.[6] Francis' arms were not belligerent, but they proved to be spiritually shattering for renovating the call to Christ.[7]

One would naturally assume that the tenor of Franciscan achievement would be in the realm of the spiritual. Undoubtedly, the case can be made (and has, *ad infinitum*) about the unique disposition of Francis' vocation and its powerful pull on the imagination. Much also has been said about what is to follow. But to rope these achievements together under the auspices of a new paradigm of Incarnational reality and further connect it to a groundswell within the Italian consciousness is the point to be made here.

Francis as well as being the great renovator of the Christian ideal became a receptacle of the emergent hopes of a new evangelism with sensibilities bent toward subverting the hierarchical (and thus despotic nature) of codified dogma.

Indicatively, and this was the case with Francis himself, it was a sensibility critical of intelligentsia, and biblio-phobic. This distaste for a learning acquired by the sophistry of the schools in Paris, Bologna, Chartres, and Oxford was also a tenet of the Cistercian spirit. Consequently, both Francis and Bernard were devotees of an experiential

---

[4] Examples are legion, one shall suffice:
"Once, when he had met a poor man and considered his poverty, he said to his companion, 'This man's poverty brings great shame on us, and is a stern rebuke to our own. For since I have chosen holy poverty as my lady, my delight, and my spiritual and bodily treasure, I feel the greatest shame when I find someone poorer than myself. And the story has gone round the whole world that I am vowed to poverty before God and men." In "The Mirror of Perfection, I, 17," *OSE*, 1142-1143.

[5] "Those who are illiterate should not be anxious to study. They should realize instead that the only thing they ahould desire is to have the spirit of God at work within them." From "The Rule of 1223; 10," *OSE,* 63.

[6] See 916 of Gerhart Ladner, "The Life of the Mind in the Christian West Around the Year 1200" in *Images and Ideas in the Middle Ages: Selected Studies in History and Art* (Roma: Edizioni di Storia e Letteratura, 1983), 903-930.

[7] See especially Brenda Bolton, "Paupertas Christi: Old Wealth and New Poverty in the Twelfth Century" in *Renaissance and Renewal in Christian History,* 95-103.

spirituality, recognizing the import of the carnal as an objectified reality to be transfigured, not obliterated. The lesson of the Franciscan and the Cistercian Orders, at least at their inceptions, was to feel a way toward the Lord. And even later, although by now such snubbing of intellectualism were untenable in the reality of such intellectuals as Duns Scotus, Ockham, and Bonaventure himself, the emphasis was always upon the stripping of the social sense, beginning with class, which tied the new men to learning or money.

The poverty debate which will be spoken about later and at length, can be seen as the codified official response to reality emphasizing the weight of the world as the underlying cause for the levity of Franciscan (and indeed evangelical) mysticism.[8] Although this discipline seems extraordinary it was unavoidable in order to strike a median path to a terrestrial perfectibility under a Christian auspice. Francis was doing only what was necessary. [9] He was tirelessly affecting a stance toward the carnal that took the carnal into account, overcoming it by naming and objectifying the flesh. This could be done only by a radicalizing love that took firm root even in the subtler minds of the early Franciscan Order.[10]

---

[8] "Disciplinati rappresentano i segni di un disagio politico esasperato nel loro ricorrere dell'idea della frattura assoluta fra il terreno e il divino.... come inevitabile il ritorno alle origine e alla poverta. " Antonio Piromalli, "Antifeudalismo Francescano" in *San Francesco e il Francescanesimo nella letteratura Italiana dal XIII al XV secolo,* Stanislao da Campagnole e Pasquale Tuscano, eds. (Assisi: Accademia Properziano del Subiaso, 2001), 75-92, p. 82.

[9] "Cependant, autre trait commune a Francois et a Robert d'Abrissel l'un et autre, tout en demeurant intransigeants dans leur ascese personelle ont su temperer a l'usage de leurs disciples la pratique d'une pauvrete concue non comme une fin en soi nais comme un moyen de perfection et d'edification qu'auraient rendu ineeficace des exces inconsideres prejudicables a la sante du corps, respectable car envelope de l'ame et la capacite d'action. "
In Jean Marc Bienvenu, *Prehistoire du Franciscanisme: Aspects Pre-Franciscains de l'eremitisme et la Predication itinerante dans la France de L'Ouest, Fin XIe et Debut XIIes* (Paris:Vrin, 1996), 31.
See also Nguyen van Khanh-Norbert, *Le Christ dans le pensee de Saint Francois d'Assise d'apres ses ecrits* (Paris: Editions Franciscaines, 1989), 10-21 esp.

[10] "Noi veniamo qualificati essenzialmente dalle nostre scelte libere: queste formano la richezza o la poverta del nostro piu intimo spessore umano, ed e mediante la vonta libera che attingiamo la nostra felicita personale nella communione con la sorgente infinita dell'amore e della gioia.
In questa celebrazione della liberta e dell amore, dei quali sorvoliamo qui l'applicazioni e gli sviluppi strettamente teologici nel mistero del Verbo incarnato e della concezione della madre di Cristo, Duns Scoto si inserisce pienamente

The profound concentration on an inevitable positioning within the world while remaining without it was mirrored in the work of Giotto, the Order's great artist, Dante, a tertiary Franciscan himself, and the pragmatism of Ockham. By then the Franciscan Rule was becoming an apparatus of functional empiricism and an arena wherein dull legality could rear its dour head. Was this not a historical inevitability? Giotto, Duns Scotus, Dante, and Ockham had to personally appropriate the singular contribution of Francis, who sought to eradicate not fulfill personal glory. By the time of Giotto, the world was too much with the Franciscans.

But this was to come later. Francis was very much part of the world and its temptations when he came to divine service. This most extreme of vocations came to him when confronting the flesh, of others, in its most decrepit and poisoned form. Leprosy taught him to put not much faith in the unencumbered flesh:

> When I was in sin, the sight of lepers nauseated me beyond measure: but then God himself led me into their company and I had pity on them...After that I did not wait long before leaving the world.[11]

Bonaventure clarifies the extent of Francis' devotion by recounting the story of the disfigured and leprous man kissed on the lips, who recovered from a grievous disease after such a benediction by the saint.[12] It was necessary for Francis to acquire knowledge and overcome fear by the same mechanism: the tangible experience. Bonaventure relates that Francis believed that it was "hard to satisfy one's material needs without giving in to the inclinations of sensuality."[13] And yet, this makes for a paradox: In understanding the lure of the flesh and corporeal existence, Francis, to a certain extent, fetishized it early in his ministry. The ministrations to the poor at first, took the form of attending to lepers. Attending need not have meant embracing them or kissing them. Francis begins his own Testament with pointing out the nauseating experience of confronting leprosy. He used this specifically corporal affliction to quicken an empathy that was to form a tentative speculum of the poor.

---

nell'alveo della prima scuola francescana, rigorizzando e portando agli estremi le profonde intuizioni del santo fondatore e del serafico Bonaventura. "
In Antonio Poppi, *Studi sull Etica della Prima Scuola Francescana* (Padova: Centro Studi Antoniani, 1996), 179-180.
[11] "The Testament of Saint Francis," *OSE*, 67.
[12] "Legenda Maior, II, 6," *OSE*, 644.
[13] *Ibid*, V, 1, 663.

Later he would approach poverty as an ordeal akin to the sacrament of marriage. Both ideals had as their basis a concentration on the relinquishing of rights over the body, and this denial became the springboard toward action. Yet the romanticizing of the concept did not survive the generation after Francis. [14] The harshness of poverty, even then, under the excellent disposition of Francis toward it, was an ugly necessity for Franciscans.[15]

Self-denial to Francis always revolved around the geometry of the flesh and the concepts of love played strongly in his ideal. To his followers, this had the effect of a new incarnation, and a new dawn for ways of thinking about Christian devotion. Francis became another Christ, put on earth to herald the novel, apocalyptic age:

> Therefore there is every reason to believe that it is he who is referred to under the image of an Angel coming up from the east, with the seal of the living God, in the prophecy made by another friend of Christ the Bridegroom, St. John the Apostle and Evangelist. When the sixth seal was broken, St. John tells us in the Apocalypse, "I saw a second Angel coming up from the east, with the seal of a living God."[16]

That Francis seemed heaven-sent could mean for his most fervid admirers he was indeed a sign to distinguish his epoch and reflect divine will once more incorporating itself into human history. Dante later echoed the *topos* of the emergent dawn of the Franciscan advent, playing on the significance of the etymology of Assisi (ascent) in this dispensation.[17]

But the eschatological excitement surrounding Francis had its roots in the mysticism of the mystical Calabrian hermit, Joachim of Fiore. It seemed that the Benedictine monk had foretold the Franciscan Age in all its glory. Ironically for the present purposes, it was Joachim whose

---

[14] "For there was no voice nor sense among the sons of Adam in that day that they might want to confer together or speak about poverty. They hated poverty bitterly, then, as they do today, nor could they speak peaceably about it to any one asking about it. " In "Sacrum Commercium, I, 5," *OSE* , 1553.

[15] "There was indeed a romantic quality in his erection of poverty to a holy virtue, in the concept of Lady Poverty, but it was no false romance he wove around her, for he and his followers knew only too well the harsh and hideous face of actual want. " Rosalind and Christopher Brooke, *Popular Religion in the Middle Ages, Western Europe 1000-13000* (London: Thames and Hudson, 1984), 128.

[16] Preface to "Legenda Maior, 1" *OSE*, 632.

[17] "Pero chi d'esso loco fa parole/ Non dica Ascesi, che direbbe corto/ Ma Oriente, se proprio dir vuole." *Paradiso*, XI, 52-54.

teachings had been condemned as anathema by Innocent III in the decrees of the Fourth Lateran Council, a document that officially set the Incarnational Age on its path. For all of the questions concerning his orthodoxy, Joachim's mystical visions approximated an early and incomplete lexicon for the Incarnational Age in Italy and clearly foresaw its advent. [18]

Joachim of Fiore was born in Celico in Calabria in or near the year 1135, a full 45 years before the birth of Francis. He was the son of a notary to the court of the Norman kings of Sicily. It is appealing to the imagination that the young boy got his taste for reading signs from eavesdropping upon the machinations of princes. But it is fairly evident that the histories of his visions supposedly began when he was a young man on pilgrimage to the Holy Land.

By 1159, he had become an itinerant lay preacher, and this led to him joining the Cistercian Order in Sambucina, Sicily. Ordained in 1168, he eventually became abbot of the Benedictine monastery of Corazzo in 1177. This election was accepted grudgingly, because the duties of abbot interfered with his contemplative leanings. Therefore he relinquished his duties as abbot and sought and was granted permission to start his own congregation in the Sila Mountains.

There he recorded (around 1183) what were to become known as the Joachimite prophecies in three major works; the *Exposition on the Apocalypse* (*Enchiridion super Apocalypsim*), *The Book of Concordance* (*Liber de concordia Novi ac Veteris Testamenti*), and the *Ten Stringed Psaltery* (*Psalterium decem chordarum*). As a casual glance at the titles suggest, the trajectory of his thought followed an increasingly poetic bent. Only one (*Book of Concordance*) was revised and actually sent to the Pope. By 1191 his community of hermits of Fiore (Flora) had been established and five years later, was given autonomy by Celestine III. By the Fourth Lateran Council in 1215, his teachings were condemned, but he himself escaped personal censure.

Although he died in 1202, his legend lived on, causing a great debate within the legacy of the Franciscan Order. Salimbene, a Franciscan who wrote what Coulton described as the "most remarkable autobiography of

---

[18] Sabatier writes eloquently on the Franciscan Incarnational Age as seen by Joachim: "These hopes were not wholly confounded. In the evening of his days the prophet of Fiore was able, like a new Simeon, to utter his *Nunc dimittis*, and for a few years Christendom could turn in amazement to Assisi as to a new Bethlehem." In Paul Sabatier, *The Road to Assisi: The Essential Biography of St. Francis,* Jon M. Sweeney, ed. (Brewster: Paraclete Press, 2004), 33.

the Middle Ages"[19], relates a curious debate which took place in Naples (1248) concerning the actual veracity of Joachimite prophecy, wherein a Brother Hugh de Digne, Salimbene's spiritual mentor, lashed out at Brother Peter of Apulia, Lector of the Neapolitan Chapter for according to Joachim no more thought than to the "fifth wheel on a wagon."[20] History has seen him in a benign light, Aquinas and Dante giving him praise (guarded for Aquinas, unreserved for Dante). His fame rests upon the nature of his prophecies. It is these that lend a prophetic insight to the "dawn" of Francis.

Joachim's doctrine depends upon the Trinity in form if not content. Very basically, the recapitulation (of second century Montanism, likewise obsessed with the imminence of the Paraclete) of a Trinitarian division of apocalyptic history occurs in Joachim, as three great periods (*status*): the First Age of the Father, presided over by the law of the Old Testament and typified by the familial connections of humanity to its God (*ordo conjugatorum*): the Second Age of the Son under the influence of the Church, and the Grace inculcated by the New Testament and its Doctrines (*ordo clericorum*): and the Third and final Age of the Holy Spirit presided over by the purified monastic order prefigured by Benedict and presumably ascendant under Joachim (*ordo contemplantium* or *monachorum*).

According to the complex numerology employed by the monk to place the prophecies in historical time, the Third Age was to begin in 1260. Joachim though never advanced the theories of the Gerard of Borgo San Donnino that proclaimed the *Eternal Gospel* . This was a hodge-podge of Scriptural writings combined with Joachim's prophecies that was heretical, and was proclaimed as such by the Fourth Lateran Council as a platform to raise the Trinatarian conceptions of Peter Lombard above the theories of Joachim. [21]

The similarities between Peter Lombard and Joachim offered a paradigm of unease to the Church as both used logic derived from extra Biblical sources to support interesting though divergent views on the Trinity. The Trinity, being a crucial *mysterium fidei*, was not really a subject fit for the perambulations of the intellectual, cross-examining Lombard and the hazy, fervent mysticism of Joachim. The Fourth

---

[19] G. G. Coulton, *From St. Francis to Dante: Translations from the Chronicle of the Franciscan Salimbene (1221-88)* (Philadelphia: University of Pennsylvania Press, 1972, reprint), 1.

[20] G. G. Coulton, *From St. Francis to Dante*, 154-156.

[21] Dupuis, J. and J. Neuner, eds., *The Christian Faith in the Doctrinal Documents of the Catholic Church* (New York: Alba House, 2001), 152.

Lateran while siding eventually with the Lombard against the presumptions of Joachim, understood that the mysteries of the faith needed to be approached on some sort of personal level. The doctrine of transubstantiation points to this need, as does the doctrine of Penance.

As Innocent III was also responsible for the official recognition of both the Franciscan and Dominican strains of Catholic spirituality, it is easy to see that the need expressed in somewhat nebulous terms by the fervency of Joachim was met by a concentrated orthodox response. Nevertheless, in the popular mind, it was Francis who was to embody the Incarnational Age adumbrated by the vision of Joachim. This was not *post hoc ergo propter hoc.* It is unlikely that Francis was aware of the visions of Joachim in their literary exposition. And even if he were, it is doubtful they would have offered a solid rubric in the heartfelt reform begun by Francis.

Joachimite millenarianism was misunderstood as apocalyptic, in the sense of Western spiritual historicism involving a definitive conclusion, rather than a reinvigoration of the Christian Spirit without doctrine. The eschatology is dependent upon a revelation toward Pentecostal reform, not destruction. The rise of the influence of the friar and the subsequent mantling of hopes upon the frail shoulders of Francis misinterpreted a subtle distinction wherein the Christian understood his relationship to Christ anew. The revelation was not, as in the Incarnation of Jesus, to come singularly, but communally:

> In the history of the Church, this interpretive understanding of the Spirit is something that develops, and according to Joachim and Bonaventure we stand at the dawning of the eschatological age, for which understanding is reserved in a special way.[22]

Joachim was used as a lightning rod and a whipping post for his followers and detractors alike, but even the Church hedged its bets on the official line against the Calabrian monk. His teachings were condemned, his followers were condemned, but Joachim himself and his monastery were left alone in the anathemas pronounced by the Fourth Lateran Council of 1215.[23]

---

110 Hans Urs von Balthasar, *The Glory of the Lord: A Theological Aesthetics. II. Studies in Theological Style: Clerical Styles.* Translated by A. Louth, F. McDonagh, B. McNeil; John Riches, ed. (San Francisco: Ignatius Press, 1998), 263.

[23] "In nullo tamen per hoc Florensi monasterio, cuius ipse Iochim exstitit institutor, volumes derogari, quoniam ibi et regularis institutio est et observantia salutaris,

What is indisputable about the "philosophy" of Joachim is that it treated the conception of the Trinity with the sense that its symbolism could be made to say things different from the official line. His disdain for the work of Peter Lombard, (the Council registers that Joachim had declared Peter "haereticum et insanum"[24]), in this arena speaks more to the poetic, indeed mystical nature of his own singular visions as opposed to the exegetical philosophy of the Lombard, based upon glosses of the Fathers rather than self-compelled.

This is an essential difference in an understanding of the Incarnational Age as precursor to the Renaissance: It relied more upon the discovery of a personal understanding with Christ rather than a learned response. Reformation and Renaissance had begun to understand Jesus through dint of intellectual effort. Joachim as precursor to Francis, and indeed as herald of the Age, was as anti-intellectual as Francis would become, and would, as Francis had already done, eventually acquire the penumbra of the holy fool. [25] This served only to underline a relationship between the spirituality of the Franciscan ideal and what seemed to be the illogic of the Pauline idea of *kenosis*, and the Incarnation as a result of the choice. [26] The novelty of the approach served to at once marginalize the ideal and garner respect for the Order, as living sacrifices to the Christian way. [27]

---

maxime cum idem Ioachim omnia scripta sua nobis assisignari mandaverit. " From "II. De erroris abbatis Ioachim" in *Decrees of the Ecumenical Councils (Nicaea – Lateran V) Volume I,* Norman R. Tanner and Giuseppe Alberigo, eds. (London and Washington: Sheed and Ward and Georgetown University Press, 1990), 232-233.

[24] *Ibid.,* 231.

[25] Francis' proclamation as God's herald to the robbers in Thomas of Celano's "First Life" garnered a beating, and a toss in the snow: "Lie there foolish herald of God. " From the "First Life of St. Francis, VII, 16," *OSE,* 242. See also Sabatier, *The Road to Assisi,* 38-39.

[26] "Francesco era destinato ad essere novissimus *pazzus in hoc mundo*, il pazzo puo singolare che ci fosse al mondo.... e forse nella sua volonta di presentarsi come *pazzus* operava il ricordo della 'follia della croce' di s. Paolo. E la follia che salva. " In Raoul Manselli, *San Francesco* (Roma: Bulzoni, 1982), 148.

[27] In Bonaventure's Prologue to his *Tree of Life*, he quotes *Galatians 2: 19*; "With Christ I am nailed to the cross", as the central axiom around which we "should, above all, strive, with an earnest endeavor of soul to carry about continuously, both in his soul and in his flesh, the cross of Christ until he can truly feel in himself what the Apostle said above. " In *Bonaventure: The Soul's Journey Into God/ The Tree of Life/ The Life of St. Francis.* Translated and introduced by Ewart Cousins (Mahwah: Paulist Press, 1978)

They must be mad, but they were mad for God; like, as Bonaventure reminds us, John the Baptist, Elijah, and Christ himself. [28]

But there is a serious difficulty arising from the presumptions of Joachimite mysticism that carted it dangerously close to other heresies of the time, which were to be met by more forceful weapons of Church and State. Joachim's expectant age of the Holy Spirit that would fulfill the expectations of the previous ages of the Father and the Son did two very dangerous things: It relegated the Incarnation as a mid point of anticlimactic fulfillment rather than the central act of the Divine on Earth; and it proclaimed celibate monasticism as the perfected ideal of the Christian life, and the only acceptable form of living within the great Age of the Holy Spirit.

This would leave faith to a hyper personal understanding of the vagaries of the Holy Spirit, an eventuality intimated by Joachim in Chapter 9, Part 1 of Book 2 of the *Book of Concordance*:

> We ought to review what we have just discussed about the three orders and the two peoples. . it was demonstrated that the Holy Spirit was sent by the Father and the Son. When he is sent, he breathes where he wishes and gives his gifts to individuals as he wishes.[29]

Such affirmation of the power and finality of the Age of the Holy Spirit denuded the faith in the eternal salvation, if such salvation were to come without the interposition of the Son's Return, to say nothing of the Church's role. Jesus was a half-time show of pedagogical importance but not the Main Event of personal salvation.

This sword of Damocles cut both ways; it cut into the suppositions of the laity who with familial ties hoped to gain heaven, and into the faith in Christ with which the clergy promulgated the necessity of the Church in the act of salvation. With the rise of Francis and Dominic, and negatively in the case of the Cathars, Joachim's prophecies, concerning an age that would see the beneficent rise of a celibate class that would purify the world, seemed uncomfortably accurate. The evident heresy of the Cathars and their dependence upon the celibacy of their Perfects dovetailed a little too nicely with this implicit heresy.

Yet by 1260, the year that would see the beginning of the Age of the Holy Spirit according to Joachim renderings of numerology predicated

---

[28] "Legenda Maior, Preface, 1," *OSE*, 632.
[29] *Apocalyptic Spirituality: Treatises and Letters of Lactantius, Adso of Montier-en-Der, Joachim of Fiore, the Franciscan Spirituals, Savonarola*. Bernard Mc Ginn, ed., preface by Marjorie Reeves (Mahwah: Paulist Press, 1979), 129.

upon Scripture, (when the Church was no longer needed as love would be the currency of personal salvation), the world seemed to be all too familiar. Indicatively the hope for a communitarian class of celibate mystics inaugurating a new age began to fade as the mercantile class gained evermore power in the *popoli commune* on the Italian peninsula. The destruction of the Cathars and the growing secular concerns of the mendicant orders began to handicap a full Christian renewal along the lines of either Francis or Joachim.

Still, Joachim's influence did not evaporate. This is the curious fate of mystical apocalypticism that supposes the end to be historically imminent. The time comes and it goes, and still the people yearn for a sign. But Joachim (it can be argued) was looking for a way, through exegesis and solitude, by which his own ardent way of understanding his faith could be sanctified, as apocalyptic. In this he parallels Bonaventure, who had centralized the perfection of fulfilled Christianity in history in Francis. Such events in personal *askesis* and prophecy could cause intelligent people to pass wildly divergent judgement upon Joachim's merits. Is it any wonder that Aquinas cautiously affirms some of Joachim but denies the rest: "Joachim... foretold some things that were true and in others was deceived"[30], and that Dante allows none other than Bonaventure to confer upon him the "true spirit of prophecy"?[31] But in either case, it must be said, (here as in Innocent's official view in Lateran IV), this is autobiography parading as objectivity. It is the difference between the intellectual citizen of the orthodoxy and the lonely poetic exile. Joachim is capacious enough to pour hopes into as well as fears.

Most interestingly for our present discussion is the nature of Joachamite prophecy in terms of inspiration. Joachim ties his visions into the sacramental infrastructure of the Church by insinuating that prophecy is akin to simple observation and in a sense, natural. The sacraments of the Christian, any Christian, could empower the same to accept and revel in the visions that permeate his imagination. This absolves him of predicting anything that is not plain to see to the contemplative:

> Thus the sacred mysteries are rightly to be understood not wholly according to what they signify, but in accordance with the Catholic faith. For it is not because a man speaks that his image speaks as well, or because a man sees and hears that his image is able to see, hear, work, eat, or walk.

---

[30] *Summa Theologica, III, qu. 77. article 2.*
[31] *Paradiso, XII,* 141.

Nevertheless, each act has meaning that enables us to contemplate in some ways a man's outward appearance.[32]

There is little in him that is pure. All philosophy shot through with poetry, all logic suffused with prophecy. The virtue of Joachim, (if virtue it can be called) is the imprecision and the nebulousness of his prophecy are put forward by the "logic" of his visions. And it is in these indistinct voices by which prophets hear and speak.

Francis, though special, was not, could not be, aloof and cloud his revelation in clouds of unknowing. Although Joachim hinted at an Italian Pentecost, the Franciscan revival, literally, got their hands dirty. This was a great paradox in the philosophy of Francis from which Christian renewal in the present dispensation can learn much: Although Francis abnegated the body's needs by mortifications and distrusted the wherewithal of personal judgement in the physical life of the flesh, yet Nature herself was to be glorified. There is a sympathy in God's creation not found in the dualist heresies that were contemporaneous with Francis. This led to the importance, in the early understanding of the Franciscan Order, of the *imago dei*, a speculum of virtue that could be provided by the imaginative (literally image-making) faculties.

The retreat, or return to Nature was not new to Francis. Monasticism in theory was predicated upon withdrawal, usually to a place marginalized for the very purpose. The consequences of Francis' solitude and contemplation, however, brought about an unparalleled, up to that point, event in Christian history: The reception of the stigmata.

According to his early biographers, on or about the fourteenth of September in 1224, during a retreat to La Verna, Francis had a vision of a six winged seraph fixed to a cross. And, as he pondered this image, according to the *First Life* of Thomas of Celano;

"The marks of the began to appear in his hands and feet, just as he had seen them a little before in the crucified man above him."[33] Celano goes on to clarify that these wounds were seen by few, but "happy Elias merited"[34] the vision of the wound in his side. The actual wounds of Christ could be offered to the world as no proof could of Francis' sanctity. It also casts the only cloud over a Christian Incarnational Renaissance predicated upon an *imitatio Christi*: It could not be replicated *ad infinitum*, conferring upon Francis the aura of actual success in his attempts to approximate the life of Christ. Incarnation was stunning and debated over

---

[32] "Book of Concordance," *Apocalyptic Spirituality*, 132.
[33] "First Life, ch. III, 95," *OSE*, 309.
[34] *Ibid.*, 310.

in part because it was an event that was repeatable only if the Apocalypse were to come.

In the natural scheme of things, it was hard to wrap the mind around it. The achievement of the stigmata caused sainthood to be conferred almost immediately upon Francis, and quite probably by popular acclaim. Renewal in this dispensation could be seen by the greater population to have very real (and painful) rewards.

The epiphenomenon of Francis' stigmatization put everything, all of his achievements in life toward Christian emulation, in jeopardy. The gift of the stigmata to Francis has since been repeated throughout the centuries, most famously in our own time with the Calabrian monk, Padre Pio. And as with this famous recluse, such 'favor' precipitated a populism that lifted what can now be termed the Heroic Incarnational, above and beyond the yeas and nays of the official hierarchy of the orthodox establishment.[35] At the same time, there was also the possibility of a terminus for the intellectualization of certain Franciscan tendencies that arose from the Order's acceptance. So the *sigillum Christie,* that was the ultimate seal of validation,[36] threatened to enervate emulation because at once it heightened the emotionalism inherent in the Franciscan ideal and fulfilled it. It also threatened a salutary relationship with the hierarchy of the official church, as the Franciscan true believer would be hard pressed to accept non-Franciscan ideas because of the obvious mark of favor that

---

[35] ". . . the citizens of Assisi 'sent an armed guard to escort him in his last illness back to his home town lest another community should seize the precious body along the way.'" From Eamon Duffy, "Finding Saint Francis" in *Medieval Theology and the Natural Body,* Peter Billers and A. J. Minnis, eds. (York: York Medieval Press, 1997), 193-236, p. 199.

[36] "The seal of the likeness of the living God, namely Christ crucified' are the words of Bonaventure in his *Legenda Maior* from the Prologue. Cousins in his edition, (p. 182, but not in Habig's *OSE*) points out this deliberate echo of Ezekiel 28:12. As this is a bone of some contention in translated texts it is best to go to the spring from which Bonaventure sipped; Jerome himself in the Vulgate: "et dices ei hac dicit Dominus Deus tu signaculum similitudinis plenus sapientia et perfectus decore". Ezekiel figures prominently later in the chapter on Dante, and I contend, as an inversion and caveat of transformative favor in the Incarnational Age. As such echoes point to the popular apocalypticism of the early Franciscan spirituals, Ezekiel's warning about Tyre has been a much-overlooked rubric in Dante studies concerning his reference in *Paradiso I* of Glaucus and Marsyas. As Cousins alludes, Ezekiel was invoked at another pivotal event-to open the Fourth Lateran Council to open proceedings (ibid.). The chapter on Dante will further investigate the connection.

Christ had shown to the Order. It was an issue of some delicacy, to say the very least.[37]

The idea that Francis himself never equated his affliction with the marks of Jesus, but probably rather with his repeated exposure to leprosy is of ominous significance.[38] The reason is simply that the negative biological consequences of mortification and exposure were transformed into a positive sign of spiritual transformation. The ideal of the Incarnational Age, Francis himself, was an example of the ultimate wedding of the dispossessed to the actual and mystical body of the Christ, represented by an idealized Christianity. It was an exhilarating example but also a daunting one, especially after the marks of Christ verified the *corpus verum* active within Francis.[39] The spectacle of the wounds caused the would-be Christian of the Incarnational Age to become a potential spectator of a miracle rather than an apostle.

In the consequential biographies of the saint, prophecy and imminence seem to meet. Bonaventure in his Prologue leaves little room

---

[37] "The supreme expression of Francis's call...his stigmatization with the wounds of Christ, a happening which his followers subsequently took as a divine imprint to his life and work. Accordingly both they and Francis took their authority directly from Chrsit." In Gordon Leff, *Heresy in the Later Middle Ages: The Relation of Heterodoxy to Dissent, c. 1250-1450* 2 vols. (Manchester: Manchester University Press, 1967), 53.

[38] See Chiara Frugoni, *Francesco e L'invenzione della Stimmate: Una storia per parole e immagini fino a Bonaventura e Giotto* (Torino: Einaudi, 1993).
In her magisterial account of the phenomenon of Francis' stigmata, Frugoni argues that the identification with Christ was a carefully calculated and executed plan on the part of the Franciscan Order (Brother Elias in particular) to propagate the mythos of the wounds which were for Francis, not relatable at all to Christ himself.

[39] ". . their (Franciscans) regard for their bodies as a substitute for society may be linked with the contemporary debate on the nature of the two bodies of Christ. The natural body, the *corpus verum* was the personal body of the eucharist in contrast with the mystical body of all believers, the church. It was claimed that Christ had intended to lead men from the example of his natural body to an understanding of his mystical body. Hence it was not inappropriate that those who wished to come closer to Christ should regard their own natural bodies as surrogates whereby, through suffering and purging, they could become part of the mystical body. The use of the body as a surrogate for the church was regarded as an integral part of the *vita apostolica.*" In Brenda Bolton, "Paupertas Christi: Old Wealth and New Poverty in the Twelfth Century," 100-101. See also Henri du Lubac, *Corpus Mysticum* (Paris 1949), 116-126 and Ernst Kantorowicz, *The Kings Two Bodies* (Princeton 1957), 193-198, (Bolton's note).

for doubt,[40] and writes half expectant of an apotheosis. Yet, such expectation can create a vacuum wherein action is swallowed up in the inexorable dictates of fate.[41]

Luckily, the saint himself allowed for the creative Christian to find avenues of expression to circumvent inaction, and this he did by creating or smiling upon mechanisms of cultural dissemination. Francis allowed for God's handiwork to be revered and appreciated, concentrating on stewardship rather than mastery of the natural world. The sermon to the birds, the mollification of Gubbio's wolf and many tales from the *Golden Legend* and *The Little Flowers* that have passed into popular legend attest to Francis' vocation to the natural world.[42] And as a grandchild to this, his own deliberate care in propagating a certain iconography of Christ and the visions implicit in the concentration on the visual helped the Franciscans along in establishing more vociferously than other Order, a mythos of images that told and defended their version of the facts.[43] Even the nebulous and intangibles of Joachamite prophecy gave birth to image – making. Indeed, the Joachamites were dependant upon a specific iconology that dated back to the legend of Joachim decorating his cell with images of the coming Mendicant Orders. Imagination operated centrally

---

[40] "Therefore there is every reason to believe that it is he who is referred to under the image of an Angel coming up from the East, with the seal of the living God in the prophecy made by another friend of Christ the Bridegroom, St. Jon the Apostle and Evangelist. When the sixth seal was broken, St. John tells us in the Apocalypse, 'I saw a second Angel coming up from the East, with the seal of the living God' (*Ap.* 7, 12). From the "Legenda Maior", *OSE*, 632.

[41] "Alla fine del XII secolo la profezia non e soltanto la capacita di prevedere il futuro, ma anche il senso remoto della Scritture e di interpretare I 'segni dei tempi' secondo la parola divina". Frugoni, 29.

[42] "He (Francis) solved in his own fashion the great problem of Christian piety: to conquer the world without debasing it." In Karl Vossler, *Medieval Culture: An Introduction to Dante and His Times, volume I*. Translated by William Cranston Lawson (New York: Frederick Ungar Publishing Co., 1929), 68.

[43] "Ideas appeared to him as images. Documents only had a secondary importance for him, and the natural medium for him to employ in conveying his ideas was the acted parable, the mime or the symbol…if we are to recreate the view of the poverty of Christ it must be in terms in which he was accustomed to think-in the primary visual images which are key to the understanding of his thought. " From Malcolm Lambert, *Franciscan Poverty: The Doctrine of The Absolute Poverty of Christ and the Apostles in the Franciscan Order 1210-1323* (New York: Franciscan Institute, 1998), 39-40, p. 65.

within the engines of the Incarnational Age, and influenced its potential for a prophetic future.[44]

Understandably, Francis' preoccupation with the life of Christ led him to view the images of the Savior with fervor. In this he was well buttressed by a tradition of piety that based itself on the suffering servant of the cross.[45] This underscored the rising preoccupation with the flesh evolving in European Art that was to have renascence within a century of Francis, so that the images of Christ reflect a growing carnal understanding that the emulation of his Presence engendered. The particular piety involved the "talking cross" of his principal conversion at the Portiuncula and the adoration of the child in the *crèche*, another product of Franciscan invention. An entire social understanding arose from just placement of hierarchy within these devotional images.[46] This threatened to submerge the apostolic bent of Incarnational ethics to decorative rather than active participation.

The Incarnational Age, as will be seen in the chapter on Giotto, eventually involved a celebration of the emulator rather than the object, so that an unhealthy desire for flesh-circumscribed piety in the art was to come about. In the end the metaphor of Christ Among Us that sustained the Incarnational Age gave way to the philosophical *a-priori* of the Measurement of Man.[47] The *imago dei* and the veneration of images began

---

[44] See Marjorie Reeves and Beatrice Hirsch-Reich, *The Figurae of Joachim of Fiore* (Oxford: Clarendon Press, 1972), 262.

[45] For one of the most complete treatments on the phenomenon of piety before the crucifixion image in this period see Hans Belting, *The Image and It's Public in the Middle Ages: Form and Function of Early Paintings of the Passion.* Translated by Mark Bartusis and Raymond Meyer (New Rochelle: Aristide D. Caratzas Publisher, 1990).

[46] "Christians have historically built into the nativity scene as they have into other powerful and sacred images, their own social and political experiences.... Look again. The whole of life seems to be at the crib...Christians arranging these crib scenes place the infant in a recognizable social order of herders, farmers, courtiers and merchants that pairs and polarizes country and court, riches and poverty, simplicity and complexity.... This realistic tendency continued so that by the time of Francis such sentiments were no longer unusual, having become a typical part of the late medieval comprehension of the crib," from Richard Trexler, *The Journey of the Magi: Meanings in History of a Christian Story* (Princeton: Princeton University Press, 1997), 3-4 & 73.

[47] See Jean Wirth, *L'Image Medievale: Naissance et developpements (VIe-XVe siecle)* (Paris: Meridiens Klincksieck,1989), 327-340.
I contend this had more to do with the populist understanding of the Age brought about by cultural shifts in recognition of the centrality of the Body of Christ in

to veer dangerously close to a Byzantine piety, whose forms had first influenced the novel art of Giotto, the greatest propagator of the Franciscan ethos in the visual arts.

In time the populism of the Franciscan movement began to participate in the overall life of official ecclesiastical authority throughout the Italian-speaking world. As has been shown, the link between official doctrines had channels through which to seep into the common life of the far-flung parishes.[48] But these responded first and foremost to the homegrown evangelical poverty of the itinerant men who spoke their language, and sang their songs. In time, the dogmatism of Franciscan ideas on want and poverty became axiomatic in a popular understanding of Christ,[49] although this did not always have the tangential desired effect. The reflex served, though, to appropriate a new *cultus*, for the Mediterranean culture to accept. The churches and their constituents began a brisk trade in relics

---

everyday life. A theory concerning the primacy of philosophical speculation as progenitor of the Incarnational Age is adumbrated by Jorge J. E. Garcia in his edited *Individuation in Scholasticism: The Later Middle Ages and the Counter Reformation, 1150-1650.* (New York: State University of New York Press, 1994), 549. Since this theory is close to the present, a summation from the text is needed: ". all doctrines (of Christianity) . . in one way or another raised questions concerning the individual and individuation. Indeed, the deep importance thst Christianity bestows on the individual, whether human or not, explains the Franciscan phenomenon. The appearance of St. Francis would be unintelligible dislodged from it's Christian background.... As already stated elsewhere in this book, the Greeks had very little concern for the individual in their philosophy. Their concern was reserved for the universal, for the principles that would ground morality and knowledge. The history of philosophy in the Middle Ages reveals that every time there was an infusion of Greek thought, there was a corresponding decrease in the discussion of individuality…Therefore it makes sense to say that, at least philosophically speaking, the individual was discovered in the Middle Ages and that such a discovery was largely due to the extraordinary influence of Christian doctrine on the thought of the period."

[48] "…many areas of medieval life were influenced by the over arching sacerdotal-sacramental world view…Inasmuch as it strove for uniformity of practice in liturgy and devotion it attempted to substitute local, regional tendencies. " In Miri Rubin, "Religious Culture in Town and Country" from *Church and City 1000-1500: Essays in Honour of Christopher Brooke,* 3-22, p. 19.

[49] "Here then we have the last essential development. Absolute poverty represented the regular way of life of Christ and the apostles. It was dispensed from time to time. Christ himself relaxed the rule for himself, as an act of condescension to the imperfect; and for his apostles, a concession in times of persecution. But the example of the perfect still stood." In Lambert, *Franciscan Poverty,* 145.

and the superstitious bent of the peoples found an easy fit with the new and vigorous "cult" of Francis.[50] In short order, such a cult was given both the masks of tragedy and comedy to wear on the stage of Franciscan ascendancy. The *Giullari* were the most jocund of the Age's revelers: The Franciscan preachers the most severe. Both depended upon a grass roots program that allowed them intimacy with the left the hopes of the average citizen in Italy. As such, both played perhaps the most important roles in dissemination of Incarnational modes of thought for they spoke to the people without the muzzle of hierarchy above their heads, even though such a muzzle was existent and active.[51]

As is common knowledge for the thirteenth century, the locus of activity within the village or town was the church. The priests of the churches were rarely literate and could not be depended upon by the officials to carefully propagate approved doctrine. The Mendicant Orders of Dominic[52] and Francis were entrusted to both combat heresy and explicate doctrine. The sermons were transformed into subtle pedagogy.

---

[50] In Italian churches of the thirteenth century "Chapters and monasteries were collections of property around cult centers and their relics, ill adapted to participate in Parisian-Lateran reform…into this elderly and rather empty, yet cluttered, stillness rushed a violent enthusiasm, the movement of friars and flagellants. The Italian church participated fully in the activism of thirteenth century Assisi. It was a church of mute bishops and listening birds. " In Robert Brentano, *Two Churches: England and Italy in the Thirteenth Century,* 347-348.

[51] "Quanto poi alla effettiva inrusione dello spettacolo giullaresco nello spazio sacro, di cui abbiamo gia visto un accenno nelle parole d'Abelardo, possono valere, come prova al contrario, le numerose proibizioni e reprimende di cui un esempio e questa decretale di Innocenzo III del 1207; ' Tavolta si fanno spettacoli teatrali nelle chiese stesse e non solo vi si introducono maschere mostruose, ma anche esponendo a turno alla scherno la loro follia, con l'oscena delirio delle loro gesticolazioni sviliscono al cospetto al popolo il decoro del clero, che dovrebbero pittosto in quell periodo alimentare con la predicazione della prola si Dio.'" In Tito Saffioti, *Giullari in Italia: Lo Spettacolo, il Pubblico, i Testi* (Milano:Xenia, 1990), 82. The admonition directly from Innocent is revealing. His attempt to micromanage even the populist aspect of the Word's dissemination points to the need for control, which, (once promulgated eight years after this decretal) should have had a dampening affect on the liberties of the players. This would not be the case.

[52] A study of the influential Dominican texts on preaching in the time under investigation is best approached by reading Leonard Boyle's magisterial "A Study of the Works Attributed to William of Pagula: with special reference to the Oculus Sacerdotis and Summa Summarum." Diss. Trinity College, Oxford University, 1956.

[53] The *Giullari* naturally gravitated toward the Order that was at once more compassionate, more understanding, and more Italian. Francis, *il giullaro di Dio* was the perfect fit for them.

Perhaps this is why the players depended upon a tenuous but essentially amicable relationship with the preachers who would give them fodder for their performances following the sermons, in exchange for jesting gazettes from the corners of Europe where they had performed. The free exchange was part of the rising mercantilism that surrounded them but from the Friars to the players, the exchange took on the color of an indulgence. To the people, the Gospel Narratives were replaced in the imagination with Passion plays with names belonging to companies or players.[54] Even if the preachers were to object, the Franciscan efforts toward Christian mimicry dovetailed nicely into the *giullari* aesthetic. Although the players could not be allowed total freedom after the comprehensive official axioms of Lateran IV, they were left remarkably alone by both the Franciscan and Dominican friars; Indeed some of the matter for the preachers was actually lifted from the words and bestiaries provided by the culture engendered under the impetus of the movements of itinerant players.[55]

The sermons of the preachers were based upon a theological synthesis around the readings in the liturgical year. Christmas time was the burning point for both sermonizing and the Christmas plays boarded, as they both revolved around specified concepts attached to the Incarnation. The reading during that time, John 1, 14 ("Verbum caro factum est") adumbrated theories of and exegesis upon, the Hypostatic Union and the Incarnation. But the sermons themselves would be gratefully devoid of scholastic metaphysics.[56] According to one scholar, the content of both

---

[53] "By transformation of the sermon, then, is meant the reorientation brought about by the revival of preaching to the laity...(this) produced the beginnings of a common religious culture which the lay men and women of the towns were able to share with the educated clergy. " In David Levesley D'Avray, "The Transformation of the Medieval Sermon." Diss. Balliol College, Oxford University, 1976, 3.

[54] Some famous ones were the later Passion of Niccolo Cicerchia and the Song of Jesus' Youth by Brother Felice Tancredi from Massa-Carrara. These would be played on a sort of evangelical rotation so that the commoner was much more likely to recognize the giullari songs than church hymns. Saffioti, *I Giullari*, 81.

[55] See *Racconti Esemplari di Predicatori del Due e Trecento*. 3 vols. Giorgio Varanini e Guido Baldassari, eds. (Roma: Salerno Editrice, 1993), II, 120-125.

[56] D'Avray, "Transformation of the Medieval Sermon," 226-227.

academic and popular sermons was "pastoral in character. It was not so much designed to solve problems as to save souls."[57]

Indeed exhortations from the official church line to the Franciscan Order, underlines a need for the Friars Minor to excite the sensibilities of their hearers rather than instruct them.[58] The most famous and adored of Francis' preachers was of course Anthony of Padua, who preached his sermons to Northern Italian cities between 1229-1231. Much closer to the intellectual ideas of his Age, Anthony, a scholar, did not eschew the polysemous levels of meaning which loomed large in explicating Biblical texts. His piety and knowledge and his devotion to Francis sum up what the ideal Franciscan became to a church beleaguered by heresy. But perhaps the greatest of influences in Italy at the end of the Incarnational Age, as far as homiletics are concerned, were the popular *Meditations on the Life of Christ* written by the preacher Giovanni de Causibus de Sancto Geminiani in the late thirteenth century. This text seemed to conflate popular stories drawn from Scripture with a contemporary time frame for the reader, so that the reality of the stories became visible and actionable within the present sphere.

It was the Franciscan idea *par excellence*, and wed a personal meditative process with the contemplative position of the audience, so that the process of meditation "signified direct participation (both imaginative and ritual) in the events of the life of Christ" so that "the urban laity of modest condition could transcend the limitations of monastic piety,"[59] by contemplation.

Whether this contemplation was active or docile, within the mendicant or the spectator, the transcendence of communitarian boundaries set by wealth or class was to make the personal a real influence in creating a perception of the self. This was ironically, a dangerous thing. Eradication of the personal, an emulation of the kenotic efforts of Jesus, was the key to Franciscan action. What the *giullari* and the preachers did under the most salutary of intentions, was to turn action to devotion.

The *Meditations* also has the implication that devotional stories not specifically scriptural have, by the preaching of the Mendicants, the same inspirational authority as Biblical authority. A different textual fidelity,

---

[57] *Ibid.*, 135.

[58] The following two paragraphs are a recapitulation of Donald Lesnick's chapter VII, "The Franciscan *Sermo Humilis*: A Practical Guide to a Spirituality of Imagination and Action" in *Preaching in Medieval Florence: The Social World of Franciscan and Dominican Spirituality* (Athens and London: University of Georgia Press, 1989), 134-171.

[59] Lesnick, *Preaching in Medieval Florence*, 171.

one vaguely held in common with the population, served devotional ends, and allowed for Scripture to be neglected as interpretation and flourish as history. [60] Franciscan piety demanded literalness if emulation with the Incarnation were to take place. Such possibilities left aside specified chapter and verse allowing the interpretive to take hold in action not in critique. Indeed an excerpt from the *Meditations* shows that Christ allowed for a myriad of possibilities to guide the Christian to salvation;

> Our Lord and Redeemer, desiring the salvation of the souls for which He had come to give His, tried to draw them to Him in all ways and extricate them from the prison of his enemies. Thus He sometimes used persuasive and humble sermons, sometimes reproving and harsh ones, sometimes threats and frights. In this way He varied the means and remedies of salvation as He saw them and was necessary according to the place and time and different people that were listening.[61]

Different people were listening, and as such, had different avenues through which Christ could ostensibly enter. The preachers were, as was said, there to exhort the faithful in order to save their souls. The players were there to entertain bodies. The union of these two forces in the play of ideas put forth under the noses of the population had an efficacious effect upon the positive potentialities of the Incarnational Age.

What it also did was create a political *sine qua non* for the Friars Minor. Such responsibility as the saving of souls within the Catholic world eventually devolved into bringing some stray sheep back into the fold. In time the predication of the Franciscans began to have a hold in the universities, a development which was to have an ominous significance, as the Friars were called upon to act in line with the orthodoxy even in the realm of the intellectual.[62] And although the Franciscans were not as responsible as the Dominicans in the crushing of the Cathar heresy in Italy and in the Languedoc, their recognition by the Papacy forced them to join, albeit by association, in persecuting the

---

[60] See Beryl Smalley, *The Study of the Bible in the Middle Ages* (Notre Dame: University of Notre Dame Press, 1964), 285.
[61] Quoted in Lesnick, *Preaching in Medieval Florence*, 143.
[62] See Laura Gaffuri and Riccardo Quinto, eds. *Predicazione e societa nel Medioevo: Riflessione etica, valori e modelli di comportamento* (Padova: Centro Studi Antoniani, 2002), especially Nicoletta Giove Marchioli, "Circolazione Libraria e Cultura Francescana nella Padova del Due e Trecento," 131-141 and Cecilia Ianella, "Predicazione Domenicana ed etica Urbana tra Due e Trecento," 171-185.

greatest challenge to the Incarnational Age, and this by the fire of heretication.

CHAPTER FOUR

THE CATHARS AND INCARNATIONAL DENIAL

Perhaps of no other period in the history of the Church has the motto been so true, that "la civilization est une fleur carnivore."[1]

In the pronouncements of the Fourth Lateran Council, Innocent III's document enjoins true believers to treat European heresies as akin to the infidels in the Holy Land, calling for a crusade to deal with those in the midst of Christendom as well as those without.[2] That a spirit of eradication had already been essayed in the Languedoc by this time (the Massacre at Beziers[3] had already occurred six years previous) makes the words of the third constitution ring like a knell upon the presumptions of difference in the thirteenth century.[4] What had happened that had resulted in making sincere Christians of one attempt at apostolic imitation and heretics of others?

A full investigation of the Italian Cathars is not possible here, nor is a minute investigation of how dualism was introduced to the West. The purpose of the following chapter is to answer the question that ended the previous paragraph and add others to it with respect to developments in the specifically Italian communal culture within the Incarnational Age.

---

[1] Colin Morris, *The Papal Monarchy: The Western Church from 1050-1250* (Oxford: Clarendon Press, 1989), 416.
[2] "De haereticus" in *Decrees of the Ecumenical Councils: I. Nicaea-Lateran V.* Norman Tanner, ed. (London and Washington: Sheed and Ward and Georgetown University, 1990), 234.
[3] For the specific crusade against the Languedoc, see Pierre Belperon, *La Croisade contre les Albigeois et l'union du Languedoc a la France, 1209-1249* (Paris: Plon, 1942), and Jonathan Riley-Smith, The *Crusades: A History* (New Haven and London: Yale University Press, 1987), 163-169.
[4] It is of interest that the Crusades themselves were probably a conduit for ideas of dualism to spread into the European heartland. See Yuri Stoyanov, *The Other God: Dualist Religions from Antiquity to the Cathar Heresy* (New Haven and London: Yale University Press, 2000), 189.

Specifically; what was considered heretical in the Age; who were the Italian Cathars; what did they believe; why were they persecuted? A proper look at the Cathar heresy of the Middle Ages presupposes that the term heresy is adequately defined. The notion of the heretical within Latin Christendom changed subtly over the centuries as the position of the Church in temporal affairs changed. By the time of Innocent III, and under his leadership, the notion was enveloped in considerations of political treason,[5] and as such, had totalistic ramifications for the heretic, who could apply no measure of law, divine or human, to ameliorate the dire results of his anathema. He was negated, legally.

The reason heresy arose as it did in the twelfth and the thirteenth-century is a matter of some dispute among scholars, as is the nature of difference within the Medieval world.[6] That it did appear, or better, that it

---

[5] Walter Ulmann. *A Short History of the Papacy in the Middle Ages* (London: Methuen and Co., 1972), 220: "As for Innocent proclaiming a crusade against Christians…the explanation may partly lie in the example which was provided by Constantinople and the papal efforts to establish papal primacy over the Byzantine Christians also labeled heretics, by, if, necessary, military means and partly in the very conception of heresy as a crime of *lese majeste*, as high treason, committed against the divine majesty…The ideological background of this was the Roman law of *lese majeste* which furnished the jurist Innocent III with the necessary legal backing and armoury…for Innocent III was the first pope to publish an official collection of canon law." See also Malcolm Lambert, *Medieval Heresy: Popular Movements from the Gregorian Reform to the Reformation* (Oxford: Blackwell, 1977), 97-98: "Innocent gave full legal justification for the crusade, based especially on his own decretal of 1199, *Vergentis in senium*, with its assimilation of heresy into the crime in Roman law of *lese-majeste* , with concomitant penalties of confiscation of goods."

[6] For the clearest, briefest, and relatively recent studies in English, see R. I. Moore, *The Formation of a Persecuting Society: Power and Deviance in Western Europe, 950-1250* (Oxford: Blackwell, 1987), and Arthur Stephen McGrade, "The Medieval Idea of Heresy: What are we to make of it?" In *The Medieval Church: Universities, Heresy, and the Religious Life: Essays in Honour of Gordon Leff* P. Biller and B. Dobson, eds. (Suffolk: Boydell Press, 1999), 111-139; and Edward Peters, "Introduction: Heresy and Authority in Medieval Europe" in *Heresy and Authority in Medieval Europe* (Philadelphia: University of Pennsylvania Press, 1980), 1-9. Also see Janet Nelson, "Society, theodicy, and the origins of Medieval Heresy" in *Studies in Church History* 9: *Schism Heresy and Religious Protest* Derek Baker, ed. (Cambridge: Cambridge University Press, 1972), 62-78, which posits the theory of theodicy by which she means 'the problem which arises within a belief system when the individual's experience involves suffering which the system fails to accommodate or explain," 66: In response to Nelson see Talal Asad, "Medieval Heresy: An anthropological view" in *Social History* II (1986),

was countenanced so ferociously is at the crux of the chapter. The fact that it could draw upon the cumulative history of the Church to be effective speaks to the consolidation of doctrine relatively early in Christian history, and the need for unity within the Early Church. The marriage of the imperial presence within the orthodoxy during the first four centuries was the ultimate cause, as the novel Christian state began to be understood as temporal as well as a divine reflex of God's will.

In order for this to be achieved, the permanence of the Christian revolution required cementing into the order of things by a corporate mentality driven by conservative, traditionalist values. This was supplied

---

354-362, in which the anthropologist makes the claim that 'heresy clearly does not represent dissatisfaction with traditional beliefs and practices (from the tenth to the thirteenth centuries the Church itself undertook far reaching reforms) nor does it signify active dissent (the Church always contained a measure of disagreement or novelty.)' 355: Bronislaw Geremek, "The Marginal Man" in *The Medieval World*, Peter Linehan and Janet Nelson, eds. (New York and London: Routledge, 2001), 347-37, states that 'It was the heretics and the infidels-that is, people of a different faith and pagans-who were excluded from the Christian community, hence from the fundamental structures of Medieval Europe. The simple fact of not accepting the truths of Christian orthodoxy was sufficient reason for a sense of difference and for exclusion.': Max Weber, "Charismatic Authority" in *The Interpretation of Social Reality* J.E.T. Eldridge, ed. (New York: Scribner, 1971), 229-235, posits the role of the individual in change and difference, making use of Francis as an exemple.: Jeffrey Burton Russell, "Interpretations of the Origins of Medieval Heresy" in *Medieval Studies* 25 (1963) 26-53, who cautions against the prejudicial pre-conditions of the historian's view. See also Scott Waugh and Peter Diehl, eds. *Christendom and its Discontents: Exclusion, persecution and rebellion, 1000-1500* (Cambridge: Cambridge University Press, 1996). Also in the Italian, Gioachino Volpe, *Movimenti, religiosi e sette ereticali nella scocieta Medioevale Italiana* (Firenze: Olschiki, 1924), and Raoul Manselli, *Secolo XII: Religione popolare ed eresia* (Roma: Jouvence, 1983). Of course, for the general work on the subject by Gordon Leff, see bibliography.

For views of heresy within the Early Church and how this informed the Incarnational Age see Peter Brown, *Authority and the Sacred: Aspects of the Christianisation of the Roman World* (Cambridge: Cambridge University Press, 1992), esp. 29-54, and his *The Rise of Western Christendom: Triumph and Diversity AD 200-1000* (Oxford: Blackwell, 1996): Walter Bauer, *Orthodoxy and Heresy in Earliest Christianity* (Philadelphia: Fortress Press, 1971):   John Meyendorff, *Imperial Unity and Christian Divisions* (Crestwood: St. Vladimirs' Seminary Press, 1989): Editor Rowan Williams in his, "Does it Make Sense to Speak of a Pre-Nicene Orthodoxy?" In *The Making of Orthodoxy: Essays in Honour of Henry Chadwick* (Cambridge: Cambridge University Press, 1989) 1-23, and his "Defining Heresy" in *The Origins of Christendom in the West*   A. Krieder,ed. (Edinburgh and New York: T&T Clark, 2001), 316-329

by the educational preparation of its political inheritors as well as by the later doctrinal philosophies of the most eloquent of the fold: Justin, Irenaeus, and ultimately Augustine. The dovetailing of these two seemingly unsympathetic forces actually fortified the new faith and propelled it to the forefront of a baffling array of religious choices for the lapsed pagan. It may be the lynchpin behind the incredibly swift rise of this once odious religion, and may be the reason, the clandestine understanding between the newly bi-cameral power of Church and Empire, that difference and debate within doctrine must be swiftly and absolutely silenced.

Intellectual difficulties arose from this pairing of paradigms. These needed to be finessed by an intelligentsia, now tried by adversity and practiced in the art of persuasion. The Early Church in the face of halting gains over the course of three turbulent centuries had perhaps come to know that the eschatology of Jesus, which seemed to promise to the earliest Christians an imminent return, had to be modified to fit a historical continuum that was now theirs to fulfill.[7] This, along with the Church being involved *nolens volens* in the governance of the Empire begged for an agreement to end factionalism, which could be done by exhorting the faithful by clear scriptural precedence for an accepted canon of doctrine from Paul, and from Christ himself.[8]

This was important for two reasons; Firstly, so that the Roman Church could be recognized by a returning Christ as his Church, *sub-clave*[9] and fulfilling his command to feed his sheep and to teach all nations.[10] Secondly, such a mission could be seen as an empirical prerogative to vouchsafe both Heaven and earth for the faithful. These reasons satisfied the temporal and the spiritual needs of the population now poised to accept Christ, ready or not, yet perhaps not satisfying their need for logic. Such was the Early Church, and with it, the first and lingering understandings of what it meant to be a heretic. The term had treasonous implications. It

---

[7] "The paradox of the church was that it was a religious revolutionary movement, yet with a conscious political ideology that aimed at the capture of society through all its strata, but at the same time characteristic for its indifference to the possession of power in this world." Henry Chadwick, *The Early Church* (London: Penguin, 1993), 69.

[8] Some pertinent Pauline precedent for the condemnation of schism or heresy are I Corinthians, 1: 10-12, 17; 3: 10-12; 5: 5, 13; 7:7; 11: 18-19; 12: 25-31; 14: 27-33; II Corinthians 11: 14. Titus 1: 10-12; 2: 1, 15; 3: 10-11; Romans 13: 1-8. Galatians 1: 6; 5: 20; 1 Timothy 6:3-5; 2 Timothy 4: 3-4.

[9] Matthew 16: 18-20.

[10] Matthew 28: 16-20, Mark 16: 15-19, John 21: 15-20.

was no longer solely an acceptable choice among competing philosophies (*haeresis*), as it would come to be distinguished within the pre-Christian Mediterranean world.[11]

With the coming centuries, events would change, and old ideas would resurface. The weight of those ideas would be augmented by the circumstances of the loss of the Holy Land itself, and the rise of the Incarnational spirit. It was now evident that an increasingly restless spirituality could not assimilate itself into the greater hierarchy. It was not so much a moral failing on the part of the population, but a spiritual challenge, which was to occur here in the thirteenth century, but would resonate until the Reformation. Further, in such a situation, the loss of the way to salvation by spiritual meretricious-ness could be immediately likened to the rising notions of Italian mercantilism and exchange. Heresy was bad for business. This in turn created a Christian paradox with ominous consequences in the early sixteenth-century. It was the notion of exchange that at once saw the birth of evangelical poverty with Francis and Aquinas compare heresy to forgery.[12]

The difference between those two times was that the centrality of Roman dogma and the will of Innocent III would not be challenged with impunity in the Incarnational Age. Another, and most pertinent distinction between the times, was that the figure of Christ, the hallmark of the Incarnational Age was not a force as much as the Word of Christ in Reformation schism.[13] Hence the Cathar heresy was as much a product of a longing for certain perfectibility within a temporal and apostolic

---

[11] For a brief discussion on the term and its meaning see Edward Peters, *Heresy and Authority in Medieval Europe*, 14.

[12] "For it a much graver matter to corrupt the faith which quickens the soul than to forge money, which supports temporal life. Wherefore if forgers of money and other evildoers are forthwith condemned to death by the secular authority, much more reason is there for heretics, as soon as they are convicted of heresy, to be not only excommunicated, but even put to death." Thomas Aquinas, *Summa Theologica*, II-II, q. 11, art. 3.

[13] See Gordon Leff, *The Dissolution of the Medieval Outlook: An Essay on Intellectual and Spiritual Change in the Fourteenth Century* (New York: New York University Press, 1976), 120-131: "The failings of the Church were interpreted as a falling away from Christ which could only be remedied by restoring the church to the pattern of (Christ's) life. It is perhaps the supreme paradox that in the criticism of the later medieval church, the figure of Christ as a man became the main threat to the divinity of the church as an institution....(this was effected by)...a spiritual failure to meet the demands of a new spirituality that could no longer be contained within the existing structure and was not permitted new outlets under the latter's aegis."

Christianity as the Franciscans. Coupled with this sincerity was an opportunism that the heretics acted upon civil unrest, especially in Lombardy. Heresy, for all intents and purposes, was insistence upon personal choice and resulted in confrontation with the accepted paradigm. The Cathars were not heretics so much by force of difference, but by degree, taking advantage of nebulous formative influences in the communes to promulgate their ideas upon the shifting social plateau.[14]

Bringing their cause into the public sphere would force a confrontation with an increasing devotion to the body of Christ, the lynchpin of the Incarnational Age. Such an event as the popular understanding of the Incarnation did not perhaps persuade the entire body of the Italian laity, but indicatively it was the persistence of Third Order Mendicants that effectively whittled away a rising tide of Cathar belief without a major crusade as the Albigensian in France taking place.[15] Priding themselves on an increasing sense of independence, the Italian communes were reluctant at first to cooperate with the central authorities, but this cooperation eventually occurred.[16]

It did not take the form of a uniform crusade with genocidal implications.[17]

The notorious *campanilismo* that kept Italy from unification until the nineteenth century was also gratefully responsible for this eventuality.[18]

---

[14] See *The Heresies of the High Middle Ages*, W. Wakefield and A Evans, eds. (New York: Columbia University Press, 1969), 151-187.

[15] "Most of the popolo seem to have been orthodox in their beliefs but of sympathy with the hierarchy of the church, whose upper ranks were closely allied with the nobility; on the other hand they favored the new piety associated with the friars with its emphasis on the practical works of charity. This is proved by the popularity of the Third Orders for laymen. The same kind of zeal was tapped by the leaders of the church when they promoted the formation of the confraternities, like the Great Company of the Virgin Mary founded in Florence in 1244, whose ostensible claim was cooperation with the inquisitors in the suppression of heresy. By the mid thirteenth-century the heretical churches were a declining influence." J.K. Hyde, *Society and Politics in Medieval Italy: The Evolution of the Civil Life, 1000-1300* (London: Macmillan, 1973), 117.

[16] See Peter Diehl, "Overcoming reluctance to prosecute heresy in thirteenth-century Italy," in *Christendom and its Discontents: Exclusion, persecution, and rebellion, 1000-1500* Scott Waugh and Peter Diehl, eds. (Cambridge: Cambridge University Press, 1996), 47-66.

[17] For a full account on a methodology of repression in the Italian communes and a few examples against the general rule of conversion rather than repression see Carol Lansing, *Power and Purity: Cathar Heresy in Medieval Italy* (Oxford: Oxford University Press, 1998), 135-157.

The protracted disputes between the popes and the Holy Roman Emperors, specifically Frederick II, also facilitated the rise of difference within the far-flung bishoprics.[19]

So too did this freedom allow for heretical or quasi-heretical inroads to be made in the nascent communes of North Italy, especially Lombardy: The Humiliati, the Waldensians, and finally the Cathars themselves. So we are confronted with the spectacle of an activated heresy inside a political body at once divided and disinterested, but active and growing. It is both a revelation and a foregone conclusion that Catharism took hold in Italy. Indeed it is not an uncommon opinion among scholars that dualism, after its introduction from the Balkans, flourished first in Italy.[20]

The Italian Cathars held many beliefs in common with other sects of dualists that had spread from the Balkans, as a remnant of the dualism of the Manicheans.[21] The basic tenet of belief was that the world was the creation of an evil demiurge, and a place associated with the classic Christian conception of Hell. Therefore the goal of their theology was to rid themselves of attachment to the world, it's cares and it's temptations. The word Cathar comes from the Greek "*katharos*" meaning pure, without stain.

Their interpretation of canonical Scripture was allegorical and they rejected all but the wisdom texts and the Prophets from the Old Testament. In their view, Christ was an angel sent by the true God to the handiwork of the evil demiurge (the world itself) to redeem the faithful by teaching the True Doctrine. Since Christ was an angelic spirit, he was neither corporeal, nor suffered death.[22] Their theology was based on an

---

[18] See Mario Ascheri, "Beyond the Comune: The Italian City-State and its Inheritance" in *The Medieval World* Peter Linehan and Janet Nelson, eds. (London: Routledge, 2001), 451-467.
[19] See Stoyanov, *ibid*.
[20] See Steven Runciman, *The Medieval Manichee: A Study of Christian Dualist Heresy* (Cambridge: Cambridge University Press, 1947), 117.
[21] See *Heresies of the High Middle Ages: Selected Sources translated and annotated* W. Wakefield and A. Evans, eds. (New York and London: Columbia University Press, 1969), 167-169.
[22] "They based their teaching entirely on the Bible accepting the whole of the New Testament, with the addition of the Epistle to the Laodiceaens, an apocryphal work attributed to Saint Paul...They rejected the Pentateuch and the historical books as the work of the evil God, but accepted the Wisdom Books and the prophets as the divinely inspired." In Bernard Hamilton, "The Cathars and Christian Perfection" in *The Medieval Church: Universities, Heresy, and the Religious Life: Essays in Honour of Gordon Leff*, Peter Biller and Barrie Dobson, eds. (Suffolk: Boydell, 1999), 5-23, 7-9.

aggressive anti-matter, and stressed the eradication of fleshy pursuits. The redemption of the Cathars, as they believed in an almost Hindu type of punitive reincarnation, lay in extinguishing the desire for procreation and teaching a rigorous abstinence in diet and behavior.[23] Such a course was not practical for the average believer (who were called the *credentes*), and as such the system of worship was divided into these *credentes* and the Perfects (*perfecti*), who, much like the original Elect of the Manichees in Augustine's time, were considered to be the carriers of the secret wisdom.[24]

The Italian Cathars were adept at textual interpretation[25] and had written texts of Cathar theology that were used across the dualist world of the thirteenth-century.[26] This engendered within the sect, a certain gnosticism that further separated the Perfects from the community, as the pre-requisites for exquisite interpretation belonged to the educated elite.[27] The central biblical text around which their theology was derived was from Ecclesiasticus: "All things are doubled, one against the other."[28] How things were doubled was the essence of their exegetical nuances, of which little survives.

So despite the relatively simplicity of their faith as compared to the official Christianity of the West, their learning needed refinement in order to properly teach a foundational theology that allowed for uniformity outside the presence of Conciliar activity in the period under discussion.[29]

---

[23] See "Cathari" in *The Oxford Dictionary of the Christian Church* F.L. Cross and E. A. Livingstone, eds (Oxford: Oxford University Press, 1997), 301.

[24] See Peter Brown, *The Body and Society: Men, Women, and Sexual Renunciation in Early Christianity* (New York: Columbia University Press, 1988), 198-200.

[25] See Lorenzo Paolini, "Italian Catharism and Written Culture," in *Heresy and Literacy* P. Biller and An. Hudson, eds. (Cambridge: Cambridge University Press, 1994), 83-103.

[26] See Malcolm Barber, *The Cathars: Dualist Heretics in Languedoc in the High Middle Ages* (Harlow: Pearson, 2000), 82.

[27] "..the Lombard Cathars sent their best minds to study dialectic and theology...Indeed despite the relative scarcity of extant Cathar writings, the existence of Cathar intellectuals was sufficiently well-known for the Cistercian, Caesarius of Heisterbach, writing in the 1220s, to use them as the basis of an exemplum for novices in his book of instruction, The Dialogue on Miracles." In Barber, *The Cathars*, 83.

[28] Ecclus. 42, 25. In the Vulgate, "Omnia duplicia, unum contra unum." See also Hamilton, "The Cathars and Christian Perfection," 8.

[29] Stoyanov relates that the "expansion of Catharism was gaining momentum, (and) at some point between 1166-1176 a crucial Cathar Council was convened at St. Felix-de-Caraman near Toulouse" which was presided over by Papa Nicetas.

The Cathar Churches of Italy that exerted any influence were all in Lombardy: The three main groups of Desenzano (called the Albanenses), Concorezzo (the Garatenses), and Bagnolo. Other churches in Tuscany, the Marches, Calabria, or Provence held fast to the rules of these three.[30] The Italian Churches were drawn against one another in their theology, especially the church of Desenzano against the Church of Concorezzo. This, although a running conflict in Italian Catharism, allows posterity to view their tenets in apologetic form not against the greater Christendom, but amongst themselves. The results of this feud provides us with the most complete formulation of Cathar theology, the *Liber du duobus principiis (Book of the Two Principles)*, written, it is believed, by the Albanensian John of Lugio.[31]

The Book of the Two Principles can be mined endlessly to see how and why the sect offended the sensibilities of the Catholic hierarchy. This would do little. More to the point is the way their particular theology offended their target audience, the Italian laity at large, which could not accept an affront to the nascent Incarnational Age, convinced, as they would be, of the "truth" of the Franciscan ideal. This and the wily persuasiveness of Franciscan inquisitors in dealing delicately with the sensibilities of the population (of Orvieto especially) assured that the Cathars could not gain a true following throughout the peninsula.[32]

One of the most complete exegetical works concerning the *Book of the Two Principles* must be taken with a grain of salt, as the author of the counter-tract, *Summa de Catharis et Pauperibus de Lugduno (Compendium On the Cathars and the Poor of Lyons)* was one Rainerius Sacconi. Sacconi converted to the Dominicans and their Catholic orthodoxy after enjoying a relatively high status with the Cathars. Therefore his testimony, although contemporary (1255), is rife with the contempt seemingly incumbent upon the sensibilities of the newly converted. Nonetheless the book offers us the most complete picture of the Cathars of North Italy.

Sacconi refers to the Cathars as "more apes than men"[33] as their sacraments mimicked the sacraments of the Church. He explains that they

---

Eventually such unity could not hold in the face of increasing pressure from the papacy, and a schism of Cathar Churches occurred by 1220. Stoyanov, *The Other God*, 195-200.
[30] Rainierius Sacchoni in *The Birth of Popular Heresy* R.I. Moore, ed. (London: Edward Arnold, 1975), 133.
[31] See Wakefield and Evans eds., *Heresies of the High Middle Ages*, 511-591.
[32] See Lansing, *Power and Purity*, 138-139.
[33] R. I. Moore, ed. *The Birth of Popular Heresy, Documents*, 133.

have four: the laying on of hands (what the Cathars referred to as the *consolamentum*), the blessing of bread, and penance and ordination. The denial of Purgatory and the denial of the resurrection of the flesh is common to the Italian Cathars, a fact echoed by the Franciscan James Capelli, who is remarkable for his restraint in his *Summa contra haereticos* of about 1240.[34]

The extreme condemnation that the Cathars aimed at the flesh and the material world, mirrored the contemporary Franciscan concern with possession. But unlike the Cathars, the Franciscans added a dimension of inevitability in their understanding of the human condition, ameliorating it by acts of charity towards those dispossessed either of health or wealth. Cathar theology can be said to have been an intellectualizing of perfection, having within it little sympathy for the material world.[35]

The attractiveness of Incarnational ideas lay in the attainability of their presumptions through effort in the temporal sphere. The hope of salvation was always present through act. The Cathars presumed that the will needed suppression lest it act out its desires, further damning the *credent* into another round of existence. The body was at the heart of their mistrust.[36]

---

[34] See W. Wakefield and A. Evans, eds. *Heresies of the High Middle Ages*, 300.

[35] "The Cathars did not fear death, they feared life. Given their premises they had reason to do so. The Good God was all loving, but he was not almighty, and he had no jurisdiction over the kingdom of darkness in which they lived. The odds were heavily weighted against their salvation: the whole universe, the vastness of the heavens as well as the earth, was the creation of the evil God, and the Cathars' souls were imprisoned in bodies made by and subject to that God." In Bernard Hamilton, "The Cathars and Christian Perfection," 23.

[36] A response will be made later in the chapter against Bernard Hamilton's reading of Cathar beliefs concerning the Incarnation. First his reading in full: " The Cathars did not doubt that the Incarnation and the sacrifice of Calvary had really taken place; they speak of Christ redeeming the Kingdom with his blood (lo nostre Segnor Yesu Christ...aisicom es scrit al vangeli, he reymu lo regne sobre dit al sio sanc.). We do not know how precisely they understood the doctrine of atonement, but in that regard it is worth remembering that no mainstream church has ever ratified one particular theory of atonement as authoritative, and the Cathars may have been like most other Christians and considered Christ's sacrifice a magnum misterium, inexpressible in human language. The confusion of modern scholars about the Cathar doctrine of the Incarnation is a consequence, I think, of their unwillingness to accept the Cathar belief that because this world was the creation of the evil God it was, in Christian terms, Hell. Christ's descent through the seven heavens of the phenomenal world to free his people thus corresponds to orthodox Christian belief in the Harrowing of Hell. Hi work in this world was indeed exemplary: he could not take a human body created by the evil God, and he could

And if the body was at the heart of mistrust, then it was only natural that contemporary Eucharistic conceptions of the Real Presence would be marshaled to combat the heresy. In response, the Cathars would have occasion to mock what they considered the absurd doctrine of transubstantiation. This is not to say that the Cathars had no referential ritual for the Eucharist. On the contrary, among the four sacraments popularly accepted by the Cathar Churches in Italy, the Breaking of the Bread was there. With the Cathars however, the ceremony was merely a commemorative one without the theophagic implications of the Latin Mass. The Desenzano sect thought that the bread itself could not be blessed as it was part of the material world. They seem to have been the most austere in their observances. This asceticism in diet was prevalent in the Cathar churches throughout where meats, eggs, and cheese were concerned. The product of animals was to be sworn off.[37]

The absolution of the Cathars dealt with a monthly public penance and then the *consolamentum* being conferred upon the contrite sinner. Cathar insistence on prayer and abstinence made both Sacconi and the normally sedate Capelli seethe:

> For puffed by awareness of their flesh to the piety and humility of the angels, they seek to convince others of what they know not…Now in order to spread false doctrine under a veil of good works, they abstain from theses foods at all times and, abstaining also in repeated fasts from wine, they crucify the flesh, as the Apostle saith, with vices and concupiscenses.[38]

They saw pride in their prayer before meals, and their absence of alms-giving. The concern seemed to be upon achieving an impossible asceticism and allowing none within their company to fall away without the societal *consolamentum* interceding upon their behalf, not so much in the sight of God, but within the sight of the community.

The mortification of the flesh was also an aspect of Franciscan piety. Capelli as a Franciscan could not have failed to note the similarities. The heretics were interested in the same approximation of perfection.

As such, the expurgated heretic was a parallel to the Incarnational man as they were both, due to different circumstances, beings who were

---

only represent his Incarnation for the edification of men, but the spiritual validity of that representation derived from the fact that the Incarnation had really happened though in another world." Hamilton, "The Cathars and Christian Perfection," 11-12.
[37] W. Wakefield and A. Evans, eds. *Heresies of the High Middle Ages*, 306.
[38] Capelli in Wakefield and Evans, eds. *Heresies of the High Middle Ages*, 306.

not. The Incarnational man was at the service of the other beside him, a speculative and active Christian, and decidedly in the present discussion acting within the legal bounds afforded society. The heretical man was differentiated by legal means, as it was ostensibly understood that there was a right and a wrong way to be a Christian in a world ruled by the purveyors of that certitude. The question becomes not why there were Cathars in Italy, but why did their practice become seen as *rightly* condemned by other Christians.

In any truly dualistic religion, the nature of the mythos splits affinities between the light and the dark. The dualism of Catharism saw the example of Christ as a doomed pedagogy as long as the place wherein the teaching was under the reign of evil.[39] The Christ of Christian hope is absent, and if hope, a theological virtue, is absent from the doctrines of an evil world, then the terrestrial become damned. Perhaps this why one scholar insists that the Incarnation was understood as being essayed in the hell of Cathar mythology, the Earth itself.[40] Yet the purpose of the Incarnation was to enflesh God so as to be a present guarantor to others of the salvation from which he comes. If in Cathar thinking, the earth is already damned, then the promise is null and void.

The Cathar contempt for the flesh and it debilitating shortcomings is best told in the story of Pietro Parenzo, a rector sent to the Italian town of Orvieto by Innocent III to combat Catharism, which was feared rife among the laity. Parenzo was murdered (it is not known by whom) and the bishop and the authorities blamed the Cathars. Parenzo's body in the meanwhile had been left in the cathedral, and had not decayed but emitted the scent of flowers, a sign of sanctity.

As the townspeople flocked into the cathedral to experience this, someone hurled a piece of rotten meat at the procession.[41] Obviously, this was a flouting of Catholic beliefs upon the corporal notions of resurrection. As Carol Lansing has reconstructed, the problems in Orvieto centered upon a mistrust of the body according to the Cathar. And such mistrust was attached to a vague disgust with the functions of the body. To the Cathars, the vehicle of putrescence could never contain the angelic purity of Christ. Even though their view of what the body was identical to

---

[39] "There is no room for Christ in a truly Dualist religion. Thus all good Christians must necessarily fight against Dualism." Runciman, *The Medieval Manichee*, 175.
[40] See Bernard Hamilton, 11-12.
[41] In Lansing, *Power and Purity*, 3.

Innocent's, the pope allowed the hope of Christ to enter and transform what was all too mortal.[42]

This also produced an uneasy alliance between the Cathar women and their theology. It stands to reason that women in such a society would approach shame when experiencing the monthly regulations of her body, and anger at being told that their children were prisons for re-captured souls. After many attempts to see the particular heresy as beneficial to women in comparison to the patriarchal creeds of Catholicism, scholars are now issuing correctives on the view that woman were better off as heretics than as Catholics.[43]

By virtue of their highly ascetic doctrine, Catharism was a difficult path for the worldly dispensation. Yet the path to follow for the awakened Christian of the Age was necessarily one of exclusivity. The need for conversion needed to be circumscribed by the dissatisfaction that arose from the orthodox practice of the day. Such a quest became, in the hands of Francis and Bernard, shamanic in that the fruits of their labors were sacrificed at the altar of the hegemonic Church, which comprised the laws of the community.

Yet life at the level of the commoner could blur distinction. It is possible that the rise of Catharism was as much a reception of Franciscan run-off and vice-versa. To an uneducated laity the Friars Minor could be considered the spiritual and ideological brethren of the Cathar *perfecti*. The poor especially would be the battleground for competing ideologies.

This was an issue of no small weight, because the idea of poverty would become one of concerns of willful exclusivity within the social order. The Franciscans, as we shall see, would lose the pace and thrust of the Incarnational Age by the imbroglio concerning poverty, but never the imprimatur of orthodoxy because they had done something that the Cathars were unwilling to do: They had embraced the notion of denial as predicated upon life within the temporal, indeed the carnal, sphere, seeing redemption only as being as worthy as the degree to which the human could imitate the divine. To the Cathars this notion was not only

---

[42] "O vile idegnita nella condizione umana, o indegna condizione della vilta umana! Osserva l'erbe e le piante; questi producono fiori, fronde, e frutti: tu produci lendini, pidocchi, e lombrichi. Esse danno olio, vio e balsamo; tu non dai che sputo, sterco ed orina. Esse spirano soavita di profumo, tu spandi il fetore della corruzione." In Innocent III, *De Contemptu Mundi* translated into Italian by Guido Battelli (Firenze: La Voce, 1924), VIII, 45.

[43] See Peter Biller, "Cathars and Material Woman," in *Medieval Theology and the Natural Body* P. Biller and A.J. Minnis, ed. (York: York University Press, 1997), 61-107.

undesirable, but heretical in itself. To the sincere poor, left out on the margins of the society, this was manna from heaven.

The acceptance and unbridled popularity of Francis and his order along with the Dominican perseverance in the grim task of Inquisition combined to have a truly catastrophic effect on the Cathar communes in Italy. But perhaps greater than either channel of orthodoxy, Catharism fell prey to the new age of mercantilism and the hope for tomorrow incumbent upon the hopes of a newly-prospering gentry.[44] The terrors and the crimes of what happened in the south of France had mercifully never happened in Italy.

In the constitutions of the Fourth Lateran Council, Innocent, along with inciting Catholics to crusade against the Cathars, had formulated and codified the doctrine of transubstantiation specifically to rebut the heresy concerning the Incarnation. He made a point to underline the continuing and active Presence of Christ in the world.[45] The effects of these pronouncements devolved into a dreadful campaign that swelled to wholesale murder. The harsh retribution against a dualism that discredited the Incarnation and the workings of the flesh in redemption is perhaps the single greatest proof that an Incarnational culture existed. It may not have heralded itself as such, but the relevance of a culture's ideals is best delineated by exposing what that culture feared as a nemesis and took pains to destroy. The Cathars in Italy, for all their predilections for living a perfected Christian ideal, condemned the mechanics of Christian salvation that was tested out on the grounds of a fallen Earth wrapped in the flesh. The creative act itself could not be seen as beneficent in the world ruled by evil.[46] The heresy contained within it the gravest error an idea can commit: It had misunderstood its time. Salvation in Incarnational Italy, would be essayed because of the flesh, not in spite of it.

---

[44] See Raoul Manselli, *L'eresia del male*, (Napoli: Morano, 1963), 330-332.
[45] Margaret Miles, *The Word Made Flesh: A History of Christian Thought* (Oxford: Blackwell, 2005), 181-182.
[46] See Arno Borst, "Die Katharer," MGH Schriften 12 (Stuttgart, 1953). It is the opinion of the German scholar that the culture of the Cathars was not stimulated enough for a creative release. In the Toynbeian analysis, the inability to confront crisis with creation spells doom for any culture.

CHAPTER FIVE

OCKHAM, GIOTTO, AND THE WEIGHT OF THE WORLD

> They would also obtain, with much cunning and worldly wisdom, all kinds of briefs and privileges from the Pope, thus not only relaxing the purity of the Rule revealed by Christ, but destroying it altogether. . . they will enter into litigation not only with men of the world, but with other religious, thus digging for themselves a pit into which finally they would fall.
> —*St. Francis' Vision of the Future.*[1]

With Francis, Franciscan achievement lay in the realm of the spiritual. The case has been made about the unique disposition of Francis' vocation and its powerful pull on the imagination. Much also has been said about what is to follow. But there was another consciousness about to usurp the momentum of the Incarnational Age, and Francis, that *fons et origo* of one became the unwitting Prometheus of the other. This consciousness was centered in the critical faculties and dealt with representing the speculum of the Incarnational idea as carefully codified idea.

After the personal achievement of Saint Francis had been made the founding mythos of the Franciscan not long after his death, the Friars Minor had to apply this peculiar fable to their everyday life. Bonaventure himself, although the great synthetic genius of Franciscan history and mysticism, left little in the way of dealing with politics outside the Order's cloistered walls.

The nature of the new individual, founded by Francis upon the tenet of poverty and reared in Christian imitation, had now to confront the very real tangible concerns of the secular arm of the Church and State. It was left to the philosophers of the Order, as in a dreary epilogue, to fight for the rights of the intentional poor. Although the actual debate on poverty (1327) began long after the death of Francis, it coincided with the work of Giotto and the dissemination of Dante's *Divine Comedy*, as another denouement of the Incarnational Age. What it achieved, especially in the

---

[1] *OSE*, 1899.

arguments of William of Ockham, had reverberations outside the call of the novice and into the Orders' nature of the individual in the political realm of the emergent fourteenth century. This had its echo in the 'new' art of their official iconographer, Giotto di Bondone, and along with the rising tide of intellectual concerns and textual understanding within the mature city-state, this served to handicap and eventual defeat the mystical and experiential bent of the Incarnational Age.

There has been much written and much said about the Franciscan role in the establishment of a language of rights. Be this wasted ink or inspired lines, the issue of conscious and careful consideration in the developing is, I trust, not one in which there is, or has been, debate. Whatever the case may be, the intent behind the earliest and last salvos fired in the debate over Franciscan poverty were not reared to offer the contemporary equivalent notion of subjective rights. Perhaps we have that spectacle with Marsilius of Padua, but historians, philosophers and antiquarians, always in obeisance to the tyrannical nature of their appetites follow Ariadne's string to daylight. Some think that William of Ockham holds the distinction of being the real Prometheus of the philosophy of subjective rights. It is from Ockham where, though inadvertently, the defense of evangelical poverty becomes ideated.

The chapter will reflect upon some notions in Ockham that, together with declarations from Bonaventure, both remained true to the Franciscan ideal and engendered (albeit unwittingly) a focus by which the individual, as we imagine him today, could begin to see himself in the crowd, and increasingly, outside of it. The actual full account of the Order's troubles beginning with Michael of Cesena in 1327 can be found elsewhere. [2] Ockham's role, in writing and defending the *Opus nonagintum dierum, (The Work of Ninety Days)* and Giotto's codification of the mythos in formal Franciscan iconography as finalizing the Incarnational Age, is the purpose of the chapter.

The arguments of Ockham in the *Opus nonagintum dierum* (1332) against the decade old claims of John XXII's bull *Quia vir reprobus* (1323) are sometimes seen to be a natural outgrowth of his nominalism

---

[2] For a sound and short treatment see Gordon Leff, "The Bible and Rights in the Franciscan Disputes over Poverty" in *The Bible and the Medieval World : Essays in Memory of Beryl Smalley,* Katharine Walsh and Diana Wood, eds. (Oxford: Ecclesiastical History Society, 1985), 225-235. For a longer treatment leading up to the debate see Malcolm Lambert , *Franciscan Poverty: The Doctrine of the Absolute Poverty of Christ and the Apostles in the Franciscan Order 1210-1323* (New York: The Franciscan Institute, 1998).

and a felicitous example of preparation put to purpose. [3] But this reading would betray the nature of the conflict by diminishing the Franciscan cause as a ready champion girt with a new weapon.

The work was not really original in its thinking and was in many ways an *ad hoc ergo propter hoc* essay into the nature of rights[4]. It was certainly not an original and fluid conception depending as it did to counter point by point the claims of the "heretical pontiff", and on the previous works of John of Pecham and of course Bonaventure which had clearly set forth a defense of the Order. What can be claimed for the *Opus* is that it summed up the Franciscan attempt at a life of poverty with thoroughly philosophical language hitherto used to codify universal theories of human and divine realities and not towards the specificity of a group found in society. The Franciscans, by the poverty debate, were forced to take themselves seriously as a social entity, very much a part of this world.

The controversy that raged in the years of the Franciscan debate perhaps can be matched by the contemporary debate over it in historical-philosophical circles. Ockham's role in the origin of natural rights has been swatted about somewhat, both rising and falling depending upon the proclivities of the scholar. The nexus of discussion involves (at least for the purposes of this brief essay) some viewpoints not altogether distinct or differentiated one from the next but particular as an ongoing and fruitful dialogue into the nature of the Franciscan achievement in the rights debate[5].

---

[3] See Annabel Brett, *Liberty, Right, and Nature: Individual Rights in Later Scholastic Thought* (Cambridge: Cambridge University Press, 1997), 49-50.
[4] See R. F. Bennet and H. S. Offler's introduction to the *Opus Nonaginta Dierum* in *Guilielmi de Ockham. Opera Politica* vol. II (Manchester: Manchester University Press, 1963), xv-xix. The editors also make the overt claim that the OND relied heavily on the *Apologia Pauperum* of Bonaventure.
[5] See Virpi Makinen, *Property Rights in the Late Medieval Discussion on Franciscan Poverty*. Recherches de Theologie et Philosophie medievales, Bibliotheca 3 (Leuven: Peeters, 2001): Roberto Lambertini, *La Poverta Pensata: Evoluzione Storico dell Identita Minoritica da Bonaventura ad Ockham* (Modena: Mucchi, 2000): Annabel S. Brett, *Liberty, Right, and Nature: Individual Rights in Later Scholastic Thought* (Cambridge: Cambridge University Press, 1997): Brian Tierney's work overall but especially *Religion, Law, and the Growth of Constitutional Thought 1150-1650* (Cambridge: Cambridge University Press, 1982): Richard Tuck, *Natural Rights Theories: Their origin and development,* (Cambridge: Cambridge University Press, 1979): Gordon Leff's work in general but here see his "The Bible and Rights in the Franciscan Disputes over Poverty" in *The Bible and the Medieval World : Essays in Memory of Beryl Smalley,* Katharine

In order to fully establish the importance of the debate it is important to stress the casual nature of the specifically political argument as the language of political discourse had not been rarefied and could be said to be a potentiality in the resulting chaos, as neither Bonaventure in his *Apologia Pauperum* (*Defense of the Mendicants*, 1269) nor Ockham in the *Opus Nonagintum Dierum* set out to offer well reasoned and objective frameworks for political theory.[6] That being said the riposte to John XXII maneuvered Ockham into arguments for what would become a framework for autonomy of a subjective notion of conscience.[7] This too echoed the AP but set forth its reasoning in a dialectical praxis.

The debate has been given full treatment, so let us, like Tuck before us, leave it to the magisterial account of Gordon Leff to set the pageant moving. Briefly, the Avignon Papacy of John XXII disestablished the foundational notion of Franciscan poverty previously defended by Bonaventure and upheld and sanctioned by Nicholas III Bull *Exiit qui seminat* of 1279. John's bull *Quia vir reprobus* of 1323, the instrument of his anathema denied the notion of use without possession and refused the Papacy stewardship of Franciscan property bequeathed to them by donation, as such actions would bolster what he considered to be the preposterous and heretical argument that they owned and could own anything.

The bull, sent to Ockham, was declared by the Englishman to be "smacking of heresy" and full of error. To prove this he wrote his *Opus*

Walsh and Diana Wood, eds. *Studies in Church History, Subsidia 4.* (Oxford: Ecclesiastical History Society, 1985), 225-235: and since Skinner's Cambridge seems to have, at least in the English speaking world, dominated the discussion, an obvious choice is *The Cambridge History of Medieval Political Thought c. 350-c. 1450,* J. H. Burns, ed. (Cambridge: Cambridge University Press, 1988), especially Antony Black on "The Individual and Society," 588-606; and Janet Coleman, "Property and Poverty," in *The Cambridge History of Later Medieval Philosophy,* Norman Kretzmann, Anthony Kenny, Jan Pinborg, eds. (Cambridge: Cambridge University Press, 1982): Also in the same volume, see A. S. McGrade, "Rights, Natural Rights, and the Philosophy of Law," 738-756, and D. E. Luscombe's "The State of Nature and the Origin of the State," 757-770. Also John Kilcullen's "The Political Writings" in *Cambridge Companion to Ockham,* Paul Vicent Spade, ed. (Cambridge: Cambridge University Press, 1999), 302-309: Finally, Joseph Canning, *A History of Medieval Political Thought 300-1450* (London:Routledge, 1996).

[6] See Coleman, 601-602.

[7] This is a rather neat way of seeing the middle ground between Brett's claim of Ockham's originality, (62) and Tuck's (Leff's) more grudging admiration for John's role in pushing the question to the inevitable answer.

nonagintum dierum (henceforth *OND*) to debate, point by point, the claims made by the Pope. Here we shall look at the OND as a final summation and codification of ideas found in Bonaventure's previous *Apologia pauperum*, (henceforth *AP*) specifically the negation of legal standing by the proclamation of the inherent personal liberties of man in the natural state. Philosophically the soundness of Franciscan doctrine was seamless within these two works, but the *OND* dependant as it was on Bonaventure, also served to codify Franciscan purpose and thereby, subtly debilitate impetus.

Bonaventure's role in the shaping of a negative personal liberty within the poverty debate was recognized earlier in this century but has, as of late, been relegated to a secondary or indeed a tertiary importance.[8] The emphasis in Bonaventure, like Francis before him was the insistence upon

---

[8] Lambertini recognizes the influence but gives pride of place as far as notional liberties before Ockham in Franciscan texts, to John Peckham's *Tractatus pauperis*. Ockham's contribution in the Opus nonagintum dierum becomes for him "una summa della difesa dell'Ordine francescano, " Lambertini, 69. Bennet and Offler are insistent upon the relevance of Bonaventure to Ockham, xv; but Tuck for one hardly mentions him whereas Brett states that the promulgation of the bull *Exiit qui seminat* in 1279 won for the Franciscans it's battle against the secularists within the Order, (Brett, 52) without mentioning that such an imprimatur made the Franciscan position inflexible and subject to a counter bull to challenge the notions covered by Bonaventure and given legal standing. Further John XXII's challenge was couched in legalistic terms making us assume that therein lay the genesis of the legal notions of liberty. Yet the Franciscan response reveals itself as having a schizophrenic legacy. By accepting arguments by John as fit for response they admit the power of one they at the same time consider as a heretical and schismatic Pope. The Ockhamite and Michaelist position therefore, as Leff says, fights the Pope on his own terms but gets the better of him by even essaying the challenge and applying notions of authority which preceded him, reminding him by this challenge of his precarious position as spiritual leader. Also, the Papacy of John was one necessarily involved with issues of ownership and possession as the move to Avignon had resulted in a dubious increase in revenue and accusations of cupidity against the Pontiff. As John was a canonists and a fine legal mind, his reign became mired in legal argument defended the overhaul of papal power. In such an understanding the sincere poverty of the Franciscans presented John with a potential enemy within the fold that could give lie to his efforts. See Tuck, 23, and Gordon Leff, *Heresy in the Later Middle Ages,* vol. I (Manchester: Manchester University Press, 1967), 250: Walter Ulmann, *A Short History of the Papacy in the Middle Ages,* (London: Methuen and Co., 1972), 286: Ludwig Pastor, *History of the Popes, From the Close of the Middle Ages,* vol. I, translated by Frederick Ignatius Antrobus (London: John Hodges, 1891), 71-72.

negation, and this of an intensely spiritual nature. The world insisted upon seeing the rights of possession, especially in the rising mercantile class, as something intrinsic to human nature. Bonaventure set out in the *AP*, at times in remarkably legal terms, a notion of liberty based on negative connotations. We must remember that although the texts may seem vague in solidifying what we would now consider the very precious idea of human liberty, the emphasis was on how to more perfectly emulate Christ, the lynchpin of the Incarnational Age. As such, as Christ thought to save the human condition by acquiescing to the harshest vicissitudes inherent to it, the Franciscans sought to achieve redemption through acting out his Incarnation.

The major points in relation to the debate from Bonaventure occur in chapters seven and eleven. Chapter XI, part 9,[9] where the Seraphic Doctor equates right with the right of refusal and ties the legal language of inheritance to the point made. The point turns on the intention of the individual and not the exchange itself. Bonaventure had already laid out the Franciscan basis for use in temporal things in part 5 of the same chapter by distinguishing four ways[10] in which those things are used—ownership, possession, usufruct, and simple use, saying earlier that only the last is permissible to the Mendicant and then, under restraint.[11]

---

[9] "His autem quae dicta sunt suffragatur legis naturalis dictamen evidenter explicatem per iura civilia. Nam lege cavetur quod non potest libertas nolenti acqueri, et quod "beneficium invito non datur" et quod nemo donatum assequi et damnosam seu lucrosam hereditatem nemo adire compellitur. Insuper, sicut rerum universitas, puta hereditas, solo animo acquiritur, ita solo animo contrario repudiatur. . cum igitur Fratres Minores animum acquirendi non habeant, quin potuis voluntatem contrariam, etiam si res corpore contingant; nec dominium nec possessionem acquirunt nec rerum huiusmodi possessors vel domini dici possunt. " "Apologia pauperum, ch. XI, pt. 9" in *S. Bonaventurae: Opera Omnia,* v. 8, (Florence: Quaracchi, 1898), 313.

[10] ". . intelligendum est, quod cum circa res temporales quatuor sit considerare, scilicet proprietatem, possessionem, usufructum et simplicem usum; et primus quidem tribus vita mortalium posit carer, ultimo vero tanquam necessario egeat: nulla prorsus potest esse professio omnino temporalium rerum abdicans usum." *Ibid,* pt. 5, 312.

[11] "Cum autem circa temporalium bonorum possessionem duo considerare contingat, dominium videlicet et usum, sitque usus necessario annexus itae praesenti: evangelicae paupertatis est, possessions terrenas quantum ad dominium et proprietatem relinquere usum vero non omnino reiicire sed arctare, iuxta illud quod dicit Apostolus ad Timotheum: 'Habentes alimenta et quibus tegamur, contenti simus. '" *Ibid,* ch. VII, pt. 3, 272-273.

Bonaventure is also at pains to separate the right of ownership and possession in a communal understanding. The group therefore has a further right above the individual because (it is implied through the example of Christ and his relationship with his apostles) use in groups supersede the one in the current paradigm,[12] and the right of the individual in respect to possession and ownership should be hobbled for the sake of his own good, as should his tethering to the greater Order.

In terms of couching his language of rights in negative terms Bonaventure uses the legal restrictions imposed upon infants and lunatics to justify the position of the Minorites. This was a point mercifully overlooked by the wily John XXII who could have turned such a point to bitter purpose.[13]

But the focus of Christ and in particular *Christus in paupertas* goes to the heart of Francis' vocation and the Incarnational Age, and clearly sets out the particular notion of redemption through an insistent poverty. This sloughing away until the bare necessities were left, corresponded to Francis' almost fetishistic view of the naked Christ[14] and worked out its implications in an interesting logic of exchange within Bonaventure's view of charity wherein a constant mortification is reflective of a more perfect dispensation. Whereas, those helping towards this through donation or gift display in a transaction, the logic of Franciscan possession; by giving way the spiritual possession remains and is active with the giver of the gift. Therefore he becomes a benefactor and an owner, as the gift, given as it was to the Order is simply used and never possessed. The spiritual ownership remains and the gift of grace is returned, whereas the Minorites, using this donation, are given the grace of

---

[12] "quod Christum at Apostolos imitari non solum quod abdicationem proprietatum, verum etiam quoad extremam temporalium rerum penuriam, quae consistit in carentia possessionum et pecuniarum non solum est licitum, sed est laudabile et perfectum. Non tamen ex hoc debet vel potest inferri, quod abdicates rerum proprietatibus, possidere aliquid in communi sit imperfectum. . et in modis perfectae paupertatis intelligendum est quamquam non sit per omnia simile hinc et inde, sicut diligenter consideranti est evidens. " *Ibid.,* pt. 16, 277.

[13] "According to Roman law, a lunatic ('furiosus') was a person legally declared to be of unsound mind who, therefore was not held capable or responsible before the law. Thus he (or she) could not rationally possess property. Such person needs a curator. For Bonaventure this text gives an example of necessity of will and intention in acquiring property over things." Makinen, 70.

[14] Lambert, *Franciscan Poverty,* 65.

continuing to follow the way of Christ and remain unencumbered by the exchange, as they keep nothing.[15]

The theory that lies in Bonaventure is that a right implies a right to refuse and hence is antagonistic and confrontational in a social setting if the social contract is pervasive. By relying on negative language it is probable that Bonaventure wished to impose less legal standing and less social standing upon the Order. His enthusiasm needed mitigating, as he was the leader of the Order busy negotiating a middle way between the extremists of absolute poverty and the more relaxed secularists. Nevertheless the bull by Nicholas settled the dispute until the arrival of John XXII.

Ockham's response to John was the final culmination of thinking on the subject and what is to our purpose here is of a narrow focus. That is concerning the concept of the dominium which one enjoys over oneself and where these rights have their origin.

The notion of any such possession and ownership stems from the loss of innocence, and consequently the right of possession becomes fraught with the implications of sin.[16] Rights in the human sphere are separated into the right of forum (*ius fori*) and the right of heaven (*ius poli*)[17], and the right of forum as it is a specified social contract informed by the just, whereas the right of heaven is a divine right which can be inscrutable under the purely natural senses but made by the jurisdiction of God attains what is known as divine right or even natural right as its benediction extends over all creation. [18]

---

[15] See Peter Fehlner, *The Role of Charity in the Ecclesiology of St. Bonaventure* (Roma: Miscellanea Francescana, 1965), 167-169; and Marino Damiata, *Guglielmo d'Ockham: Poverta e Potere Evangelica e Francescana nel sec. XIII e XIV. Origine nel Pensiero Politico di G. d'Ockham,* anno 75 n. 1-4 (Firenze: Studi Francescani, 1978), 147.

[16] "Dominium ergo illud vocatur proprietas nullo modo fuit in statu innocentiae, nec fuisset unquam, si primi parentes non peccassent, quia nulla res taliter alicui personae singulari vel collegio speciali appropriata fuisset. " Guilelmi de Ockham, "Opus nonaginta dierum, ch. 26, 54-58" in *Opera Politica,* vol. II, R. F. Bennet and H. S. Offler, eds. (Manchester: Manchester University Press, 1963), 484.

[17] "hoc nomen ius a aliquando accipitur pro iure fori, aliquando pro iure poli...habetur eadem distinctio. Ad istius autem distinctionis evidentiam est sciendum, quod ius fori vocatur iustum quod ex pactione seu ordinatione humana vel explicta constituitur." *Ibid.*, chapter 65, 34-35, 39-41.

[18] "Ius autem poli vocatur aequitas naturalis, quae absque omni ordinatione humana et etiam divina pure positiva est consona rationi rectae, sive sit consona rationi rectae pure naturali, sive sit consona rationi rectae acceptae ex illis, quae sunt nobis divinitus revelata. Propter quod hoc ius aliquando vocatur ius

This seems to be a rather straightforward Augustinian notion of separate jurisdictions but they are not absolute and by his language concerning human reason, his own nominalism can be seen to creep in. The result, in this, as in most of his writing on politics, Ockham's notions are sketched out, and not blueprinted.[19] When Ockham comes to define rule (*dominium*), he distinguishes the senses of rule, both actuality and potentiality. Jurisdiction is not only an understanding in the social sphere but an act of identity and as such agrees or disagrees to join in the discourse. Ockham says flatly that by right reason when someone rules over the self, he can be regent over himself and those doing so in perfect accord with poverty do so as one of the Elect.[20] The implications are astonishing within this text as it was a public response to a Pope.

The Ockhamite achievement may seem warped if viewed through the strictly political or philosophical notion of right. The triumph here is psychological and firmly in keeping, though by a circuitous intellectual route, not only with Bonaventure but also with Francis himself. At the same time, the blow struck was a birth pang into the wider world of overt ecclesiastical and canon law, and hence, legalism. The Incarnational Age was suffering a legal acceptance, which could only mean that the apostolic bent of evangelical poverty would become submerged in apologetics.

But this was a foregone conclusion. What mattered was that the Incarnational Age and it's precepts were beginning to make sense of legal notions of individualism were being essayed. The competing notion of rights stemming as it does from specified readings into the life of Christ cannot be separated from the notion of individual as Christian.[21] Abrogation of Christianity to these men meant heresy, and heretics were outside the notions of both the City and the Church.

As has been noted in the problem of Catharism, the heretic or the exile was tethered negatively to the cosmos of the Medieval juridical process, and this negativism is mirrored in the Franciscan insistence to

---

natural...Aliquando vocatur ius divinum; quia multa sunt consona rationi rectae acceptae ex illis , quia sunt nobis divinitus revelata, quae non sunt consona rationi pure naturali." *Ibid.,* Chapter 65, l. 76-83,   574.

[19] In *William of Ockham. A Letter to the Friars Minor and other Writings*, John Kilcullen and A. S. McGrade, eds. (Cambridge: Cambridge University Press, 1995), xii.

[20] "Aliud est regimen, quo quis seipsum ac motus ac actus suos ratione recta regit: et ab isto regimine quilibet rationabiliter vivens rex poterit nuncupari.   Unde et propter hoc beatus remigius omnes Christi electos asserit reges. " *OND*, ch. 93, l. 128-131, 673).

[21] Leff, *Heresy in the Later Middle Ages*, 226.

remain possession-less. The Incarnational Age demanded a preliminary negation in the hope and expectation of full communion with Christ. The negative existence then is a real and germinative influence on what would become later empirical notions of what or what is not an individual and more importantly how does the individual see himself as a potential negation, a contradiction more in terms, than in the actuality of the Incarnational Age.

The insistence upon the right to refuse the natural propensity to possess or own was given buttress not only by the appeal to a *vita pauperum* couched in the necessary ecstatic language used by apologists such as John of Peckham and Bonaventure, but also in legal language of Ockham. The development of rights language became an outgrowth, a seminal one from the debate over property and use. This much is clear. More importantly to my understanding is that the legalism of the language that was to find its way into intellectual and legal texts, was at first a *lingua franca* of artifact made visible by the inculturation of the Franciscan Order within the *communitas* of the Middle Ages.[22]

The popularity of Francis, the forceful example of the early Minorites and their swift rise to prominence seeded the jealousy that the order encountered at the University of Paris, and to which Bonaventure responded. The example of the intelligentsia perturbed by the argument of worldly denial can be seen as either a reflex over the threat of it to their lifestyle or an example of indignation over apparent hypocrisies that they might have witnessed in the life of the Franciscans. The second is less likely as the early arguments against the Minorites did not appeal to emotional accusations over hypocrisy but concerned itself with the theological and legal implications of the lifestyle. As such the debate began an episode that progressed into an event that has been seen in hindsight to be a seminal moment in the identity of the individual within the world.

If this is so, then the remarkable thing about it is that the rights language it engendered stemmed, as has been shown, from quasi heretical leanings that attempted to adumbrate the separation of the Two Cities by allowing, nay insisting upon, the possibility of perfectability within the

---

[22] See Leff, Ulmann, and Lambert as overall studies and Antonio Piromalli, *Antifeudalismo Francescano in San Francesco e il Francescanesimo nell Letteratura italiana dal XII al XV secolo*, Atti del convegno nazionale, (Assisi, 10-12 Dicembre 1999), Stanislao da Campagnole e Pasquale Tuscano, eds. (Assisi: Accademia Properziano del Subiaso, 2001), 75-92.

temporal sphere.[23] Francis, as we have seen, inaugurated this age by his insistence on reflecting, as perfectly as he could, the Incarnation, down to the wounds of Christ. The new Christological event that Francis represented led to the apocalyptic theologies of such Franciscans as Ubertino da Casale and prefigured by the afore-mentioned prophecies of Joachim of Fiore. As the ingrained notion of the corrupted post lapsarian world could not be shaken, the appearance of a second Christ such as Francis pushed the idea that the perfect life could be essayed only as a harbinger of real change.[24]

The real change here was the End of Times, and the fervor of the zealous within the Order now had, by any accounts, crossed the line and had entered heretical terrain. The extreme anti-papalism of the Franciscan response to the Avignon Pontiff John XXII and the new ecclesiology of the apocalyptic texts of the Joachamites and the ideas of the Spirituals, were clearly signs that the Friars Minor not only saw themselves as unique, but had given their Rule a theological and social structure that ventured upon a mythos encompassing both the community and the individual.[25]

These things all resulted from the denial, the vehement denial, to be included into the nature of the new society that had conquered feudalism by the growth and power of exchange and profit. As possession and dominium and use of fact had very real meaning in such a culture of exchange the Franciscan recoil necessitated a defense against an increasingly hostile view of their idea of evangelical poverty. The essays of Bonaventure and Ockham were then part of a larger intellectual and cultural movement that attempted a paradigmatical shift of ideas in individuality. The attempt, although unconscious in the beginning, became a real force to newly reckon the personal. The Incarnational Age was a threat, and the efforts toward affecting a true Christianity, although

---

[23] See the irrepressible Gordon Leff, *The Dissolution of the Medieval Outlook: An Essay on Intellectual and Spiritual Change in the Fourteenth Century* (New York: New York University Press, 1976), 120.

[24] See Antonio Poppi, *Studi sell'Etica della Prima Scuola Francescana* (Padova: Centro Studi Antoniani, 1996), 178-180.

[25] "The Spirituals saw the poverty of Christ conflict as proof of the arrival of the evil Pope of Joachamite prophecy even of Antichrist, and of the deepening of persecution preceding the opening of the seventh seal. John's actions reinforced their eschatological awareness and strengthened their will to resist." Malcolm Lambert, *Franciscan Poverty,* 263. See also the seminal study of Marjorie Reeves, *The Influence of Prophecy in the Later Middle Ages: A Study in Joachimism* (Oxford: Clarendon Press, 1969), 109, 208-210.

assailed began to be reckoned in legal and cultural terminology. Firstly, by the influence of the Franciscans, both positive and negative, within the newly established universities.[26] Secondly, by the pervasiveness of their preaching and their use of penitential privileges bestowed upon churches founded by the Friars.[27] Thirdly by the iconography established to attest to both the Life of Francis and the poverty of Christ.[28] The attempt at *speculum* by the force and sincerity of the movement engendered a personal search for perfection outside of both the legal and theological laws of that world.

The attempt to find a way toward Christ on his terms became a way of justifying the self through the act of denial, as has been essayed in the investigation of Francis. The difference between Francis and his followers lay simply in the needs for code in the maturing Order that would conform to the needs of the growing outside society. Speculum had transformed into speculation, and by the codes forged previously in the scholasticism that preceded Ockham, speculation demanded answers. However nominal those answers became, their debatable contingencies laid the groundwork for the movement to become atrophied and official. Such orthodoxy condemned the Franciscan ideal to calibrate itself to the weight of the world, and their primary exegetical master in this was not a mystic, nor a philosopher, but an artist, and not even a tertiary at that.

The frescoes of the Upper Basilica of Saint Francis in Assisi by Giotto can be tentatively dated between the years 1298-1305. This is a matter of some dispute. But it is obvious that the iconography of Francis and his Life, the subject matter of the frescoes, helped (as much as Ockham did with the lawyers and the intellectuals decades later), to codify the Incarnational Age into a reflex better assimilated by the people, and thereby successfully integrating it into the rising mercantilist and bourgeois class from which Francis sprung, and rejected.

Giotto's contribution to the Art of the Western World is not in question. The fact is, in this debate, the iconography of Giotto and his

---

[26] See Michael Robson, "Saint Bonaventure" in *Medieval Theologians: An Introduction to the Theology in the Medieval Period.* Edited by G. R. Evans. Blackwell: Oxford, 2001, p. 190-192.

[27] See Brett, 24, and J. K. Hyde, *Society & Politics in Medieval Italy: The Evolution of the Civil Life, 1000-1350* (London: Macmillan, 1973), 117.

[28] See Walter Ullmann's *The Individual and Society in the Middle Ages* (London: Methuen & Co, Ltd., 1967), 104-105; and Joanna Cannon, "Giotto and the Art for the Friars: Revolutions Spiritual and Artistic," in the *Cambridge Companion to Giotto* A. Derbes and M. Sandona, eds. (Cambridge: Cambridge University Press, 2004), 103-134.

school is only of interest in the effect it had upon the popular imagination concerning Francis, an effect that could not be disseminated by even the popular tales and mendicant preaching that circulated concerning Francis.[29] Indeed the rubric of divesting and investing the flesh, the spiritual transformation of the Franciscan ethos, would be made visible by Giotto and in no way bettered by succeeding generations of artists. It was the instance of the right artist for the right time.[30]

It should be noted that there are vociferous voices that doubt the authenticity of Giotto's hand in the frescoes at the Basilica of Saint Francis in Assisi altogether. A more cogent dispute, to my mind, would be the actual dating, for it is probable that Giotto had been at Assisi to execute the *Life of Francis* for the Basilica, as early art historical references and documents point this out. It is doubtless a work of his late youth, and probably predates his *magnum opus*, the Scrovegni chapel.[31] As it is probable that the work in Assisi was early in his career, it is instructive to see how the idea of Francis worked it's way into his consequential maturity as a pictorial master.

The spatial volume of Giotto's figures and the singular manner in which the individual is represented, reflects upon a negative corollary of

---

[29] "Narrative paintings of St. Francis' life and miracles had somewhat different audiences than the written lives.... Thus which stories to include and how to represent them were in part determined by what the patrons and the friars wanted the general public to know about St. Francis and, by extension, the Order he founded." William Cook, "Giotto and the Figure of St. Francis," in the *Cambridge Companion to Giotto*, A. Derbes and M. Sandona, eds. (Cambridge: Cambridge University Press, 2004), 135-156, esp. 138.

[30] "La nueva espiritualidad aportada por Francisco de Asis viene designada por la preoccupacion por lo exterior especificando en la atencion al volumen. Giotto al prestar acusado interes al volumen refleja la manifestacion plastica de los nuevos modulos de relacion con Dios.... . Al traslador a la iconografia religiosa las nuevas categorias de enjuiciamiento surge la original plasmacion de la figura de Cristo...Cristo delos ojos abiertos...vestido de lujosas telas...signos de la derrota y muerte...La humanidad abstracta es sustituida por la humanidad tangible. " In Juan Canto Rubio, *Giotto y la Secularizacion*. (Madrid: Alicante, 1975), 46, 52-53.

[31] For a short yet thorough account of the debate see Creighton Gilbert, "Giotto: The Assisi Debate" in "Giotto," Grove Art Online. Oxford University Press, [13 February 2007], http://www.groveart.com/. For more in depth readings see Alastair Smart, *The Assisi Problem of Giotto* (Oxford: Clarendon Press, 1971); Hans Belting's "Assisi e Roma," in *Roma anno 1300*. *Atti della IV settimana di storia dell'arte medievale dell'Universita di Roma* (Roma: La Sapienza, 1980), 199-209; and in the same volume Enzo Battisti, "Body Language nel ciclo di San Francesco di Assisi," 675-688.

the Incarnational Age; the theme of seclusion and abandonment, previously discussed. Yet the natural world in Giotto is not as forbidding as it is secondary, indeed tertiary, to the significance of the human figure. The act of negation thereby, in the Franciscan frescoes in the Assisi Basilica and beyond in the work of Giotto, is made manifest by figural solidity and grandeur, hinting at an existentialism imbued, perhaps unconsciously, within the ramifications of the doctrine of evangelical poverty. This insistence on the individual is not celebratory as it is exegetical, and that specifically toward the kenotic tendencies of the Incarnational Age.[32]

The pedagogical efficacy of the frescoes and of Franciscan iconography altogether cannot be overestimated, especially the degree to which Francis was made to appear upon that most central of Christian images, the crucifix itself. Such depictions underscored a specified spirituality that dealt with the flesh and it's suffering. Indicatively although the Dominicans and the Franciscans were simultaneously founded, the followers of Dominic rarely, if ever, put their patron on the same threshold of physical suffering as Christ. The influence of the Franciscan legend of the stigmata, as previously discussed, served as a welcome reflection to be aggressively pursued in the art depicting the saint.[33]

---

[32] "Giotto a admirablement reussi a representer las liens psychologiques unissants les personages de son monde imaginaire. Mais sa reforme mit fin a l'idee de la reunion des fideles dans les eglises medievales. Giotto etait le premier artiste europeen qui s'imagina l'homme dans la solitude (Joachim allant chez les pasteur). L'homme abandonne par tout le monde est devenu plus tard un motif tragique dans l'art des temps moderne. " In Michail Alpatov, "Giotto: Traditions, Creation, Reforme,"in *Giotto e il suo Tempo: Atti del Congresso Internazionale per la celebrazione del VII centenario della nascita di Giotto 24 Settembre-1 Ottobre 1967, Assisi- Padova-Firenze* (Roma: De Luca, 1971), 340-342.

[33] "The focus that this type of image provided on the actuality and reenactment of Christ's sacrifice, was appropriate both to Franciscan and Dominican spirituality and might be seen equally by both as a tool with which to shape the devotions to the laity.... On the other hand, there was a difference in content between crucifixes painted for the two groups of friars, for St. Dominic was almost never shown at the foot of a monumental crucifix. Unlike Francis, he was not viewed as a second Christ by his followers. " In Joanna Cannon,"Giotto and Art for the Friars: Revolutions Spiritual and Artistic," in *The Cambridge Companion to Giotto*, 112. For Dr. Cannon's assessment of Dominic's artistic character see her "Dominic Alter Christus? Representations of the Founder in and after the Arca di San Domenico" in *Christ Among the Medieval Dominicans: Representations of Christ in the Texts and Images of the Order of the Preachers*. Kent Emery Jr. and

Giotto was reared in a milieu that saw art as instructive, and specifically scriptural. His choices of gesture and form would be a lot more careful than an artist from the Renaissance proper, when the speculum of the Middle Ages and the import of the Incarnational Age would have had a loosening hold upon the mind of the artist. Saying this leaves Giotto confined by gesture and craftsmanship as much as Dante was by the rules of rhetoric and his *terza rima*; within either dispensation, the creative act was circumscribed by form and carried immense significance.[34]

For one, the liturgical purpose of the art would be reflected in the substance of the iconography. The populist and pedagogically minded images would need the Mass itself as an echo chamber for it's significance. Further, such considerations within an understanding of the central importance of the Eucharistic celebration within Incarnational understanding places Giotto's choices in a more hallowed realm than just a pure imaginative visualization of the Franciscan ideal.[35] His gesticulating

---

Joseph P. Wawrykow, eds. (Notre Dame: University of Notre Dame Press, 1998), 26-48.

[34] A most succinct and useful explanation of the artistic ideas that informed the age can be found in a little book on Dante. Here the author is quoted at length along with the sources to best explain the aesthetic informing Giotto and for that matter Dante. "The medieval conception of art as 'reason of doing or making' (ratio factibilium) is essentially non aesthetic. There are three points to bear in mind. First, the principal distinction in the mind of the medieval philosopher falls between the liberal and the mechanical arts. The former serve the spiritual part of man and the latter the material (see Aquinas *In metaph.* I lect. 3 n. 59, Hugh of St. Victor, *Didascal.* II 21, Bonaventure, *De reduct.* 2). ..Considerations of craftsmanship and expertise prevail over those of a specifically aesthetic kind. Secondly the literary pictorial and plastic arts are intended to instruct rather than delight. Honorius of Autun speaks of painting as the *laicorum litteratura* (*De gemma animae PL* 172 c. 586)... Bonaventure agrees; for him pictorial art is justified 'propter simplicium ruditatem, propter memeoriae iabilitatem, propter affectus tarditatem (*III Sent.* 9. 1. 2). The idea of art as a spur to love is taken up by Aquinas who notes its usefulness in common worship: "Et in ideo quaecumque ad hoc utilia esse possunt in divinas laudes congruenter assumuntur" (*Summa Theol.* IIa IIae 91. 2 resp.). The aesthetic is throughout secondary to the didactic and the liturgical. Thirdly there is the generally finalistic conception of art in the Middle Ages. Like nature, whose purposefulness is everywhere manifest, it is to be accounted for in terms not principally of beauty but of efficiency. It is a means to an end. " In J. F. Took, *L'Etterno Piacer: Aesthetic Ideas in Dante* (Oxford:Clarendon Press, 1984), 42-43.

[35] See the seminal study of Mosche Barasch, *Giotto and the Language of Gesture* (Cambridge: Cambridge University Press, 1987), 7-11.

figures carry sacerdotal weight and conform to an aesthetic dependant upon sermon and site rather than the vagaries of artistic inspiration.[36] Hence, the imagery of Giotto is a concrete example of the interface between the popular understanding of the Franciscan ideal and the intentions of the Order towards that understanding. It is not too much to say that Giotto was hired to set down for once and all, a pictorial narrative giving primacy of place to Francis and his Order within the quest to best follow Christ.

That such a scheme would take hold and work itself seamlessly within the Mass was a foregone conclusion. The developments of Eucharistic Presence along with the penitential privileges bestowed upon the Friars Minor, previously elucidated, would naturally lead the Christian to see within the images a proper understanding of place as taught by he closest to Christ, namely Francis.

The Incarnational leant itself to the increasingly anthropomorphism of theories regarding the Trinity, and as such telegraphed it's submersion beneath the weight of the human.[37] The volume and weight of the figures, the conflation of history bringing Christ and Francis within the same visual space, the careful gestures of the figures mirrored in the actual gestures of the living, these all combined to create a sphere of influence upon the Divine which would naturally impress the penitent. Even a spiritualist like Bonaventure did not eschew the power of the image.[38] Giotto created an art that would, like Dante's, complete the Incarnational

---

[36] See Marilyn Aronberg-Lavin, *The Place of Narrative: Mural Decoration in Italian Churches, 431-1600* (Chicago: University of Chicago Press, 1990), esp. 15-42.

[37] "En un mundo secularizado antropocentrico recalcar el aspecto humano de Jesus era satisfacer una de las misiones esenciales del arte la cual se cifra en fotografiar el alma de los pueblos y de los tiempos. Ese narrar la vida de Jesus como algo tangible es acercar a Dios a los hombres, es fijarse mas en el caro (hombre) quen el Verbum (Dios)." Rubio, 53.

[38] "Easier to apply to our understanding of art and the friars are his brief but illuminating remarks summarizing the justifications for the presence of images in churches: 'First, for the instruction of the simple people, because they are instructed by them as if by books. Second so that the mystery of the Incarnation and the examples of the saints may be the more active in our memory through being represented daily to our eyes. Third, to excite feelings of devotion (ad excitandum devotionis affectum) these being aroused more effectively by things seen than by things heard'. Cannon, "Giotto and the Art for the Friars," 124.

and herald the human, asserting itself in ways unimagined, and perhaps unwelcome, by these masters.[39]

Giotto's role should not be seen as completely docile and subservient to the ideal. His work in Padua, his masterpiece in the Scrovegni Chapel, shows him in all his scintillating splendor. There was, as any art historical survey will tell, a refreshingly novel approach to painting that Giotto inaugurated in Western Art. Born poor, he became the most sought after artist of his day, so that his contemporary, Dante memorably trumpeted his popularity in the *Purgatorio*.[40] He died in 1337 aged about seventy years and proclaimed *magnus magister* by the city of Florence a little while before that. He had, by all accounts died rich.

This was an artist of the first rank and of the highest social station. An artist, it can be said, who lived already within a milieu which remembered his name. The insistence upon simplicity, the distinction of the solitary individual, the barest traces of the natural world, the immense weight and volume of the human were all trademarks of his art, and in a sense of the Incarnational Age. But as for distinguishing the individual by setting him apart, the purpose of this in the evangelical bent of the Incarnational Age was to negate him. Giotto's paradox in achievement is that he was informed by a spirituality whose purpose it was to more perfectly follow Christ by abandoning the self in the very real Presence of Christ. By doing so, the penitent circumvented personality by seeking Another. Giotto's achievement in the Upper Basilica of Assisi denied the denial of Francis it's humility and sent a mixed message that would be resolved by the Order in finally joining the establishment.[41]

---

[39] See Giovanni Fallani, *Dante e la Cultura Figurativa Medievale* (Roma: Minerva Italica, 1971), 159. "La capella padovano e il poema dantesco hanno in commune principalment il tema cristologico…L'umanita nell opera di Dante e in quella di Giotto ritrova se stressa, non e spettatrice degli avvenimenti, participa per l'altro all'azione, si sente protagonista in funzione religiosa, dell storia. Negli episodi..si scorgono gli uomini degli Evangeli, che vestono I panni e dichiarono le loro passioni, secondo l'uso e il carattere cittadino e popolare del Trecento."

[40] "It was thought that Cimabue in painting/ held the field, now Giotto has the cry/ so that his fame is overshadowed. " *Purgatorio* XI, 94-96.

[41] "It was all there to be found in pamphlets of 1309-1312…Franciscans…in remaining true to Saint Francis remained loyal to Christ. Poverty thus had for themj a cosmic significance which their opponents did not share. It was part of a mystic union with God, which had to be lived, not legislated for." Gordon Leff, *Heresy in the Later Middle Ages*, 154.
See also Eamon Duffy, "Finding Saint Francis" in *Medieval Theology and the Natural Body,* Peter Billers and A. J. Minnis, eds. (York: York Medieval Press,

Giotto's art as well as Ockham's defense, served to celebrate and establish precedent and uniqueness in Francis's quest. It was developments of which Francis would not have approved. Yet it was to be that the personalities that formed the artistic-philosophical statements of the Franciscan Order dealt a blow to the Incarnational Age by elevating the *poverello* from Assisi.

Instead of the metaphor of the *homo viator*, of Christ himself wandering homeless throughout Europe, a victim of Hattin and not where to rest his head but in the hearts of men, a New Jerusalem reared itself quite concretely upon the Italian earth in a small town in Umbria. And it served as a Bethlehem as well for the *alter Christus* who was buried in a magnificent church bearing his name. The hosannas that emanated from that place echoed throughout the Christian world, and in the coming age men would disremember what the diminutive friar could not; that he was the least of men.

1997), 193-236, esp. 198-200, as well as Rona Goffen's *Spirituality in Conflict: St. Francis and Giotto's Bardi Chapel.* (London: University Press, 1988), 214-215.

CHAPTER SIX

THE FIRE NEXT TIME: DANTE, TRANSFORMATION, AND INCARNATIONAL CODA

> And thy niche was prepared for thee when thou wast created; a cherub thou shouldst be, thy wings outstretched in protection; there on God's holy mountain I placed thee, to come and go between the wheels of fire.
> *Ezekiel*, 28: 14

Human perfectibility is at the heart of the Incarnational Age. Attempting to mirror the ultimate act of sacrifice for service to the human condition was the goal of Franciscans and the Cathars. Both entities were set upon courses seeking to destroy notional existential systems: The new class identities springing from the use of an exchange of currencies, and the seemingly natural impulse to procreate. Both shared a desire to marry or deny carnal identity with that of a spiritual reality.

Yet the artist had to suppose an identity before creation and then conjure his dreams into waking reality. Dante's *Divine Comedy*, the most representative literature of the age and hence an Incarnational text *par excellence*, at once set up an interface with these new paradigms and sought to transform what it meant to be human in the realm of letters.[1]

---

[1] The influence of Dante throughout the centuries as a figure of seminal importance in Western Literature is not debatable. The strains of discussion found in this section and as a recapitulation and summation of the ongoing thesis is heavily indebted to the following books whose influence hovers over the entire chapter: Marcia Colish, *Medieval Foundations of the Western Intellectual Tradition, 400-1400*: Ernst Robert Curtius, *European Literature and the Latin Middle Ages.* Translated by William Trask. (New York: Pantheon Books, 1953): Karl Vossler's *Mediaeval Culture: And Introduction to Dante and His Times:* Helen Flanders Dunbar, *Symbolism in Medieval Thought and its Consummation in the Divine Comedy* (New Haven: Yale University Press, 1929): John Freccero, *Dante: The Poetics of Conversion* (Cambridge: Harvard University Press, 1986): Guy Raffa, *Divine Dialectic: Dante's Incarnational Poetry* (Toronto: University

Dante Alighieri would create the new cultural man according to the tenets of transformation found first in the old myths, customs and men, fully forming under the aegis of the new condition discovered and disseminated by these masters. The methodology would become a grammar of transformation for Western Literature, and has hardly been bettered in the long years since its genesis.

The Incarnational *materiel* of the poem is widespread throughout the three worlds of the *oltretombe,* but there are significant, (and signifying) episodes within each canticle that I believe, are the anteroom to the full ethos of the Renaissance method. By which is meant, that the cultural infrastructure based upon the centrality of Christ is shifted to the self in an aggressively personal and individual ethos that will eventually inform an aesthetic that was to culminate in what Paul Zweig called "the heresy of self love."[2]

The three episodes all involve the dialectic of transformation to occur within the presence of fire, and finally to underline the knowledge of self and the apotheosis of a personal Incarnation with imagery that unites the elemental with the divine within us and without. The entirety of Christian salvation history takes place in Dante.[3] These three episodes are intimately bound with Dante's sense of self and as such are barometers for the course

---

of Toronto Press, 2000): William Anderson's *Dante the Maker* (New York: Crossroad, 1982). *Dante: The Critical Complex.* 8 vols. Richard Lansing, ed. (New York: Routledge, 2003): Charles Singleton, *Dante Studies 2: The Journey to Beatrice* (Cambridge: Harvard University Press, 1967): Edmund G. Gardner, *Dante and the Mystics* (London: J. M. Dent and Sons, 1913). Commentaries on the *Divine Comedy* are primarily by C.H.Grandgent, Mark Musa, Natalino Sapegno, and Charles Singleton. The text is the editorial work of Umberto Bosco and Giorgio Petrocchi. Translations are my own. Encyclopedias include *L'Enciclopedia Dantesca* Umberto Bosco, ed. (Roma: Treccani, 1978), which is the indispensable resource. The best single volume is the *Dante Encyclopedia,* Richard Lansing, ed. (New York: Garland, 2000).

[2] Zweig uses another (we shall see) Ovidian story to support his thesis of the historical and literary instances of subversive individuality. Dante mentions Narcissus, Zweig's central myth, in the *Inferno* (XXX, 128) when he refers to his mirror, water. See Paul Zweig, *The Heresy of Self Love: A Study of Subversive Individualism* (Princeton: Princeton University Press, 1968).

[3] "The descent of the divine Logos into humanity as Erich Auerbach, Charles Singleton, John Freccero, and Marcia Colish have argued is the controlling model for Dante's depiction of the otherworld...Colish shows how Dante fashions his renowned mimetic realism out of this union of word and flesh thus making his Commedia 'the poetic corollary of the Incarnation.'" Guy Raffa, *Divine Dialectic: Dante's Incarnational Poetry*, 4.

that European man will take after the Incarnational Age. At once the summa and the coda, Dante is as Ruskin once alluded, a central man. These episodes from the *Comedy* can be seen as clues to the trajectory from the Incarnational to the Renaissance, hence transformational, in Western literature.

There is in the character of Ulysses in the twenty sixth canto of the *Inferno* (as in most cantos and personages), a variety of possible interpretations or glosses that can elucidate it as something quite integral to the text. The infinite avenues that can be taken due to the efflorescence of modern and contemporary literary criticism sprouting from peripheral disciplines are interesting in their own way, but not concerned with the lesson Dante is trying to teach. What lesson is Dante teaching, and what exactly is the sin for which Ulysses is punished?

The answer to the second is fairly obvious: Obvious because Dante tells us by geography which sin is being punished. It is so obvious that it has led some commentaries to think that such a powerful story in this *bolgia*, that encompasses much more and demands more of the reader is a bit too obvious. Yes and no. The sin is the sin of fraudulent counsel. That much is certain. Virgil is explicit: Ulysses and Diomedes are punished for the Trojan Horse, for enticing Achilles to war and for the stealing of the Palladium,[4] events mentioned in Virgil and Statius. It can be, and has been argued that the most egregious of the examples of Ulissean fraudulent counsel is his final disastrous harangue enticing his men to their doom.[5] But this is not implied, nor is it convincingly made to be so as Ulysses is open as to explaining the cause of his death, as commanded by Virgil.[6]

Once the story comes out we are promptly divided as to the merits of his desire and the justice of his fate. Pro and contra camps spring up in the critical literature arguing over Dante-Pilgrim's own feelings toward

---

[4] *Inferno* XXVI, 55-63.
[5] See Teodolina Barolini, "Ulysses" in *The Dante Encyclopedia*, Richard Lansing, ed. 884; Emiliano Mariano, *Il Canto XXVI Dell' Inferno* (Firenze: Le Monnier, 1962), 22; and G. Singh's "Inferno XXVI: A Personal Appreciation" in *Dante Commentaries: Eight Studies of the Divine Comedy*, David Nolan, ed. (Dublin: Irish Academic Press, 1977), 56-57. In this last example, Sigh takes a rather capacious view of fraud as an 'unscrupulous astuteness' and accuses Ulysses of using the art of poetic persuasion and the dialectics of moral and philosophic reasoning to a poetic end', 56. Is there then no difference between Churchill and Hitler, at least rhetorically?
[6] *Inferno* XXVI, 78-84.

Ulysses.⁷ A vehement minority led by Fubini claim that there is nothing in the canto that dispels the notion that Dante has nothing but admiration for Ulysses.⁸ That recognizing his own quest for things unknown, Dante implicitly regards the Greek as a mentor. More cautious commentary, (perhaps in the majority) agree with this last insight on Dante's perception of his own intellectual hunger mirrored in Ulysses, but use the Ulysses canto as Dante-Poet's self imposed cautionary tale placed toward the beginning of his ascent to Purgatory: ostensibly, the mountain that Ulysses sees before he is covered up by the sea by the will of a god greater than his old nemesis Poseidon.⁹

Dante has these sinners punished by flame, and yet dependent upon it to communicate. Dante describes the sinners enveloped in a flame that "hides its own theft by castigating the sinner it holds in thrall." ¹⁰ The viewing of this almost topples Dante over and Virgil explains that the flames holds those it burns.¹¹ Dante had already divined this as the *contrapasso*¹² of this particular *bolgia*, being now adept at seeing God's inexorable justice. The flame of Ulysses and Diomedes is in itself an inversion of the sacred flames of Holy Spirit that descended upon the Apostles to give them the gift of tongues to speak to all nations.¹³ The gift

---

⁷ Buti (14th century) takes a moralizing position, Benvento, Fubini, Sapegno, Pagliaro, Forti, say that Dante admires him. Nardi argues that Ulysses' sin is Adam's and Lucifer's for going past the mark, (trapassar del segno, *Par.* XXVI, 117.) See Teodolina Barolini's "Ulysses" in *The Dante Encyclopedia*, 843.
⁸ See Mario Fubini, "Ulisse" in *l'Enciclopedia Dantesca,* vol. 5, 803-808. Fubini feels Ulysses compromised by an excess of commentary, and like De Sanctis before him, admires Ulysses as a typified "eroe Dantesca", who is ill served by the commentaries that cannot understand "quest' ordine nel mondo dantesco, questa misura del suo eroe," 808.
⁹ Valli sees the peril of Ulysses as symbolic of the peril within Dante himself. . . the propensity of intellectual pride, anticipating Freccero Thompson and Corti. "It seems more likely that Ulysses reflects instead Dante's conscious concern for himself. . within the Commedia, Ulysses is reflected not only by Dante Pilgrim, who as Scott and others have shown, is related to Ulysses as an inverse type but also by Dante Poet who "transgresses the boundary between life and death, between God and man. " See Barolini, *The Dante Encyclopedia,* 845.
¹⁰ "tal si move ciascuna per la gola/ del fosso, che' nessuna mostra 'l furto,/ e ogne fiamma un peccatore invola," *Inferno* XXVI, 40-42.
¹¹ *Inferno* XXVI, 44-48.
¹² "Contrapasso" in *Inferno* XXVIII, 142; 'retribution': the law of retaliation, according to which the penalties are meted out in Hell. " Grandgent, 256.
¹³ See Mario Aversano, *Dante Cristiano: La selva, Francesca, Ulisse e la struttura dell'Inferno.* (Roma: Il Calamaio, 1977), 125; "un e contrapposto a due. Questo puntualizzare crea un rapporto di antitesi tra la fiamma di Ulisse-Diomede e quella

of persuasion and of blessings went with it. Here the flame is made to castigate and punish those whose persuasions purposely led to disaster.[14] Dante is preparing us to steel ourselves for Ulysses, as Ulysses himself did for the passage of the Sirens.

A word here must be said about the "small oration"[15] that Ulysses has given to his "small company"[16] during the now last moments of their "slight (or short) vigil of the senses"[17] the oration that consensus says is the last example of wily Ulysses and his powers of persuasion. Firstly, that the oration is indeed calculated. Dante uses *picciola* to describe the speech, the company, and life itself. *Picciola* can be seen as tripartite use that modifies the meaning quite deliberately and malevolently. Ulysses does this with false modesty once we hear the now proverbial speech, which has been taken to herald the spirit of Pico's Oration and the Renaissance itself.[18]

I say hear because that is what Dante wants us to do; to follow in his footsteps, and lest we forget, Dante in this instance is specifically an auditor away from the exchange. Since we now share common ground with the Pilgrim it would be best to remind ourselves where we are. Despite the noble thoughts expressed by Ulysses with the full power of rhetoric, we are listening to a sinner. A sinner who perhaps is not contrite, but one who remains convinced of the truth of this, his almost romantic narrative.[19]

---

dello Spirito Santo disceso sugli Apostoli: formata quest'ultima, non da due…in un sol foco'. . ma da una in un fuoco doppio." Aversano goes on to lay the influence on Dante on Prosper of Aquitaine where the telling phrase *charismatum dona dispensans* comes in reference to the flame.

[14] Fubini's remarkable explanation for the flames merits inclusion here; "la fiamma. . non ha qui altro effetto per Ulisse che di nasconderla, di farne un puro spirito, una voce che s'innalza sicura e serena. " The flame hiding the calm and placid voice of a purer spirit lends weight to the quality of seduction argued later, although Fubini perhaps blinded by a critical animus toward a damning Nardi on the subject of Ulysses, would not have seen it our way. See Fubini, "Ulisse" in *l'Enciclopedia Dantesca, vol. V*. 803.

[15] "questa orazion picciola', *Inferno* XXVI, 122.

[16] *Inferno* XXVI, 101-102.

[17] *Inferno* XXVI, 115-116.

[18] "A questo punto accettiamo l'identificazione di Ulisse con Dante, in sede, vogliamo dire, di una prospettiva storica che nel XXVI canto si affaccia al Rinascimento." In Emiliano Mariano, *Il Canto XXVI Dell'Inferno* (Firenze: F. Le Monnier, 1962), 27.

[19] "The essential characteristic of Ulysses' rhetoric is that it is completely self-serving dedicated to a heroic enterprise. " In John Freccero, *Dante: The Poetics of*

Why should we believe Ulysses? It is a question rarely put to the canto. Is not a fundamental aspect of fraudulent counsel to be that the counsel given is known by the counselor to be false? Can it not be a condition of Hell that the sinner is unaware of sinning and diligent in continuing to follow his damnable nature? If this speech was given maliciously, then Ulysses was himself the last willing victim of his rhetoric. He is at pains to make us aware that he was unable to rein in their enthusiasm,[20] but lets us know (perhaps with hindsight) that the enterprise was daft. [21] The brief enticing view of a mountain, taken to be the Mount of Purgatory[22] in the critical response, sends them into paroxysms of joy turned to grief. The waters suck them into a vortex and "closes over them, pleasing another."[23] This "another", is presumably God.

The common gloss of the Poet-Pilgrim and the sinner being both guilty of voyage outside of the boundaries set for mortal men is too obvious to refute and so shall not be. [24] Some thoughts must be indulged under this rubric, such as the voyages taken are poetic expressions of

---

Conversion, 144; Also, "Questa e la malizia, la frode che il Dio cristiano punisce nella bolgia di Ulisse. La frode affidata alla parola, alla lingua," Mariano, 14.

[20] "Li miei compagni fec' io si aguti/ con questa orazion picciola, al cammino/ che a pena poscia li avrei ritenuti," *Inferno* XXVI, 121-123.

[21] "de remi facemmo ali al folle volo," *Inferno* XXVI, 125.

[22] John Scott in *Dante Magnanimo: Studi sulla Commedia* (Firenze: Leo Olschki, 1977), 165, explains the sight of Purgatory as a lever by which to mechanize an interpretation that parallels Ulysses mission with that of Aeneas. Whereas Ulysses overcame Circe, Aeneas leaves Dido, "e come Ulisse riesce a intravedere la montagna del paradiso terrestre cosi Enea si avvicina alla terra promessa. " Scott's treats Ulysses as a sort of *exemplum oppostum* with Aeneas, Dante himself, and Cato of Utica. The basic gloss is that Ulysses is a model of hubris to Dante, mirroring those things that Dante had suffered by seeking them out; "Un opposizione fondamentale distingue indubbiamente l'autore della Commedia dal suo grande personaggio. Dante era stato mandato in esilio contro ogni giustizia; Ulisse, invece diventa un avventuriero," Scott, 139. Dante also used what he thought was the historical proof of Seneca that "the immortal gods had given (Cato) to us as a true exemplar of the wise man than earlier ages had in Ulysses and Hercules. " To Dante the proximity of the Christian revelation and the greater restraint and sacrifice of Cato merited a distinguished place in the Purgatorio whereas Ulysses is damned. See also John Scott, *Dante's Political Purgatory*, (Philadelphia: University of Pennsylvania Press, 1996), as well as Barolini, " Ulysses," 844.

[23] "com' altrui piacque." *Inferno* XXVI, 141.

[24] See Barolini, "Ulysses," 846.

presumably real events. With Sapegno, we are compelled that Dante is telling us the truth.[25]

But with Ulysses the story is different. Indeed it is implicit in the canto that Dante leaves us plausible reasons to discredit the entire tale as false. To do so would be advisable of good Christians who wish to learn not the stories of pagans but the truth of salvation. For one, Ulysses cannot speak to one whose language displeases him. The language, the *volgare* of the Dantean smithy, will be good enough for Heaven but not Ulysses. His thoughts require the circumscription of Virgil's High Style and the Latin poet deigns to this.[26]

It is within this arena where Ulysses can do his best as a raconteur, and his worst as a counselor. For if he is counseling anyone it us through Dante-Pilgrim, through Virgil. His message appears to be cautionary but who is not moved by the impulse to live as God made us and not as brutes? Ulysses poison works quickly because it appeals to our pride. The tone is, according to Fubini and Torraca, one of serenity and of perfect diction as Ulysses is telling the story of someone else.[27] The language itself becomes an obstacle for Christian virtue, as it reveals and hides the truth of the sinner's character and story.[28]

---

[25] " secondo (Sapegno) 'era nell'intenzione del poeta di segnare con questo strano contrasto, il trapasso che qui si attua, dal mondo del mito a quello della cronaca attuale. " In Antonio Pagliaro, *Ulisse: Ricerche Semantiche sulla Divina Commedia, t. II* (Firenze: G. D'Anna, 1966), 438.

[26] "Speech in this context is by no means language. . In other words, the language that Virgil and Ulysses share is a common style, the high style of ancient epic, whose qualities are unappreciated in the vulgar company of hell, where the language is the *sermo humilis* of Christian comedia. " In John Freccero's *Dante: The Poetics of Conversion*, 1986.

[27] See Fubini, 84.

[28] Here we must quote Freccero in full: "The episode of Ulysses thus provides a moral exemplum metalinguistically as well as a poetic representation of such gravity that it both warns against and atones for a poetic excess beyond the poems didactic needs," Freccero, 145. The pedagogy of the poem however demands the exercise of even the sinner's excesses for the praxis of reader to text to have the salutary effect upon the soul. This should place in spite of (or even because of) the affinity the Pilgrim or the reader has with the fallen; "La condanna divina scende inesorabile, quando Ulisse con le sue stesse mani sciupa questo bene supremeo e usa per ottenerlo un'eloquenza di frode. Questa e la moralita del canto di Ulisse, e Dante, all inizio aveva rivolto proprio a se stesso l'ammonimento che vale come implicito solenne riconoscere una radice di simpatia, d'affinita'. " In Mariano, 18.

Unlike the Pentecostal flames of the Acts of the Apostles that compels the disciples to seek out and save others, this forked tongue advises us to pursue "virtue and knowledge" (seguir virtute e conoscenza, l. 120) for ourselves. Ulysses knows the weakness of men, and the ways to seduce them.[29] He has, after all been victimized by seduction; of glory, of virtue of war. Dante knows this to be folly, but he holds his tongue, perhaps for a secret sympathy he holds for this bold enterprise.[30]

Ulysses speaks of the mad dash for glory, but why should we believe this? Perhaps he died an old man, away from the swirling ocean and the sinking ship, and the distant mountain. It would be prudent to do so, if we are to save ourselves from misunderstanding the Dantean mission toward redemption by conflating it with the protean nature of the storyteller enveloped in flame, and subject to the vicissitudes of the wind. Perhaps as Barolini insists, Ulysses "holds up a mirror to the poem's principal voyager, Dante himself, whose ambitions were no less grand."[31] But it would be a disservice to the Christian Poet for us to lionize a soul in Hell. And if Dante's voyage is one of discovery, and we are expected to learn from it, then it is well we take the forked tongue of Ulysses and place it firmly in cheek. It would be apropos that the inversion of the tenets of the Incarnational Age, the active Christian in service of kenotic *exemplum*, would be the meretricious claims of a voyage much praised but remaining untried.

In this instance the fire enveloping the sinner is as meretricious in its properties as the Greek is in language. The fire in Ulysses torment is not so much a part of the torment as much as it is an accomplice in deceit It serves to lull Dante into giving an ear to the lies of Ulysses while wreathing his words with the *magnaminitas* reserved in Hell for a Farinata, him too wreathed in flame. By the time we arrive at the cold of Caina, all notions of heat or warmth are eradicated. There is something alive in the fire, and something purposeful. As we ascend with the Poet,

---

[29] "Ma il tocco che completa il ritratto di Ulisse e gli da il carattere che lo distingue sopra gli altri eroi dell'antichita, e l'eloquenza il bello stile fondato sulla eetorica. Quando Ulisse parla, capovolge le situazioni piu difficili;egli conosce l'art di dire le parole che persuadono; e ottiene, in questo modo, cio che desidera. " Mariano, 14.

[30] "There is a comparable intensity of commitment behind what they set out to achieve. Moreover it is Dante's awareness of such kinship that makes him implicitly realize the difference between his own lot and that of Ulysses," Singh, 48.

[31] Barolini' "Ulysses," 846.

we become aware of how the fire transforms the baser alloy of our humanity into the stuff from which gods come.

The description of a stasis that is Hell inevitably condemns the poetry of Dante to remain mired there by the absence of a full development. The damned seek only to justify themselves and to explain away their sins. This ultimately betrays them. The actual poetry in the *Inferno* is bent upon one end and by a series of different means to arrive at that end, which is the damned's own inadvertent confession and *contrapasso*. The poetry therefore becomes, in the mouth of the sinners, suspect, cajoling, seductive, or treacherous. Dante succeeds in imparting upon the reader, after careful reading, that such punishment may be horrible, but it must be just. Dante becomes convinced that even his sojourn has threatened his gift. So although the observation of Schnapp, that

> Poetry is reborn by the ascent into *Purgatory* whereas it suffered by the complicity of the crimes in *Inferno*. From cacophonous babble it is purged and resurrected (Qui la morta poesi resurga [*Purg. I, 7.*]) by allowing it harmony,[32]

Brings the focus clearer. What should not be missed are the metaphors of elevation, of flow (*miglior acque alza le vele,*[33] *salire al ciel*[34]), which focus on the nature of the poetry itself and on this world of the *oltretombe*. Indeed Schnapp goes on to remark on the urgency of the souls, the tone set by Cato in the beginning of the canto, and the perpetual eagerness and mobile nature of the Canticle, that seeks expiation with movement. The properties of fire here shall not be wasted, nor will they be false.

The rituals of penance with which the souls seek to fulfill in order to be destined for salvation, makes this the most human, the most accessible of the canticles. It should not be forgotten that Dante Pilgrim, far from a casual observer, must himself fall to ritual, must himself be marked, and must himself, at least casually, be prepared for *Paradiso*. This is true for Dante Poet as well. All that is dross cannot stay, and Dante knowing this, must shed himself of anything that may hold him back.

By the twenty-sixth canto, he must and does come to terms with his poetry's purpose and take the necessary steps to sanctify it, as well as him. The *Purgatorio* throughout prepares us for Dante's concerns with relinquishing the concept of artistry and the vainglory of worldly fame

---

[32] Jeffrey T. Schnapp, "Purgatorio' in *The Dante Encyclopedia*, 723-727, esp. 723.
[33] *Purgatorio* I, 1.
[34] *Ibid.*, 6.

concerning the poetry that has made his name, although he tends to resort to a concession to his pride nestled deep in the heart of his similes.

Cosi ha tolto l'uno a l'atro Guido
la Gloria de la lingua; e forse e nato
chi l'uno e l'atro caccera' del nido. [35]

This would not seem so shocking if Dante did not say it on the First Terrace where the proud are punished. We could, if we wish to defend our poet, say he did not unequivocally state that he was greater than Guido Cavalcanti and Guido Guinizzelli. The word *forse* implies uncertainty. But Dante will always be Dante.

By this point, any careful reader is aware of Dante's contest with his fellow poets. His worth in relationship to his Pagan predecessors is a simpler matter in the sense that they are men reared in a world ignorant of the Incarnation. In a poem that attempts to discover the nature of ultimate salvation in the intellectual love of God, the artistry of a Virgil, Statius, Lucan, Homer, Horace, or especially an Ovid cannot be seriously considered as proper vehicles. Indeed their *communitas* serves to establish pedigree, not purpose, and works as a customs stamp to get past those disbelieving of Dante's attempts and suspicious of his claims. They also serve to establish the Latinity of both the aesthetic and political corpus from which the pretensions of Dante spring. [36] Indicatively, though both Virgil and Statius are present in the twenty-sixth canto, they are by and large, silent.[37] His contemporaries are another matter.

This struggle is one that stretches itself out over several cantos going back to the *Inferno*. By the *Purgatorio* Dante prepares us for the *agon* of the twenty-sixth canto, where the last of his obstacles, Arnaut Daniel, is shown dispatched by burning. The ends are justified by the schemes, not of an overt moral, but of a covert, aesthetic judgement. Dante's justice is meted out along a now continuous idea of theology and poetry in which the refinement of the poets poetry go hand in hand with the weightier

---

[35] "So one Guido took from the other/ the glory of the tongue; but perhaps is born/ one who will throw both from their nests." *Purgatorio* XI, 97-99.

[36] See Schnapp, 724. For the finest short study in English on the relationship of Dante to Medieval traditions of Classical authors see Peter Dronke, *Dante and Medieval Latin Traditions* (Cambridge: Cambridge University Press, 1986).

[37] See Teodolinda Barolini, *Dante's Poets: Textuality and Truth in the Comedy* (Princeton: Princeton University Press, 1986), 85-87; and Antonio Corsaro, "The Language of Love: Purgatorio XXVI" in *Word and Drama in Dante*, J. Barnes and J. Petrie, eds. (Dublin: Irish Academic Press: Dublin, 1993), 127.

matters of the Blessed Realms.[38] The language of Dante is put to the calisthenics of rigorous ascent, and the poet's stylistic shift is as much as a self-purgation as a necessary mutation for the poetry itself to meet and to overcome the specters of Guido Guinizelli and Arnaut Daniel. [39] Dante's personal and self-reflective transformation will occur finally in the first canto of the *Paradiso*. There his language will be self consciously representative. Here it is still contaminated, as we shall see, by baser alloys. There the Incarnational power of his genius subverts the very Age he represents.

Dante prepares us carefully for his supremacy. We need look to Casella as part of the proof. A musician in life and Dante's dear friend the Poet asks Casella to sing a song to "solace the soul,"[40]. In the realm where Psalms are sung for salvation, Casella sings one of Dante's own verses, so sweetly that all within earshot (including Virgil) are transfixed by the sound. Dante does not constrain Casella to sing one of his songs; the musician *chooses* to sing "*Amor che ne la mente mi ragione*", from Dante's *Convivio*. The musical salve that heals at the start of Dante's new travels is one of his own verses that attempt to reconcile Love and Reason in the Poet's mind.

The lesson is to be driven home later when, at one stroke, Dante separates himself from his mentor and his contemporaries. It is on the Sixth Terrace of the *Purgatorio* where the Gluttonous are punished, specifically the twenty–fourth canto. There he sees Bonagiunta da Lucca, a poet, who asks the Pilgrim if he is indeed the poet of the famous "*Donne ch' avete l'intelletto d'amore*". Dante does not mention his ancestors, his name, or his city. He famously says (and this must remain in the original)

E io a lui: "I' mi son un che, quando
Amor mi spira, noto, e a quell modo
Ch'e' ditta dentro vo significando.[41]

Dante takes notation on the breath of love that moves him to signify the beloved. That to Bonagiunta seems to explain the *dolce stil nuovo,*

---

[38] See Robert Hollander's "Dante Theologus-Poeta," in *Dante Studies* 94 (1976), 91-136.

[39] The concept is not a new one but despite a book length treatment by Barolini on the poets in Dante, my debt for interpreting this canto remains greatest to Aurelio Roncaglia's "Il Canto XXVI del Purgatorio" in *Nuova Lectura Dantis*, A. Chimenz, ed. (Roma: Signorelli, 1951).

[40] *Purgatorio* II, 108.

[41] "And I to him: I am one who, when/ love inbreathes me, takes note, and in the way it dictates within/ I go forth speaking." *Purgatorio* XXIV, 52-54.

but Dante will show that the Lucchese will have misapprehended the spirit of what it is that moves him. He cannot see that that which Bonaguinta recognizes as the pure knot is something which needs be transcendent by belief in purpose, not only of technique.[42] Here, after Virgil's halting discourse on love and his inability to reveal it *in toto,* Dante explains that this selfsame love that Virgil cannot comprehend is Dante's *raison d'etre.* Dante Poet and Pilgrim is in possession of the one ingredient mysterious to both Bonaguinta and Virgil; the unfolding revelation of caritas within and without; the Christian Incarnational attitude. But he was not alone in discovering this.

The heart of the contest between Dante's past is in the twenty-sixth canto and with Guido Guinizelli and Arnaut Daniel. Here, on the Seventh Terrace of the Purgatorial Mountain, the Lustful are condemned to dance in purgatorial fires. Once more, the fires are reserved for the most important obstacles to Dante's ascent, and once more, fire is meted out to storytellers, one of Dante's own, as it were. Dante is saved from the pain of the castigating fires because he is insistent upon telling the truth, and will do so in corporality.

Dante begins by again stating his carnal nature, implying his sustenance in the aesthetic contest. In a beautiful phrase, he is "a wall against the sun"[43] to the amazed souls. The allusion here is to physicality, contrasting strongly with the condition of the penitent. This is not accidental. Dante's not dead; he is not inconsequential to the trajectory of his art. Indeed he is the manifestation of the way to be traveled for salvation. By retaining this he fulfills the most important prerequisite of the Incarnational Age; he is alive and effecting change through his humanity. He is literally *poeta im corpore* and as such, holds a power that has been abrogated by his "betters" by their deaths. This is nowhere more evident than in the conscious exorcism of Dante's greatest influence, and hence strongest threat in the realm of the love poetry of the *volgare,* Guido Guinizelli. Dante gives him lavish praise, naming him "the father / of me and of the others-those, my betters-/ who ever used sweet, gracious rhymes of love."[44]

---

[42] "una fedelta espressiva sempre piu stretta all intima dettato d' Amore-sottintendono una fede assoluta nella transcendenza della ispirazione amorose." Roncaglia, 5.

[43] *Purgatorio* XXVI, 23.

[44] *Purgatorio* XXIV, 97-99. "Until this moment in the poem, Dante has acknowledged only two characters as fathers-Virgil and Brunetto...the precise nature of this relationship clearly deserves careful attention." In Corsaro, 128.

Christ Among Them: Incarnation and Renaissance in Medieval Italian Culture

We must remember that in this encomium, Dante alludes to the *dolce stil novisti*, a school to which he once belonged. Yet by this point in his travels, Dante cannot expect to ascend to realms that do not require these gracious rhymes of love. In a few short cantos he will recount a vision and compare his powers of description to John of the Apocalypse and Ezekiel.[45] This is of paramount importance in the third and final *exemplum* of transformation. Dante then must here and now, disestablish the centrality not so much of the *stil novismo* as the inherent impotence within it. It fails because it considers *eros* too strongly and gives a dull ear to *agape*. The placement of Arnaut Daniel and Guido Guinizelli within this terrace underlines the inadequacy of the poetry itself to approximate the vision of love that waits and demands a purified aesthetic.[46] The canto also succeeds in concluding a historical poetic process specified to adumbrate roots now ever after irrelevant to the Poet, the Pilgrim, and the reader.[47]

In order to make us fully understand the *Dolce Stil Nova's* impotence, Dante must take on its champion. This is by no means a simple proposition as the residual honor of Dante's youth toward Guido informs this canto. Dante's ambiguity is evident to a degree greater than even Virgil. It seems with his Christian predecessors, indeed with the shades of his near contemporaries Dante is on less sure footing in approaching a way to address and finally relegate them to their proper proportion.[48] In doing so Dante relies on a historicity, precise quotation and names that work to divide the poem around Dante himself.

Guittone and Bonaguinta from the earlier in the *Purgatorio* have served to remind the poet that he indeed draws the spirit of the *dolce stil nova* from a purer source than did or do his predecessors and his contemporaries. By the twenty-sixth canto the groundwork has been laid to claim for Dante a central place in the realm of poetry. The canto then is a Dantean canto to a high degree as its answers serve to justify the poet,

---

[45] *Purgatorio XXIX*, 100-103.
[46] "It contains both verbal references and conceptual allusions...within the semantic fields of love and lust. . they shape Dante's story into a complex scheme in which the literary preoccupation (the language of love) is inextricably linked to the ethical subject matter (the sin of love)." In Corsaro, 123.
[47] See Bruno Porcelli, "Il Canto XXVI" in *Letture sul Purgatorio* Vittorio Vettori, ed. (Milano: Marzorati, 1965), 257-258.
[48] For a thorough reading of the relationship between the poets, which veers from the ambiguous to the hostile (on Dante's part) see Vincent Moleta, *Guinizzelli in Dante* (Roma: Edizione di Storia e Letteratura, 1980), especially 121-123 for the particular contention above.

Dante, as a potentiality in the salvific process.[49] Here we see the beginnings of the transformative personal power of Dante leaving the Incarnational Age as much as Francis represented it. As Anselm noted, God does not save his people through dialectics. Dante begins to do just that and the salvation is for and within himself. But we are still in early in the canto and still in Purgatory, where such misapprehension can be forgiven before the ascent.

Guido though is by no means the inferior technician. This would be much for Dante to claim, for those reading should know the glories of Guinizelli in their original scintillating beauty. This would even be too much for Dante Pilgrim.[50] The needle of this is threaded theologically, and Dante uses the crippled moral system of the *Dolce Stil Nova* as the primary reason for Guido's purgatorial residence.[51] Such judgements,

---

[49] ". . . we realize that in the Comedy Dante does indeed while creating an undifferentiated poetic chorality as a backdrop. . accords a special status to his own named nova rime…Dante thus claims for himself the title of poet of rectitude, whose purpose is to direct the wills of others." In Teodolinda Barolini, *Dante's Poets: Textuality and Truth in the Comedy*, 85-108.
The poetry of rectitude stems from Dante's selfsame claim to that title in the *de Vulgari Eloquentia II,ii, 9:*
Circa que sola si bene recolimus illustres viros invenimus vulgartur poetasse, scilicet Bertramum de Bornio arma, Arnaldum Daniellum amorem,…Cynum Pistoriensem amorem, amicum eius rectitudinem…Amicus eius doglia mi reca lo core ardire. The friend of Cino who can speak on rectitude is obviously Dante who wrote the famous lines. Barolini establishes that the Magnalia of the DVE is of Dante's own aesthetic informed as much by his Age as by his reading. The worthy topics are prowess of arms, love's kindling, and the directing of will. Of course Dante is fit for this.

[50] "Anzi questo contappunto stilistico, intenerito com'e di ricordi e nostalgie, apre lo spiraglio sulla natura lirica e autobiografica di tutto l'episodio, quail che siano state le ragioni della decisione di Dante di porre Guido tra I lussuriosi. Nell ultimo incontro col maestro e precursore Bolognese riemerge ancora urgente e commossa…il Guido si trasforma in mito e simbolo di una giovinezza fiduciosa e operosa, che volle e seppe rinnovare e costruire, ora contemplata e guidicata alla luce dell' eternita. " In Mario Marti, "Guinizzelli" in *l'Enciclopedia Dantesca*, v. III, 323-333.

[51] "By canto XXVI Dante's doctrinal system has expanded and the Guinizellian element in it has been relegated to an area of lesser importance (he has)…a diminished regard for Guinizelli's moral system." See Corsaro, 131. But this moral system is no by no means a set of platitudes easily delineated as Edwards is at pains to underline: "Another technique is to develop a philosophical and analytical language within lyric poetry that combines several medieval lines of thought…the ideological framework of the Dolce Stil Nuova does not present a

coming as they do in Purgatory must be just and must be based upon the conception of overcoming the obstacle of the idea of poetry, rather than the actual poems and styles of the poets under discussion.

Dante cannot throw away the *modus operandi* that will bring illumination; what he can do is summarily encapsulate its history by his own vision of aesthetic morality, and isolate it, away from the reader's imagination, saving him from the temptation of shortsighted pleasure, and bringing him along to the refinement that await.

Now we see a shift back to the Incarnational as what he is doing is systematically disowning what nurtured his youth, and in doing so, is coming to concord with other systems predicated upon the Incarnational Age, namely the Franciscan and the Cathar. Neither believed in the lust that compelled the troubadours could survive the first full flush of frenzy. Dante agrees that ascension, even divine verisimilitude, cannot be predicated on unalloyed love for the purely carnal in the opposite. What Dante does further is take the presumptions of the poets of his sweet new style seriously enough to go beyond the point of their own comprehension. This may seem hypocritical, but Dante is obeying the theology of the poetry, looking beyond what both Arnaut and Guido became trapped in.[52] He is the master of the metaphor not a disciple of the subject, and hence can acquire the vision intended by a poetry used to measure devotion.[53]

His realities on the terraces of Purgatory demand not abandonment of the form of his wonted poetry, but of its corruptible essence. Dante's chiding is both contextual and formal in that it ostensibly critiques the form of expression as well as what is being expressed. Arnaut in particular, is relegated because he is subject to a misapprehension not so much of lust and love, but of poetry. His attempts to form desire had become not only an art by him, but essential to him, a god within a god,

---

consistent philosophy so much as a framework for speculation," (pp. xxii-xxiii), in the *Poetry of Guido Guinizelli*. Translated and edited by Robert Edwards (New York: Garland, 1987).

[52] Dante si sentiva superiore a quei due poeti, consente che la coscienza di tale superiorita sia implicitamente affermata senza sminuire il valore e il calore delle parole con cui Dante proclama esplicitamente il suo debito e la sua ammirazione." Roncaglia, 6.

[53] "l'attenzione letteraria-sempre nobilmente sostenuta-e evidente nella ricerca tecnostilistica che infittisce qui le sue prove; rime difficili-ed equivoche...vocaboli insoliti. . metafore...perifrasi...allusioni erudite. . E tutta una serie di compiacimenti della proprio perizia tecnica...(Ha un) tono aristocratico d'un dialogo fra artisti che dominano con sicuro padronanza ogni piu sottile virtuosismo letterario. " Roncaglia, 14-15.

which like a sickness must and will be burned away. The fire shall be honest this time around.

Guido points out "the better craftsman"[54], Arnaut Daniel to Dante, affirming that he was the greatest of the artisans of the mother tongue. Here Dante's irony is delicious. After nearly seventy cantos of Italian, Arnaut Daniel expresses his sentiments...in Provencal.[55] The language to set down the New Revelation of Dante is Italian. The implication is that although Daniel was a wonderful poet, he erred twice: He spoke Provencal, and he misunderstood the love that compels Dante. Indicatively Dante states that Daniel then "he hides himself in the fire which refines him."[56] The Frenchman thereby becomes part of the obstacle, elementally so, blocked by his misapprehension.

Daniel becomes the final obstacle for Dante Pilgrim Poet in the arena of both poetry and love. His presence is an *idee fixee* in the poem and although placed in Purgatory, seems to be stationary, not static. This means only that the turbulence of the movement of the Lustful is in Daniel, contained essentially within both his literary and spiritual bodies. The fire, previously a problematic, even deceitful element in the *Inferno*, here takes on the significance of real Dantean intent by both containing and burning away influence on Daniel and from Dante.[57] The refining fire of the poet in which he hides and emerges acts as a quarantine for Dante's inspirational gifts. It gags and binds a dangerous influence while at the same time condemns him to a penance.[58]

It is not insincere on Dante's part to do this to such a poet, for he loves him, and knows that the spiritual interests of Arnaut are bound, by now, to be at the forefront of his necessary evolution.[59] It is evident that Dante deserves to go past, through this fire, and running, unscathed. The fact that he can view and pass indicates his prophetic role beyond the

---

[54] *Purgatorio* XXVI, 117.
[55] *Purgatorio* XXVI, 140-147.
[56] "Poi s'ascose nel foco che li affina." *Purgatorio* XXVI, 148.
[57] "e su quell motivo del fuoco ch'e tra le metafore piu banali dell'ardore amoroso, e che qui in Dante ne diviene l'ovvio contrapasso. . con particolare energia fantastica che sulla metafora imprime un marchio personale, e illumina cosi d'un riverbero diretto, d'un preciso riferimento ad personam lo stesso contrapasso dantesco. " Roncaglia, 21.
[58] "Dante. . finds in Arnaut an intensity of amorous commitment that prefigures his own. . who displays throughout his verse an overt link between eros and praxis, eros and knowledge. " Barolini, *Dante's Poets*, 113.
[59] Sono amici che partengono alle piu disparate condizioni sociali, al mondo delle professioni borghesi. . ma sopratutto artisti e poeti legati intimamente alla cerchia di interessi spirituali di Dante. " Porcelli, 271-272.

provincialism of Arnaut's language and sentiment, and in doing so shed the dead skin of his past to enter a sacred arena where he is expected.[60]

In the *Paradiso* the refining fire, and a double mythos, end Dante's fumbling towards self-realization, coming together with a sharp and glorious shock in the opening canto. Dante essays what cannot be essayed because he has gone beyond the human. The famous neologism *trasumanar* represents a defeat. Language itself has caught up with what Dante perceives to be active in him, and is found wanting. "To go beyond the human (*trasumanar*) by words/ is impossible: but the example will do/ for any whom grace will allow the experience."[61] It is a desolate conclusion at the burning point of emphatic experience. The first canto of the *Paradiso* is a paradigm gotten through hard experience that at once prepares us for the best and resigns us to the common. This indeed can serve as a working definition for what was the Incarnational Age. The Poet must confront the experience and by allowing the divine to be represented by his poetry he performs the exchange that is the heart and soul of the Incarnational Age; the divine working throughout the human. Why then such mythology as the mythology Dante uses at the start of the *Paradiso*?[62]

The referential problem revolves around Dante's choices that eschew overt Christian mythology and goes directly to two strange stories that only serve to underline Dante's intent and his adumbrated relationship to the kenotic theory inherent in Incarnational understanding. Before teasing

---

[60] See Schnapp, 726.

[61] "Trasumanar significar *per verba*/ Non si poria; pero l' essemplo basti/ a cui esperienza grazia serba." *Paradiso* I, 68-72.
Freccero sees in the *Paradiso* and in this line in particular, "the technical problems involved in finding a stylistic correspondence to this transformation (which) reaches insoluble proportions by the poem's ending, for it demands straining the representational value of poetry to the ultimate," Freccero, 211.

[62] "The wondrous change in Dante's condition is explained by the fact of his purification, which has taken place in the Earthly Paradise. In his new state, he is to ascend through Paradise and gradually acquire understanding of Divine Love. Thus he already enjoys a condition far beyond mortal limitations and in this sense he has become superhuman. Dante has crossed an essential threshold; what he is about to experience during the rest of the journey must by it's very nature exceed the intellectual grasp of mortals. To those deserving, the experience of sanctification will come only after death. For the present, the Poet can only approximate his extraordinary adventure by calling up the example of Glaucus. " In Mark Musa's "Paradise: Commentary" in *Dante Alighieri's Divine Comedy* 6 vols. (Bloomington: Indiana University Press, 2004), 11.

out meaning, the stage will be set in this last canticle and its opening canto.

Dante invokes his Supreme theme and calls upon Apollo and the Muses to sustain him. In such an invocation Dante asks Apollo "to enter into my body, and inspire/ as when you unsheathed Marsyas/ from the cage of his limbs."[63] The vision of Beatrice as seen from Dante, herself contemplative, engenders a relational metaphor to another Ovidian myth, that of Glaucus; He looks upon her and it has the effect within him of "what happened when Glaucus, in tasting the herb/ became sea-espoused to the other gods. / To go beyond the human (*trasumanar*) by words/ is impossible: but the example will do/ for any whom grace will allow the experience."[64] Dante cannot comprehend this change and Beatrice explains to him that what he feels is the speedy rise of his soul toward Empyrean. This purity seems to Dante to manifest itself in weightlessness. They pass through the Sphere of Fire and Dante hears the Music of the Spheres.

This is the raw *materiel* of the canto, and once more the fire of spiritual transformation is present. In Heaven such a fire is effective through Presence and not through Essence: That is that the contemplative potentiality within *Paradiso*'s flames are not the elemental properties that serve to castigate and inform. The fire has become symbolic, yet this should not deter the reader from understanding that such symbolism may yet be active, if not upon the Pilgrim, then the reader herself.[65]

---

[63] "Entra nel petto mio, e spira tue/ Si come quando Marsia traesti/ de la vagina de le membra sue. " *Paradiso* I, 19-21.

[64] "qual si fe Glauco nel gustar d l'erba/ Che 'l fe consorto in mar de altri Dei. / Trasumanar significar *per verba*/ Non si poria: pero l'essemplo basti/ A cui esperienza grazia serba. " *Paradiso* I, 68-72.

[65] "To appreciate the *Paradiso*, it has been said, a state of quiescence and submission is necessary. It is true in a sense that progress has no place in the *Paradiso*, which in its representation of infinity contains the ground of all progress: On the other hand, neither has quiescence and submission, except as one of two opposites which there are unified, where contemplation and action are as it were the inbreathing and outbreathing of the soul, equally exigent to life and to each other." In Helen Flanders Dunbar, *Symbolism in Medieval Thought and its Consummation in the Divine Comedy*, 461-462; or more to the point is Anderson: "If fire, flame, and light have been one of the fiercest means of punishment and refinement up to this point, they now in *Paradiso* become both the means and the manifestation of the souls of the blessed and their environment of delight. It is the same divinely created element that tortures one soul and irradiates another: thus flame is a permanence both in the cosmology of the poem and in Dante's creative

Dante uses two mythological allusions (which point to other latent biblical connections) that are necessary for understanding Dante's position in his *détente* with the Incarnational Age. That the myths are invoked while Dante is surrounded by fire is not accidental. Even in the *Paradiso*, at the start of his purified journey, there are symbols still tethered to a temporal, incomplete notion of fulfillment. We shall see that this metaphoric usage serves to teach and to warn of the apocalyptic nature of such revelation. This conflation rolls magnificently into a personal mythology reflective of Christian history, reminding the reader that personal intent, and hence personality itself, cannot be divorced from God's alchemy in the Incarnation.

The myths used by Dante are taken from Ovid's *Metamorphoses* and both deal with the desire of the mortal for the divine, the stories of Marsyas and Glaucus.[66] Dante has repeatedly used the Latin author to underline the conversion and transformative tropes within the journey. That he uses the Ovidian metaphor here points to the tacit admission that it only within the famed mythological stories of transformation that, later in the poem, the carefully learned in their own small ships following in Dante's wake, can grasp the Vision without foundering.[67]

Marsyas and Glaucus are explicitly points of pedagogical reference. There are there to specifically instruct. Their potentialities are aimed at a god and a human: Apollo and the Christian. The reader at this point is ostensibly affiliated to ideas of Christian salvation. So the opening canto of a Christian Paradise as a fulfillment and vestibule to final illumination

---

imagination; it is the human character that undergoes transformation within its nature. " Anderson, *Dante the Maker*, 396.

[66] The myth of Marsyas can be found in Ovid, *Metamorphoses* VI, 382-400, and the myth of Glaucus can be found in book XIII, 898-968. For Dante's use of Ovid see Barolini, Dronke, and Curtius respectively. A most thorough investigation can be found in C. A. Robson's *Dante's Use in the Divina Commedia of the Medieval Allegories of Ovid* in *Centenary Essays on Dante* (Oxford: Clarendon Press, 1965), 1-38. "Allegory pursued in this and in countless other ways formed a common denominator for widely disparate domains of thought and experience. Biblical and pagan histories were seen in an identical perspective, and both, conceived as a storehouse of symbols, tended to compete in Dante's poetry with 'real world' personages and recent events.... Dante speaks with enthusiastic approval of Apollo's flaying of Marsyas and with strong religious feelings of Glaucus' transformation into a marine deity.... the material itself is very carefully assembled and pieced together from the books of the Metamorphoses and arranged in two great cyles, corresponding to the realm of Virgil and the realm of Beatrice. " Robson, 2-5.

[67] *Paradiso* II, 1-7.

at once refers both to the human and the divine. This is the final flourish of certain Incarnational ideas of reconciliation that calls for the human to be completed in transformation.

Apollo is reminded of a gruesome victory over the presumptions of a satyr, wherein the defeat of the demiurge involves a stripping away from the *'vagina'* (literally) of his limbs. A transmutation by mutilation: *Mutatis Mutilatio*. Dante must undergo this type of inspiration, a harrowing one, before being made worthy. The story as told in Ovid is as follows in the full Loeb translation:

> Another recalled the satyr whom the son of Latona had conquered in a contest on Pallas' reed, and punished. "Why do you tear from me from myself?" he cried. "Oh, I repent! Oh, a flute is not worth such price!" As he screams, his skin is stripped off the surface of his body, and he is all wound: blood flows down on every side, the sinews laid bare, the veins throb and quiver with no skin to cover them: you could count the entrails as they palpitate, and the vitals showing clearly in his breast.[68]

The story concerning Glaucus is much more involved and, for reasons of elucidation, a full transcript must be given.[69] Glaucus, as explained by Ovid,

---

[68] "…satyri reminiscitur alter/ quem Tritoniaca Latuos harundine victum/ adfecit poena. 'quid me mihi detrahis?' iniquet;/ 'a! piget, a! non est' clamabat 'tibia tanti. '/ clamanti cutis est summos direpta per artus,/ nec quicquam nisi vulnus erat; cruor undique manta,/ detectique patent nervi, trepidaeque sine ulla/ pelle micant vanae; salientia viscera possis/ et perlucentes numerare in pectore fibras. " *Metamorphoses* VI, 383-391.

[69] Since the amount of text is considerable in this instance, translation of text and the Latin following was not taken from the Loeb classics but from the University of Virginia's Internet Latin texts. See www.etextvirginia.edu/latin/ovid/trans/Metamorph13.htm. Downloaded on 17 February 2007. "discedunt placidisque natant Nereides undis /Scylla redit; neque enim medio se credere ponto / audet, et aut bibula sine vestibus errat harena /aut, ubi lassata est, seductos nacta recessus /gurgitis, inclusa sua membra refrigerat unda:/ ecce fretum stringens, alti novus incola ponti, / nuper in Euboica versis Anthedone membris,/ Glaucus adest, visaeque cupidine virginis haeret /et, quaecumque putat fugientem posse morari,/ verba refert; fugit illa tamen veloxque timore/ pervenit in summum positi prope litora montis. /ante fretum est ingens, apicem conlectus in unum/ longa sub arboribus convexus in aequora vertex:/ constitit hic et tuta loco, monstrumne deusne / ille sit, ignorans admiraturque colorem/ caesariemque umeros subiectaque terga tegentem,/ ultimaque excipiat quod tortilis inguina piscis. / sensit et innitens, quae stabat proxima, moli /'non ego prodigium nec sum fera belua, virgo,/ sed deus' inquit 'aquae: nec maius in aequora

comes, skimming the water, a new inhabitant of the sea, his form recently altered, at Anthedon opposite Euboea Seeing the girl, he stood still, desiring her, and said whatever he thought might stop her running away. Nevertheless she ran, and, with the swiftness of fear, came to the top of a mountain standing near the shore. It faced the wide sea, rising to a single peak, its wooded summit leaning far out over the water. Here she stopped, and from a place of safety, marveled at his color; the hair that hid his shoulders and covered his back; and his groin below that merged into a winding fish's tail; she not knowing whether he was god or monster.

He saw her, and, leaning on a rock that stood nearby, he said: 'Girl, I am no freak or wild creature, but a god of the sea. Proteus, Triton, or Palaemon, son of Athomas have no greater power in the ocean. Mortal once, but no doubt destined for the deep, even then I worked the waves: now drawing in the drag nets full of fish, now sitting on a rock, casting, with rod and line. There is a beach, bounded by a green field, one side

---

Proteus/ ius habet et Triton Athamantiadesque Palaemon. / ante tamen mortalis eram, sed, scilicet altis/ debitus aequoribus, iam tum exercebar in illis;/ nam modo ducebam ducentia retia pisces, / nunc in mole sedens moderabar harundine linum. / sunt viridi prato confinia litora, quorum altera pars undis, pars altera cingitur herbis/ quas neque cornigerae morsu laesere iuvencae,/ nec placidae carpsistis oves hirtaeve capellis;/ non apis inde tulit conlectos sedula flores,/ non data sunt capiti genialia serta, neque umquam / falciferae secuere manus; ego primus in illo/ caespite consedi, dum lina madentia sicco,/ utque recenserem captivos ordine pisces,/ insuper exposui, quos aut in retia casus/ aut sua credulitas in aduncos egerat hamos. / res similis fictae, sed quid mihi fingere prodest? / gramine contacto coepit mea praeda moveri / et mutare latus terraque ut in aequore niti. /dumque moror mirorque simul, fugit omnis in undas / turba suas dominumque novum litusque relinquunt. /obstipui dubitoque diu causamque requiro,/ num deus hoc aliquis, num sucus fecerit herbae:/ "quae tamen has" inquam "vires habet herba?" manuque / pabula decerpsi decerptaque dente momordi. / vix bene conbiberant ignotos guttura sucos, /cum subito trepidare intus praecordia sensi /alteriusque rapi naturae pectus amore; / nec potui restare diu "repetenda" que "numquam /terra, vale!" dixi corpusque sub aequora mersi. / di maris exceptum socio dignantur honore, / utque mihi, quaecumque feram, mortalia demant, / Oceanum Tethynque rogant: ego lustror ab illis, et purgante nefas noviens mihi carmine dicto / pectora fluminibus iubeor supponere centum; /nec mora, diversi lapsi de partibus amnes / totaque vertuntur supra caput aequora nostrum. / hactenus acta tibi possum memoranda referre, /hactenus haec memini, nec mens mea cetera sensit. /quae postquam rediit, alium me corpore toto, / ac fueram nuper, neque eundem mente recepi: /hanc ego tum primum viridem ferrugine barbam /caesariemque meam, quam longa per aequora verro, / ingentesque umeros et caerula bracchia vidi / cruraque pinnigero curvata novissima pisce. / quid tamen haec species, quid dis placuisse marinis,/ quid iuvat esse deum, si tu non tangeris istis?' /talia dicentem, dicturum plura, reliquit /Scylla deum; furit ille inritatusque repulse/ prodigiosa petit Titanidos atria Circes. " *Metamorphoses* XIII, 906-968.

bordered by sea, the other by grass, that horned cattle have not damaged by grazing, that placid sheep or shaggy goats have not cropped. No bees intent on gathering This pollen plundered the flowers there; no garlands came from there for the heads of revelers; no one had ever mown it, scythe in hand. I was the first to sit there on the turf, drying my sea-soaked lines, and laying out in order the fish I had caught, to count them, that either chance or innocence had brought to my curved hook. This will sound like a tale, but what would I get from lying? Touching the grass, my catch began to stir, and shift about, and swim over land as if they were in the sea. While I hesitated and wondered, the complete shoal fled into their native waters, leaving behind their new master, their new land.

I stood dumbfounded, for a while not believing it, searching for the cause. Had some god done it, or the juice of some herb? "Yet what herb has such power?" I asked, and gathering some herbage in my hand, I bit what I had gathered with my teeth. My throat had scarcely swallowed the strange juice, when suddenly I felt my heart trembling inside me, my breast seized with yearning for that other element. Unable to hold out for long, crying out: "Land, I will never return to, goodbye!" I immersed my body in the sea. The gods of the sea received me, thinking me worth the honor of their company, and asked Oceanus and Tethys to purge what was mortal in me. I was purified by them, and, cleansed of sin by an incantation nine times repeated, they ordered me to bathe my body in a hundred rivers. Immediately streams from every side poured their waters over my head. So much I can tell of you of those marvelous things, so much of them I remember: then my mind knew no more. When later I came to, my whole body was altered from what I was before, and my mind was not the same.

Then I saw, for the first time, this dark green beard, my hair that sweeps the wide sea, these giant shoulders and dusky arms, these legs that curve below into a fish's fins. Yet what use is this shape, or that I was pleasing to the ocean gods? What use is it to be a god, if these things do not move you?'

As the god spoke these words, looking to say more, Scylla abandoned him. Then Glaucus, maddened, and angered by her rejection, sought the wondrous halls of Circe, daughter of the Sun.

The story is replete with significance if taken in context at this point in the *Comedy*, and has not been sufficiently mined for it's strange and strong allusions to the Dante's poem.[70] The woman being chased, the purification by nine incantations, and the one hundred rivers, along with Glaucus' recognition of his transformation and it's ineffectual response in

---

[70] See Charles Singleton, *Dante Studies 2: Journey to Beatrice*, 28-29. As Singleton points out in his Commentary on the Paradiso, the allusion "clearly points to verb "trasumanar" in the next verse as this applies to the pilgrim," in Singleton, *Paradise: Commentary*, 18.

the beloved, his anger at the rejection and his seeking Circe (Ulysses' bane) named here as the daughter of the Sun can be paralleled with the earthly Beatrice in her Florentine life, the nine circles of hell, the one hundred cantos that complete the journey, and his transformation when looking at Beatrice in the Sphere of Fire. For the Incarnational Age and its unraveling, this passage and the Marsyas episode, are the Dantean confessions of "going beyond" not only the human, but beyond the parameters of the afore-established Christian speculum by continuing mythological parallels.[71]

An important distinction between Marsyas and Glaucus lies in their vocations: One, art; the other love. It is the exact double bind that has compromised the soul of the aforementioned Arnaut Daniel and as such points to the stubborn echoing past of Dante as he essays to perfect himself. Dante, as has been noted, was made fully aware that he was and to a certain degree remains, part of the camp that made the philosophy of the troubadour an acceptable, and seductive, paradigm. The way this became so was to deny the primacy of place to the immortal element and concentrate upon the aggressively personal aspects of the beloved. Transforming and, by the imaginative faculties, completing the mythology of a third testament of language[72] which the Comedy becomes apart from Scripture, involves in it a certain sense of hubris. Dante's achievement therefore is one of betrayal to the greater faculties and potentialities that have given him the grace to rise to such heights.

In short, as Dante goes forward he continues to divest himself not by emptying, not by the kenotic theory of Incarnational speculum, but by transformation. This is necessary when the human enters the sphere of

---

[71] Daniel Murtaugh's conclusion about this episode is enticing but in the end a bit misleading; " The example that must suffice is the story of the metamorphosis of the sea-god. It is the sort of *bella menzogna* (beautiful lie) that lies ready to a poet's hand, but is inadequate to the pilgrim's experience. As with so many of the similes and analogies of the Paradiso, the final point of the story of Glaucus is its unlikeness to the experience of Dante. It is a provisional structure, a vantage point from which we can judge the great distance that separates our poet and us from the pilgrim in Paradise. It must suffice for us and for him until the promise of grace is fulfilled," 278 in "Figurando il paradiso': The Signs that Render Dante's Heaven", in *PMLA*, vol. 90, No. 2 (March, 1975) 277-284. The analogous in Dante is rarely if ever used to point out unlikeness or dissimilarity in Dante. The point can be taken that it is insufficient, but the Glaucus analogy, like the famous Neptune analogy, in the last canto, use specified mythological allusion to point to what exactly must be rendered for identification.

[72] See Harold Bloom, *The Western Canon* (New York: Harcourt, Brace, and Co., 1994) 72-98.

the divine. For the philosopher this provides a scandal of disunity that cannot be reconciled for the main thrust of Dante's fabrication is the poetic not the philosophic,[73] causing criticism to bifurcate along lines of literary and metaphysical camps.

But especially in the *Paradiso*, the divine empties, the human fills, and when filling in Empyrean, the light eradicates the need for speculum. Indeed here in the first canto, Beatrice reassures Dante that his purification has vouchsafed him a position closer to God.[74] He is, after this canto, made swift by transformation. The reason that Dante is such a central figure in both the apotheosis and the denouement of the Incarnational Age is because he has mirrored the actions of Christian salvation within a sphere (at least imaginatively) that does not need the sacrifice. The act of movement through Heaven is as philosophically scandalous as movement through Hell. All sinners and saved are pre-determinate beings who retain a place in separate spheres, disallowed (with the exception of Virgil) a freedom that comes naturally to the mortal. That Dante moves through them signifies that the unique position afforded Dante must be had during suspension of the laws of salvation.[75] Since this cannot be so, the laws of salvation must be understood to be active within Dante.[76]

---

[73] The best book and recapitulation on the theme of the metaphysical problems within the Comedy is T. K. Seung, *The Fragile Leaves of the Sibyl: Dante's Master Plan* (Westminster: The Newman Press, 1962) and his essay, "The Metaphysics of the *Commedia*" in *The Divine Comedy and the Encyclopedia of Arts and Sciences,* Giuseppe Di Scipio and Aldo Scaglione, eds. (Amsterdam and Philadelphia: John Benjamins Publishing Co., 1988), 181-222.

[74] *Paradiso* I, 130-142.

[75] "It is the question of striving for absolute fidelity to the inner imaginative process and reality that are his own, but are also beyond him-that are moments perceived as the god speaking in the vessel he has chosen....Dante's special capacity to experience and record the more than earthly stems from the fact that the more than earthly had been revealed to him in an unparalleled way: through the highest moments of earthly love.. and (he) realizes that if anyone can bring him to heaven's blessedness it is she (making his mission)..a true one, not one spurred by of grandeur of his own." Dronke, 4-5.

[76] "In the postlapsarian world we reason by a limited and eliminatory logic which Dante tells us, over and over, cannot hold in the 'real world'...Dante's Christianity yields numerous contradictory verities, and the Paradiso itself offers a carefully orchestrated sequence of unfathomable events that we cannot hope to understand, and can ultimately only accept." In F. Regina Psaki, "The Sexual Body in Dante's Celestial Paradise" in *Imagining Heaven in the Middle Ages: A Book of Essays* Jan Swango Emerson and Hugh Feiss, eds. (New York: Garland, 2000), 47-61, 58.

And since Dante is guilty of dissimulation, he must convince himself and the Incarnational world he has inherited, that the mirrored image portrayed is based upon a *similar* mythos; that is to say he understood that humankind cannot bear very much reality, and would needs be lulled by his fantasy to accept the heretical notion that Dante believes himself to be the *locus* of his salvation.[77] Such a conclusion begs the comparison to be made by each reader, indeed Dante, aware of the unique claim inherent in the journey, warns the reader to follow carefully within the *Paradiso*.[78]

This realization is responsible for the guilt that compels his fear, anger, wonder, awe, and transcendence at his own creation. He is proud, and fearful of his pride[79] yet this does not compel him to retire, but to squeeze the juice of his creation until he drains himself of himself, to prepare the husk of his identity for God; the God of Dante's wonder. This is the step shod in Renaissance leather which Dante took out of the Incarnational Age, and such an ending, in the Christian understanding, denotes eschatology.

Why? Because the conflation of Dante's wonder with his explanation of its working within him, reflect a transformation from the wandering pilgrim-poet invested with the desire for true speculum, to adjudicator of destiny.[80] In short Dante inverts the achievement of the Incarnational Age by returning to the trope of God the Judge from the human Christ. The ability to fulfill, *knowingly* fulfill, a life with its grace-given purpose should be the property of an omniscient judge, the God of the Dark Ages. The human Christ has been along with this Divine Judge swallowed up in the pretensions of the voyager. Scriptural examples of this achievement and the punishment incumbent upon such extravagance is powerfully set forth in the book of another prophet of eschatology, Ezekiel. That Dante knew this is shown in his letter to Can Grande.

---

[77] See Aaron Gurevich, *The Origins of European Individualism*. Translated by Katherine Judelson (Oxford: Blackwell, 1995), 231, wherein the Russian scholar states that Dante assumes a quasi-heretical but original notion of salvation by recounting his journey in a state of clear consciousness.
[78] *Paradiso* II, 1-20.
[79] *Purgatorio* XIII, 136-138.
[80] Guy Raffa, *Divine Dialectic: Dante's Incarnational Poetry*, 127, 115: " Dante shifts his representational mode from exposition to *ekphrasis* by lifting the veil off his incarnational poetry as the wayfarere…(he) both performs and challenges the predominant figuration of Christian hermeneutics in the medieval imagination… Dante who envisions the Incarnation as both dialectical process and product holds nothing back in celebrating the mystery of his supreme theological event."

This letter to his patron in Verona, briefly includes the prophet as one who has understood the material purpose of heaven, and as such uses Paul as the New Testament parallel to couple with Ezekiel to lend force to the illustration. In the letter (which I obviously take as authentic), Dante dedicates the canticle to his patron and offers a methodology by which to interpret the entire poem.[81]

Dante's recognition of his own hubris begs the sincerity of the poet to form an eschatology of self. This being operative, reference to biblical apocalyptism must then be voiced. When adumbrated, only a referential figure that can parallel the terrestrial experiences of the Poet will be adequate to the task. Within this epistle, Ezekiel is invoked twice; once referring to man's perfected genesis in his lamentation over Tyre (Ezekial 28: 12-13), and the vision of election (Ezekiel 1: 28) that is compared to the transhumanizing experience of the Pauline vision in Corinthians (II Corinthians, 12: 3-4).

The Pauline model, another reference in the epistle, has been well illustrated in the scholarship,[82] but Ezekiel forms a more cogent parallel. Dante has used the example of Ezekiel previously in the Comedy (*Purgatorio* XXIX) to recall Ezekiel call to prophecy during Dante's own election for the edifying visions to come.[83]

Ezekiel's eschatology was quickened, like Dante's own, by the powerful experience of exile. This exile for Ezekiel was punctuated by the destruction of Jerusalem's temple.[84] Dante's reference cues the consummation in the literature of the Incarnational Age of its purpose; the embodiment of God within a defeated people after the expulsion from Jerusalem, and Dante as the High Prophet who performs the mighty task of codifying the metaphor into a literary and personal reality. It was the

---

[81] For the text of the letter in the Latin, see "Epistole" in the *Appendice* volume of the *Enciclopedia Dantesca* Umberto Bosco, ed. (Roma: Treccani, 1978), XIII, 813-817; for the English see Charles Allen Dinsmore, *Aids to the Study of Dante*, (Boston and New York: Houghton Mifflin, 1903), 263-286.

[82] See Joseph Anthony Mazzeo, *Structure and Thought in the Paradiso* (Ithaca and New York: Cornell University Press, 1958), 84-110.

[83] For the eucharistic and penitential significance of this canto and interesting ties to later processional developments see Grandgent's coomentary on *Purgatorio* XXIX, 591-593.

[84] For recent scholarship in English concerned with the theology and allegory of exile in Ezekial see Thomas, M. Raitt, A *Theology of Exile: Judgment/ Deliverance in Jeremiah and Ezekiel* (Philadelphia: Fortress Press, 1977): John F. Kutsko, *Between Heaven and Earth: Divine Presence and Absence in the Book of Ezekiel* (Winona Lake: Eisenbrauns, 2000): and Andrew Mein, *Ezekiel and the Ethics of Exile* (Oxford: Oxford University Press, 2001).

terminus of the road first approached in the allegorical methods of the heightened, Franciscan apocalyptic spirituality of the Joachamites.[85]

To concentrate upon Ezekiel's lamentation over the King of Tyre recalls Dante's own predicament both within the debacle of Florentine politics and in the transhumanizing event of Dante's ascent. The biblical passage has been also assumed to refer to Lucifer, as the king of Tyre, a city no longer in God's favor (read both Florence and Rome under Boniface VIII to Dante) and its king is lamented. But the interest in the comparison is quickened when Ezekiel refers to the "ill day" of the king when his "proud heart proclaimed that thou wast a god, enthroned god-fashion in the heart of the sea."[86]

The king is cast down because he spurns the honor of exaltation, the honor of "God's garden to take thy pleasure in." But God becomes as punitive as he was beneficent to the king. While reading the text of Ezekiel, the ascent of Dante in the supernatural world and his fortunes in the physical world must be kept in mind, at least until this point of the poem:

> From the day of thy creation all was perfect in thee, till thou didst prove false; all these traffickings had thee false within, and for thy guilt I must expel thee, guardian cherub as thou wert from God's mountain: between the wheels of fire thou shouldst walk no longer....such a fire I will kindle in the heart of thee as shall be thy undoing, leave thee a heap of dust on the ground for all to gaze at. None on earth that recognizes thee but shall be dismayed at the sight of thee.[87]

With typical adroitness Dante has subsumed the lamentations over the traitorous king with the myths of Marsyas and Glaucus to make the reader aware that although the achievement of the poet is to go beyond the

---

[85] "ne soltanto per Dante o per Ezechia comincia la commedia, il drammma, ma per ogni uomo che viene quaggiu..tra le veglia di Gesu Cristo nella preghiera e nel sudore di sangue, ed il sonno e il torpore della morte spirituale da parte degli apostolic nell orto di Getsemani. Si tratta di un rapporto dialettico in senso idealistico, ma da un punto di vista cristiano ci si trova davanti al drama divino e umano della Passione il quale non si compiuto una volta sola ma continuamente si rinnova sacramentalments e spiritualmente." In Camillo Paoli, *Il Riformatore Veltro: Giochinismo e Francescanesimo nell' allegoria fondamentale della Divina Commedia* (Pisa: Giardini, 1971), 81-82.

[86] *Ezekiel* 28: 2 in the Ronald Knox translation. "eo quod elevatum est cor tuum et dixisti, Deus ego sum in cathedra Dei sedi in corde maris, cum sis homo et non Deus" in the *Vulgate*.

[87] *Ezekiel* 28: 15-19.

human, such a dispensation is recognized as being above his desserts. Also, that the telling of the dispensation to the living is not only forbidden in a sense, it is also, to a great extent fabricated.

> For the comprehension of these things it must be understood, that when the, it did not remember what human intellect is exalted in this life on account of the natural relation and affinity that hath to the separate intellectual substance, it is exalted to such a degree that after the return the memory waxeth feeble, because it hath transcended human bounds And this is suggested to us by the Apostle where in speaking to the Corinthians (II Cor. 12: 3-4) he saith: "And I know such a man (whether in the body or out of the body), how that he was caught up into Paradise, and heard unspeakable words, which is not lawful for man to utter." Lo then! When the intellect had transcended human bounds in its exaltation then had passed exterior to it...And in Ezekiel (Ezek. 1: 28) it is written: "and when I saw it, I fell upon my face."[88]

Like Ezekiel, Dante is offering a paradox of exile, wherein God must be made present and the Temple reestablished within a wilderness.[89] It is through the memorial power of the poet of the Incarnation that the Incarnation must be recalled rather than acted out, because Dante has subsumed the exile and the God within himself. The man god has been swallowed in the fire of transhumanization, made indeed a god "among the wheels" of fire in which he and Beatrice now revel.

So the greatness of Dante lies in the awareness with which he brings the ramifications of his pride to devolve upon himself. He is exiled, like Ezekiel, like Lucifer, like Christ in the Incarnational Age, to a sphere wherein the terrain must be habitable by the primary duty of the exile; the

---

[88] Dinsmore, *Epistol.* XIII, 28, 282-283.
"Ad que intelligenda sciendum est quod intellectus humanus in hac vita, propter connaturalitatem et affinitatem quam habet et substantiam intellectualem separatam, quando elevatur, in tantum elevatur ut memoria post reditum deficiat propter transcendisse humanum modum. Et hoc insinatur nobis per Apostolum ad Corinthios loquentem, ubi dicit: 'Scio hominem, sive in corpore sive extra corpus nescio, Deus scit, raptum usque ad tertium celum, et vidit arcana Dei, que non licit homini loqui.' Ecce, postquam humanam rationem intellectus ascensione transierat, quid extra se ageretur non recordabatur...Et in Ezechiele scribitur: 'Vidi, et cecidi faciem meam.'"
Jeffrey Schnapp relates the events described here to the canticle as a reference to the Transfiguration. See Jeffrey Schnapp, *The Transfiguration of History at the Center of Dante's Paradise* (Princeton: Princeton University Press, 1986), 106-107.
[89] See Kutsko, *Between Heaven and Earth*, 155-156.

rebuilding of the Temple, either literally or metaphorically. The interior and the exterior of the foreign land must be made amenable to his god; a "Rome where Christ is a Roman."[90]

This is the duty of the citizen in any Christian dispensation. It is not a narrow view, but a capacious one; understandable as a paradigm because it comes from the yearning of displacement.[91] Is it any wonder, then that Dante has invoked Marsyas and Glaucus, those two who had approximated the divine with different consequences. With Beatrice looking upon him, with the ramifications of his journey apparent was the world not a bit too much with Dante still. The purgatorial flames and the waters of Lethe perhaps had not been as attendant upon the imagination as they had been on the experience.

The Sphere of Fire in Paradise was the final axis wherein, like a god, Dante could hold the reins of mythic identity and steer the chariot of his hopes into the road wherein the exile transforms his fears of eternal displacement into the joys of a true home; the Celestial. In his glance toward the Sun, reflective and reactionary of Beatrice's own glance, (*Paradiso* I, 46-54) we see also the hopes of the exile to attain a place,[92] a stationary place, among the wheels of fire.[93] This is also an echo of Ezekiel recalling the lost hopes of Tyre, and lamenting the idea of fallen perfection.

Dante does not write to be interesting; he is convinced of the veracity of his poem. The achievement lies in the eradication of the painfully personal by the transformation of the baser dull alloys of his humanity by the alchemy of his art. It is the only way he makes sense of his position. He is guilty in the end of a transgression that animated the pride of Marsyas. He is guilty of the love that compelled a sea change in Glaucus. He is guilty of hoping against hope for home. Like Ezekiel, for the sake of others he consecrates a Temple within himself.[94]

---

[90] *Paradiso* XXXII, 102.
[91] See *Dante and Governance* J.R. Woodhouse, ed. (Oxford: Clarendon Press, 1997), especially John Took, "Justice and the Just Ruler," 139, and Peter Hainsworth, "Dante's Farewell to Politics," 157.
[92] "E si come secondo raggio suole/ uscir del primo, e risalire in suso,/ pur come pellegrin che tornar vuole.." *Paradiso* I, 49-51.
[93] "...inside the simile the reflected beam is a pilgrim desiring to return home and doing so, which is just what Dante and Beatrice are desiring and doing at the moment." C.S. Lewis, *Studies in Medieval and Renaissance Literature* (Cambridge: Cambridge University Press, 1998), 73.
[94] Raitt, *Theology of Exile*, 198.

His actions arise from the same goad that reared the Scrovegni Chapel, the Brancacci Chapel, and even Michelangelo's *Last Judgement*; guilt. The powerful impulse that led Leonardo to paint enigmas rather than arrivals, that led Raphael, that most hedonistic of painters, to give order to a riotous School, that had Donatello sculpt finally a Magdalene, who prays more for him than for us. By subsuming the entirety of the Incarnational Age, Dante at once prefigures and (in true Dantean fashion) fulfills the art of the Renaissance. Artists without the conviction of the possibility of the Incarnation will never know enough to attempt to approximate the eternal. Their art will remain mired in the baser elements of human concern. Incarnational artists attempted a speculum and by this approximated a notion of *kenosis*.

Dante inverted the quest and divined what was human in God, and how the terrestrial concerns can storm Heaven. The consequences of the human within the sacred sphere, is the *menschendammerung* caused by the transgressed Augustinian notions of the separate systems at work in Christian History. The clear line of demarcation had been erased and all things were now possible in Christian Art, even it's suicide. By Dante's magnificent metaphoric manipulations, the divine and the human began to breathe the air designed for the other. It was at once the most miraculous and the most definitive expression of the Incarnational Age.

Only a year before Dante's birth (1264), the former Jacques, archdeacon of Liege (Urban IV), by his *Transiturus de hoc mundo*, extended the celebration of the Feast of Corpus Christi to the entire Latin Church.[95] The official obligations occurred across Christendom beginning only in 1317, a mere four years before the Dante's death. Within the lifespan of the poet, the song of Christian Incarnation was sung by the processions of simple folk who felt obliged to both carry aloft and reverence a god sacrificed and transformed into themselves. Dante had indeed understood this sentiment, for he had, to a great extent, embodied his time. Perhaps it was no accident that the great Poet went to his grave clothed reverently in the habit of a Franciscan friar. The seraphic love[96] with which the poet described Francis was finally his, for he had, in attempting to mirror it, swallowed its fire.

---

[95] Gavin I. Langmuir, "The Tortures of the Body of Christ" in *Christendom and its Discontents: Exclusion, persecution, and rebellion, 1000-1500* S. Waugh and P. Diehl, eds. (Cambridge: Cambride University Press, 1996), 287-309.

[96] "L'un fu tutto serafico in ardore," *Paradiso* XI, 37.

Epilogue

Under God, In the Flesh

> It is true that all that did happen is a presentation of what is happening; all the historical events, especially of this category, are a pageant of the events of the human soul. But it is also true that Christendom has always held that the two are indissolubly connected; that the events in the human soul could not have existed unless the historical events had existed...The union of history and the individual is, like that of so many other opposites, in the coming of the kingdom of heaven, historic and contemporary at once. It was historic in order that it might always be contemporary; it is contemporary because it was certainly historic.[1]

The phenomenon of Incarnational speculation gripped the Italy in the thirteenth century with the force of a cultural gale storm. The time strikes a strange chord against our current concerns, as these are deferential to a God kept discreetly quiet among the cluttered furniture of accumulated ideology. To understand the time in question, it is not the sacrifice of Christ, the event that concerned those in question, with which we are to concern ourselves. Instead, it is that gentlest of saints, the *poverello* of Assisi who seduces us with his vocation and his life to begin a rapprochement with the more questionable aspects of his age.

Can our current culture sustain another spiritual force on the scale of Francis of Assisi? Saint Francis was a reed with a strong wind blowing through him, and the music from that meeting spoke to the feet as well as the soul. The fractured age in which he lived, as all fractured ages do, sought an incarnation of what it hoped to be. All too often this corporal reality materializes wearing motley. If the age is particularly ill starred, the charlatan is also a sociopath, intent on disabusing the time of any predilection for a moral order. Francis was neither, but he wasn't exactly the prototype that everyone had in mind. The ubiquitous merchant (which he started out as being) was more of a realistic paradigm for the rising

---

[1] Charles Williams, *He Came Down from Heaven* (London: Faber and Faber, 1950), 12-13.

middle class. That's most of us, all children of the least common denominator.

Poverty, a much closer reality to the median of Francis' time, was for a time a contender to the psychological aspirations of that emergent middle class. Indeed, wealth and a rising in class, however illusory to the vast majority of men, always acted out its presumptions against a background of a guilt gilded by the dull colors of poverty. Poverty was for a time, a hope of the hopeless, and surrounded by the concomitant halo of *bona voluntas* bestowed upon it by a Church at once critical of financial abuse and conversant in the Gospels.

And yet the impetus behind the embrace of evangelical poverty was a negation of the systems of the state that had begun to foist an emergent mercantilism on the feudal idea. It was a willful exile from the concerns of the duties of the world. The previous exclusionary process of the marginal men and women of the Middle Ages was not self-inflicted. Perhaps this understanding wreathed the mendicants in a begrudging admiration from the distracted world.

At first, even the Church, although the greatest temporal power, saw the inherent worth in an act of an individual's real renunciation of the world. The bishop's clothing of Francis, naked before his father, assumes at first that the mantle was given in deference to public modesty. Instead the symbolism is apparent that the benediction of the orthodoxy fell upon a social choice that bucked the trend towards a class formation within Europe. The Franciscan rule, at first, was a subversion of authority that could be smiled upon by the Church because the critique was not understood as aimed against the spiritual authority, but against the predilections of the merchant class.

By now, poverty was used by the Church as a bulwark against the unseemly appetite of the energized mechanisms of trade, and exchange and profit. The situation became untenable by the time of the Franciscan debate on poverty, which came to a head in the early fourteenth century. This event decidedly refigured poverty's role even in the life of the Christian. From thence onwards, it became a problematic endeavor to pursue self-denial to its logical extremes and live within a tidal change in how Western man was to see himself. Poverty became an evil to be remedied rather than an ideal to be attempted, and would remain a crisis to be avoided in the collective and personal western body and mind. The sincere withdrawal from the world on the part of the Christian after the Reformation was as bizarre to the common man as the "insane" person of the Foucaltian exegesis of the seventeenth century, resulting, no doubt, in the gradual abnegation of an absolute moral duty owed to the "least of these."

If one were to attempt a sloughing away today, the quest for absence would be irretrievably tangled in the web of the exclusively spiritual. The results of corporal denial are sought specifically for their corporal properties. Only today do we encounter the "virtue" of absence in the affluent when they starve themselves to approximate a purely physical beauty. The understood virtue of poverty in the thirteenth century was to deny the self for the ultimate goal of mystical and spiritual fulfillment. Today, in the industrialized world, the results of starvation are seen as specifically impinging upon appearance. A fast has lost its spiritual reward and masquerades now as a cleansing of impurities in the body rather than the soul.

In Islam, the distinction is still made. But they are a younger child than Christianity, and are seemingly now at war with the modern world, one that they will, in time, lose. One can argue that it is the legacy from the Enlightenment that informs us outside of any considerations to what preceded it, yet the struggle that has allowed poverty to be the enemy to be destroyed rather than the goal to be attained began in earnest after its possible virtues were essayed. Yet divesting all that ties us to the world to attain spiritual fulfillment seems like a great idea today precisely because the possibility of succeeding has been made increasingly remote. People aren't expected to try it in an age when an automobile is a necessity rather than a luxury. This has been the case for centuries.

It is in the recent decades that the understanding of the Medieval quest for a spiritual fulfillment has been seen through the lens of a clinical mind, and Francis can be explained as suffering from a certain psychosis. Our microscopes are precisely worthwhile to our age because we have become drunk on progress: Chaos theory and butterfly wings are the idealistic paradigms for a world intent on accelerating information. The Middle Ages dared to see the big picture (a trite concept to us) because they sought illumination. If one were asked to differentiate our divergent world-views, we can say that for Medieval man, the world was to be explained by poetry, not math.

This essay has attempted to bring to light some of the physical presumptions of medieval man made by emergent conceptions of the Incarnation. Whatever recent biblical criticism thinks of the life of Christ, and contemporary American Christianity has now supplied us with a prosperity gospel, the Middle Ages looked upon Jesus as a poor man. This is true even of those who enjoyed wealth within the Church and Empire. There was no attempt to better Christ's temporal circumstances in the medieval mind in order to pacify the egos of the newly moneyed classes.

Indeed *Christus paupertas* fit the age well, as the defeat of the Crusades and the penumbra of that failure hung over Western Europe. Guilt was a by-product of the historical comparison between mercantilism and *christianitas*. And it was to be accepted as an axiom that the accumulation of money was something unseemly for the faithful, expiated only by the good works of those unfortunate enough to have the stigma of wealth attached to their names. That in microcosm resulted in the patronage of Renaissance Art. The thirteenth century had come to know the phenomenon in its infancy. It was born in its shadow, but didn't learn to walk for a century.

What was active, and remained so, was the establishment of Christ as *Rex mundi*; the attempt to reconfigure the fulfillment of the Christian hope in line with a Jewish understanding of the Messiah before Jesus' arrival. Only then could his honor be slighted, (or his kingdom threatened), although he himself was adamant in his testament to the authorities that his kingdom was not of this Earth. The combined will of the papal propagated Crusades, which was manifested by the European lords, voiced its solidarity with the cry of *Deus vult*. Such assurance was more a release of the collective unconscious than a manifestation of the deity. God's participation had already been essayed historically, and on the same ground over which the bloody contests of the Crusades were to rage for centuries. Accordingly, the land itself attained the sanctity once bestowed and hitherto continued upon the rich legacy of relics that flooded Europe after the Crusades.

The disastrous Christian loss at the Battle of Hattin and the subsequent capitulation of the Holy City affected the same collective unconscious that had saddled the European warriors with the fervor and zeal to take Jerusalem. Christ's presence, previously quickened, but then confined to the sands of Jerusalem, joined rather than abandoned the spirit of defeat that preyed upon the Medieval warrior. As a result, Christ reentered Europe humbled. Once again, the man of sorrows had to carry his cross.

This time it was as a *homo viator*, throughout Europe. This time it was the metaphor that was important. Even the relic of the True Cross remained in the hands of the Mohammedans. The mysticism and theology of the thirteenth century attempted to compartmentalize experience according to the Incarnation like no age that preceded it.

By the first two decades of the fourteenth century, Dante had swept aside the hazy ruminant imagination of the accumulated Christian mythos and established the definitive version of what was to come. This was only possible by a surety inherent in the personal experience of a *homo viator* privy to the experience of Christ outside of the orthodoxy; again made possible by an historical humiliation, like a Pentecost following the harrowing days after the Crucifixion and Resurrection. There was no choice for the Christian warrior after the Fall of Jerusalem than to identify with a metaphorical Presence. Indeed, the knight errant had lost his purpose by the receding horizon of sacred glory and began to play a private trade in heroism.[2] Before Dante and after Hattin, the theology of it was to be landscaped by Innocent III and his imprimatur on transubstantiation at Lateran IV.

One nuance needed massaging, and that for the despair prevalent after the news of Hattin. Christ had not abandoned his kingdom: The fault lay with the absence of faith. The danger became that a conscious acceptance of a collective fault could result in a societal schizophrenia that could turn European man against himself. The genius of Innocent III lay in this stroke of subversive psychology: To offer gracious acceptance to a seemingly truant mendicancy and understanding that a natural inclination toward inner reflection needed sanctioning. This he did by tying Penance to the Eucharist, and calling for a vindication of the previous defeat in Jerusalem, (among other things) in the documents of the Council. Identity and idealism were the bouquet from the strange garden of Lateran IV.

Indeed, identity and the ability to analyze is another relic of the age. This is a case much disputed, yet it here we should say something more about the sacrament of Penance. Its sanction to precede the acceptance of the Eucharist implicitly blessed the idea of a personal psychology within the orthodoxy. It subjectified the self against a numinous (or at least a problematic) reality. Within this psychology a transaction of real worth was taking place.

The miracle of the Eucharist to the medieval mind (and to the observant Catholic today) does not only lie in the substantial alchemy active in the sacrament; it is in the re-enactment of sacrifice outside of the realm of human justice. It is a debt re-paid to a debtor who obviously does not deserve the remuneration-Lord I am not worthy to receive you, but only say the word and I shall be healed. It is a love that the healed

---

[2] "..with the rapidly slackening of the crusading spirit, there arose in the literature of the second half of the twelfth century that fateful image of the knight errant who must seek out the hostile forces of the world and find his own self in a ceaseless course of avanture." In Gerhardt Ladner, "Homo Viator: Medieval Ideas on Alienation and Order," 956.

penitential heart, caressed by its refining fire, is allowed to receive in its most concentrated strength. It is indeed the hearts mirror that pumps the blood anew. This was only possible by eradicating a center by concentrating on its refinement. They stared at their sins until they were not there, until they were made holy.[3] In the Eucharist, medieval man saw himself through Christ, as Christ.

The poetic nature of the preceding paragraph owes its genesis not to any evangelical purpose on the part of the author, but to the realm of *speculum* so prevalent in the Middle Ages. This was how the common man saw the reception of the Eucharist; perhaps not in such language, but without doubt with the concomitant devotion implied by such prose. The annual reception of the sacrament only added to the *mysterium tremenda*. Could such an event, open to all, and all being equal under its auspices fail to have an effect upon its society? If properly comprehended, how can it not?

The ecumenical nature of the Eucharist's new official Incarnational understanding caused a reflex of zeal. As much of an influence that the Council became, there was the challenge of Joachim of Fiore, himself repudiated within its pronouncements. His influence relied upon the sweeping zeal on the Italian peninsula during this incredibly fluid time. Some awaited eschatology without the hope of the Second Coming. Others engendered prophetic visions that used their contemporaries as *dramatis personae* of a hoped-for *parousia*. Francis himself was not eschatological in his ministry, but Joachim was only too happy to see the humble monk as close enough to the Master to quicken another paradigm.

Yet there were others concerned with shoring up the existing political paradigm of the Christian state by narrowing the field of orthodoxy. Christ's 'official' earthly representative, Innocent himself, needed to establish laws of *lese majeste* when concerned with divergent ideas upon doctrine. Heresy was treason, in the political sense, and those who dared to establish rival religions (such as Mohammed in Dante's vision) were not differentiated faiths, but schismatics, whose transgressions did violence to the temporal body politic.

A subtle but important difference in the Christian eschatology of those times and ours was that their Age understood the Second Coming as a reward for the attempt to perfect, or Christianize the world. Of course Augustinian theology underscored the impossibility of such an endeavor. Our age waits as things get worse before we take out our prophetic glasses. Christ would have come to reward medieval man, because the

---

[3] See 1 John 3: 2, 3.

world would be, by then, Christian. Today, when Christ comes, he'll know his own in the turmoil, where nary one would be found with the faith. Our age, surprisingly, harbors a much more pessimistic Christianity than the one of the Middle Ages. Medieval man was much more comprehensive in his theories on salvation. It could afford to be during a time when heterodoxy was absent during the previous five centuries. That is why heresy was treated so harshly in the case of the Cathars.

The Albigensian Crusade remains an unforgivable act of aggression, a blot upon European history. Indeed, it has been argued as the genesis of genocide within Western Europe. Only the despair of defeat, and the terror of dissolution on the part of the Empire and Papacy can be used in an attempt to make sense of it. Tragically, it is perhaps easiest understood in the simple axiom provided by Jesus and misapprehended by the Latin Church: "let them all be one."[4]

To the heirarchy, the Cathars were not another interpretive paradigm. The time for this understanding (a compassionate one at that) was long past. Yet, the Church allowed for regression into heresy to be forgiven. What it could not countenance was the stubborn zeal and unblemished faith of the Cathars. This withdrawal from the views of their fellow European established them as a society choosing the interpretive paradigm just for itself. One look at the city of Carcassone underlines the notion that the people of the Languedoc were attempting to approximate a utopia based upon secretive, exclusionary rites. These were nothing more than appropriations from older discarded notions of dualism still growing wild among fringe elements in a decayed orthodoxy, usually based in towns far from strong centers of Roman episcopacy.

The Cathars were outside the realm of identity because of their "obstinacy", and such stubbornness was not adumbrated by their previous position in European life. After the tentative end of the Crusader states in the *Outremer*, their unique position on salvation needed scrutiny if the sins of the West were to be expurgated. Once excommunicated, they were made invisible. If continuing obstinately in heresy, they were made to disappear. This disappearance, ironically so sought after by the presumptions of what we know about the Cathars, was obviously only welcome by realizing their physical and spiritual negation themselves. The incursions by the Roman Church upon the Cathars, although partially explained by the ubiquitous concomitant greed, is better understood as a clash of hopes concerning an understanding of human destiny. In the end,

---

[4] John 17: 21.

the forces arrayed against them could not digest heterodoxy of their size. Why?

The central concern was what was perceived to be a challenge to the orthodoxy along the lines of the Arian heresy in the Early Church. The Cathars could not be risked to persevere, as their mythos understood the carnal implications of the God-man to be ridiculous. In a grim paradox, Catharism represented an affront to the natural inclinations of the bifurcated Christian world although the Cathars were a sect of thoroughgoing dualists. They, however, understood dualism neatly, without the "embarrassment" of the crucifixion.

This could not do, not even to a populist Christian in those times, who identified with the process of salvation specifically because it involved the God in suffering. To risk a God aloof from the human condition would have done violence to the nascent conception of the self. Identity, to be understood, needed to be crucified in the Middle Ages. Catharism saw the world as evil, the act of a demiurge, and the flesh as something to be overcome. The finality of the ramifications of their doctrine did not allow for a choice to be made by a sympathetic God to reserve the time to save them. The assumptions of their doctrine called for a cessation of procreation, a self-induced extinction.

Understood by Roman dogma, this attitude toward the command to "be fruitful and multiply" was arrogant and debilitating for the obvious reasons. But one reason not so obvious was that the society of Cathars protested the necessity of the flesh in the act of salvation, as much their own flesh as Christ's. Further, to eradicate existence subverts an understanding of eschatology of return and salvation. It puts the hour and the place in the hands of those to be saved. *Maranatha* seemed more like a command by their actions than a request. And yet the quest for identity was as strong in their nihilism as it was in the Franciscan ideal. The simple act of proclaiming difference in a world shattered by defeat and clamoring for unity was something they all shared.

The development of an ideal outside a greater collective was also the fountain from which flowed the chivalric code, the *dolce stil' nuova*, and, specifically, Dante; and what Dante meant to the Age was completion. His long poem has rightly been understood to sum up and to systemize the aggressive imaginative flora of the *zeitgeist*.

Dante's Vision (and the Arthurian mythos for that matter) assailed the neat division between the terrestrial and the spiritual and located the latter in the benighted world of the forest, away from the encroaching civilization of an accepted order.

In Dante (and Wolfram), it was the errant and fallible, the penitent, who understood the hidden salvation and became the Savior. No longer the great central and obvious hero, like the Cid or Roland, the tendencies of the spiritualized quest opted for a hero of flesh and blood, susceptible to the whims of carnality: A Lancelot, a Parsifal, a Tristan, a Dante. Even the singers of their songs achieved a mystic potency as if their songs were incantations as ritualistic as the Mass itself.

Dante specifically and in a deep and strong poetry, roped the transformative power of the self to an ethos sprung from the Incarnational Age's penchant for common sacredness. In the final canticle we have seen that the impetus of the Incarnational Age has been veiled and recapitulated as a mythos, and as such susceptible to an apocalyptism not for the world, but for the self. This is always the hope the exile who cannot stitch himself to the world. Christian salvation is active and reflective in the individual, because (and especially in Dante) the Temple needed building in the body if the body had been ejected from the Temple. A subtle heresy was Dante's when he alluded as such; the Florentine saw himself as the salvation itself.

The completion of the *Divine Comedy* brought a close to the Incarnational Age; not only did it apotheosize it, it regulated it. By a tacit reversal of aesthetic intention Dante betrayed the quest for identification with the kenotic, and held faith with transformation of the mortal within the divine. This was an achievement of the imaginative faculties confined to text. And textual regulation spoke to the coming Renaissance and its child, the Reformation. The speculum became the self, and understood itself as such, in no uncertain terms. [5]

In this mythopoeia in which the thirteenth century rejoiced, these artists created utopia as pedagogy, at once deferential to the temporal

---

[5] Gregory B. Stone's explanation on the demise of the troubadour involves a prophetic nature inherent in the artist of the late Middle Ages to foresee the Renaissance as a loss, "a destruction of a philosophy of anonymity that had been one of the great positive gains of medieval thinking," 3. According to Stone, the anonymous is the central maxim that distinguishes the mature and substantial thought of the Medieval mind. Yet to my thinking, anonymity could also be broached by criminality or heresy, making it therefore a negative- negative value. The Incarnational model presupposes negation in submersion to the ethos of a speculative Christianity, and models itself on Christ. In other words, Christ as salvation is good reason for the loss of identity, perhaps the only reason. This aside there is much to commend in Stone's work as a fertile influence on the present essay. See Gregory B. Stone, *The Death of the Troubadour: The Late Medieval Resistance to the Renaissance* (Philadelphia: University of Pennsylvania Press, 1994).

systems in place but free enough to create an insulated understanding of personal salvation. Despite a prevalent notion of these newly forged codes as antitheses to the orthodoxy, their genesis depended upon the shared desire to vulgarize the European mind along lines of Christian salvation.

The debate later, over the rights and uses of Franciscan poverty, was also a death knell to this illustrious Age of the Spirit. As much as we honor Ockham for his acuity and Giotto for his profundity, the sense of their efforts to establish a Franciscan piety in law and image finally does a disservice to the Age that bore the *poverello* from Assisi. Indeed the debate itself was inevitable following the re-politicized temporal interests of the Church that stretched back to Innocent III. Francis was now an idea, not a man, just as Christ became an idea, not a *homo viator*. From this to the Renaissance was but a step.

The term Medieval is usually used pejoratively to signify something backward or infantile, Paleolithic in its assumptions and no friend to the human spirit. There is no doubt that some things can be demonstrated to support this view. But at its core the condemnation rings hollow. For the official movements towards adumbrating differentiated concepts of religion were the results of a truly populist movement speculating in salvation. The zeal flowed like a torrent throughout Italy, especially in the thirteenth century, but became dammed and tamed with the succeeding generations of nominalists and humanists. For a brief moment, the center would not hold because thirteenth century man sought, as Meister Eckhart eternally testifies, to place the center everywhere.

The distinction is a badge of honor in a muddied epoch: It is the legacy of the Incarnational Age that men felt responsible enough to prepare the Way of the Lord. And not as slaves, but as disciples: Not groveling in obeisance, but rejoicing in sacrifice: Not dissecting the world, but attempting to save it: Not singing of themselves as cogs in a mechanistic universe, but reveling in the flawed aspects of their humanity. God as man, Jesus, was someone to be emulated as well as worshipped, portrayed as a neighbor, as a friend, no longer the severe judge.

With the solidification of the Calvinist doctrine as the *coup de grace* of Reform theology and the subsequent counter reform of a bloated Roman Curia against its own excesses, Renaissance and Reformation man became interested in the textual worship of God rather than the demonstrable emulation of Christ. In short, after the Reformation men became Christians of understanding. During the halcyon days of the thirteenth century in Italy, they were apostles of action. The difference lay in the much-misapprehended difference between faith and works, which by the time of Luther, had become so misunderstood as to be split into a dualistic understanding. This is not to say that the concerns of the Renaissance and the Reformation were purely classical-critical concerns. They were not. Indeed, as has been adumbrated, the concerns of the New Age dealt with Christian critique. As the Classical served, so it was about the Classical.[6]

The faith of one such as Francis began with an act upon the self, before the act upon the other could flourish into faith. Faith, in the thirteenth century, was a transaction, sacramental, as much a part of those unbelievers acted upon as it was a reflex of those acting. It did not end in understanding, but in crucifixion.

The crossing of the beams as it were, was a necessary devotion for sacrifice. Paradoxes existed in the age because the spirit in the flesh is a living paradox. In order to approximate the spiritual, in order to transgress the Augustinian parameters between the earthly and the heavenly pilgrimage, a break needed to occur: A radical one. It is precisely this that relegated the sincere quest for sanctity through poverty, true mendicancy as radicalized flesh, as ridiculous in the consequential post-reform moment of textual criticism. It became necessary to know Christ through knowledge, not be Christ through act. Feeling was much too susceptible to charlatanism.

And so, the friar in literature and art became a butt of jokes, preyed upon by the temptations of the world and easily mocked. Saints were not

---

[6] "As Haskins, Thorndike, Panofsky, and Kristeller knew, more significant by far than the established institutions political power center, ecclesiastical temporalities, professions, economic organizations (all drastically and sometimes catastrophically important) were the elements of consciousness: ideas purposes, feelings, behavior, beliefs, hopes and fears." Trinkaus goes on to say that "the secularization of culture and the deification of man grew out of the movements and attitudes that were present within medieval Renaissance Reformation Christianity (?) itself rather than being the program of a secularist opposition to medieval Chrsitianity...Let us propose that what was going on was a tendency to secularize the sacred while sacralizing the secular." Charles Trinkaus' "Humanism, Religion, Society: Concepts and Motivations of Some Recent Studies." *Renaissance Quarterly* 29 (1976): 676-713, esp. 685-688. Although the text is somewhat dated, the problems remain and the crux of them with Renaissance historians who wish to conflate the specifically thirteenth century achievement with the Quattrocento's classicized enlightenment. Whereas Trinkaus has pinpointed the consequences of a theory engendered through a Christian dialectic, he is too generous with allowing the achievement a far later birthdate. See also his "Renaissance Ideas and the Idea of the Renaissance." *The Journal of the History of Ideas* 51, (1990): 667-684.

special, nor could they be, if an entire political state was to be reared upon an evangelical base. All accepted *propter hoc* into this experiment were part of the salvation process within the political sphere. The quest for the spiritual became the arithmetic of the state, not a mystical, personal quest. Individualism in this age reveled in reflections unfettered by strictly spiritual concerns. The Arena Chapel was propitiation to the divine in us: The Pazzi Chapel an expectation of the human in God.

With the advent of the brief Renaissance, it seemed, in Central Italy at least, that the gods of commerce were benevolent to the Christian ethos. A watershed date in this history is 1492. On the eve of the sixteenth century, the turmoil that gripped Florence after the death of Lorenzo de Medici resulting in the rise of the Jeremiah-like Savonarola, prefigured a darker détente to be played in the European mind until the Peace of Westphalia. The terrestrial had resented the incursions of the spiritual upon its self- estimation. The empirical world had been disallowed, indeed hobbled, in its quest to rear a lexicon of identification for itself, and by itself.

The poetry, the mythos of a united Christianity became a gilded and obese joke, underlined by the excesses of a Church intent on saying yes to a world which was as insistent on saying no to the spiritual. Finally, almost in tandem with the Peace of Westphalia, Western Europe, wearied of the swords of religion, became as contemptuous of their language and arranged an epistemological break. Calvin's state became an ideal prop to pry the excited commercial ventures that were pulling the West away from the antique and faintly ridiculous moorings of the thirteenth century, overgrown as they were with fantastic creatures spawned by an incense-haunted imagination.[7] The Word was now translated, and spoke in as many different tongues as had reason enough to differ. Debilitated by the whimsy of local inflection, Scripture lost its primacy in the debate between the state and conscience, until the disseminated Bible became what could be called a personal guide of ethical platitudes.

---

[7] "With Calvin, the hierarchical dichotomy that characterized our field of consideration comes to an end: The antagonistic wordly element that individualism had hitherto accommodated disappears entirely in Calvin's theocracy. The field is absolutely unified. The individual is now in the world, and the individualist value rules without restriction or limitations. The inworldly individual is before us." See Louis Dumont, "A Modified View of our Origins: The Christian Beginnings of Modern Individualism" in *The Category of the Person: Anthropology, Philosophy, History* M. Carrithers, S. Lukes, and S. Collins, eds. (Cambridge: Cambridge University Press, 1985) 93-122, 113-114.

The argument can be made, and has been made, that this was a result of jettisoning base superstitions used to hold the free man in thrall. The victory of Renaissance and Reformation man lay in making himself accountable for the evils of the world, and the goods. The dour face of frowning salvation had to be tickled into oblivion if man was to blame himself for anything. The devil cannot stand mockery, and as such was mocked away. A result of smiling at the Devil was the laughter that drowned out the voice of God. In the trajectory of human history, revolution is the name given to the inevitable event. As precipitous as the Renaissance was and as earth shattering, it takes a brave automaton to argue that it was an uncomplicated act of progress. There were many things lost in translation.

Can the Crusades be defended? Can the pogroms be denied? Can the massacre of heterodox groups be ignored? Can relics be seriously considered to be a balm for the sick? Can prayer seriously alleviate suffering? Can renunciation from the duties of the world activate participation in an amelioration of its conditions? On the other hand, can the renunciation of want in the name of progress sustain any sympathy with those, as Jesus has said, will "always be with us"? Is Darfur or Tianamen or Auschwitz or Pol Pot the responsible and progressive reflex of man un-tethered to "religion?" As far as prayer and the power of faith, one need only understand the complexities of chemotherapy to curb the assurance of science in the face of the kneeling penitent in a hospital chapel.

It would be foolish to claim that we are not physically better off now than we were then. Hygienically we've done wonders. People don't die so easily anymore. People are allowed to enjoy more than a modicum of freedom and comfort. Air conditioning and grocery stores immediately come to mind. Unfortunately, so does television.

Our present century is immediately apprised of events that happen half a world away. At times a response, aid or prayers or sympathy, comes if an event is spectacular in its devastation. Most of the time, the voyeur within is exercised without. Perhaps later in the arithmetic of our hyper-speed age we will be able to act upon subtler information. The amount of information, though, militates against this. So the information age remains just that; informative, and the suffering goes on with the addition of spectacle to contribute to a sense of the inauthentic in our collective consciousness. Like the victorious general in Imperial Rome, we too need the slave at the back of the chariot as we canter majestically through hyperspace, saying in a fierce whisper above the drone of our technology "Information is not illumination. "

We then really can't assume that we haven't lost anything by rearing such structures, to allow us to divorce ourselves from nature and from what the thirteenth century called God. The God of their paradigm resembled them to a startling degree, in all their humanity. When the divine is spread upon the earth, the speculation of what are the divine properties are academic if the zeal enflames a population prepared for action. Cathedrals, as the old saw goes, are not built by opinion.

Today, in America, the religious and scientific are enslaved by the notion of empirical truth, an arena wherein religion dare not tread. This debate becomes an exercise in a common language reared by a desire to destroy the mystical. The real concern should be if the current ethos can be courageous enough to be spiritual in the face of the rational, and to carve Jung's axiom in hearts and minds as deep as he did over his door: *Vocatus atque non vocatus, deus aderit.*[8]

Such courage demands sacrifice. Such courage demands a wish to see the world as a sacred place because it has been stripped, like we ourselves should be, of the baser alloys of expectations. The Incarnation, to the desiring, does not exculpate us from the adventure of life. Nor should it make the faithful arrogant and relaxed in the face of human misery and cruelty. The Incarnation, the God-event in Western historical consciousness should not cease to activate a fascination within a mind that can prepare the Way of the Lord, even if today, this lord flowers from within.

The impossibility of comprehending fully the purpose of nature in a paltry century of life should not hobble the efforts of the noblest among us who try. Understanding need not assume a metaphysical mantle; nor can it speak exclusively in mathematics. This is not a precise science. It is an art that need only be awake and careful. For no matter our length of days, a single moment of compassion recognizing a brother or sister in someone alien to the tangible self, can redeem us. These mysteries are to be felt first. Rejoice if this can be explained, but the world is not a lock to be opened, it is the key itself. When it is comprehended as such, it lies naked to the opportunity of a love unfettered by limitations and measures, sustained by the one law in these physics: the weight of glory.

> Who says that all must vanish?
> Who knows, perhaps the flight
> Of the bird you wound remains
> And perhaps flowers survive
> Caresses in us, in their ground.

---

[8] Bidden or unbidden, God is present.

It isn't the gesture that lasts,
But it dresses you again in gold
Armor – from breast to knees –
And the battle was so pure
An Angel wears it after you. [9]

---

[9] Rainer Maria Rilke. Translated by A. Poulin.

BIBLIOGRAPHY

Primary Sources

Anderson, Roberta and Dominic Aidan Bellenger. *Medieval Worlds: A Sourcebook.* New York, London: Routledge, 2003.
Alighieri, Dante. *Dante's Divina Commedia.* Commentary by C.H. Grandgent. Boston: D.C. Heath and Co., 1933.
—. *The Divine Comedy.* 6 vols. Commentary and translation by Mark Musa,. Bloomington: Indiana University Press, 2003.
—. *The Divine Comedy.* 6 vols. Commentary and translation by Charles Singleton. Princeton: Princeton University Press, 1961.
—. *La Divina Commedia.* 3 vols. Commentary by Natalino Sapegno. Firenze: La Nuova Italia, 1985.
Allen, S.J. and Emilie Amt, eds. *The Crusades: A Reader.* Peterborough: Broadview Press, 2003.
Aquinas, Thomas. *Summa Contra Gentiles.* Paris: J.P. Migne, 1863.
Augustine of Hippo. *De Civitate Dei Contra Paganos.* In 7 volumes with an English Translation by George McCracken in the Loeb Classical Library. Cambridge: Harvard University Press, 1957.
Baldassarri, Guido, G. Varanini. *Racconti Esemplari di Predicatori del Due e Trecento.* 3 vols. Roma: Salerno Editrice, 1993.
Bernard of Clairvaux. *Sancti Bernardi Opera.* 5 vols. J. Leclercq and H.M. Rochais, eds. Roma: Cistercian Editions, 1963.
Biblia Sacra Iuxta Vulgatam Versionem. Stuttgart: Deutsche Bibelgesellschaft, 1994.
Bosco, Umberto, ed. *Enciclopedia Dantesca.* 6 vols. Roma: Treccani, 1978.
Brundage, James A. ed. *The Crusades: A Documentary Survey.* Milwaukee: Maquette University Press, 1962.
Contini, Gianfranco, ed. *Poeti del Duecento.* 2 vols. Riccardo Ricciardi: Milano, 1961.
Coulton, G.G., ed. and trans. *From St. Francis to Dante: Translations from the Chronicle of the Franciscan Salimbene (1221-1288), with Notes and Illustrations from Other Medieval Sources.* Introduction by Edward Peters. Philadelphia: University of Pennsylvania Press, 1972, reprint.
Di Benedetto, Luigi, ed. *Rimatori del Dolce Stil Novo.* Torino: Unione Tipografico, 1925.

Dupuis, J. and J. Neuner, editors. *The Christian Faith in the Doctrinal Documents of the Catholic Church.* New York: Alba House, 2001.

Durando, Gulielmo. *Rationale Divinorum Officiorum.* Naples: Joseph Dura, 1859.

Edwards, Robert ed and trans. *The Poetry of Guido Guinizelli.* New York: Garland, 1987.

Eschenbach, Wolfram von. *Parzival: With Titurel and Love Lyrics.* Translated by Cyril Edwards. Cambridge: D.S. Brewer, 2004.

Gabrieli, Francesco, ed. and trans. *Arab Historians of the Crusades.* Translated from the Italian by E.J. Costello. New York: Dorset Press, 1969.

Habig, Marion A., ed. *St. Francis of Assisi: Writings and Early Biographies: English Omnibus of the Sources for the Life of St. Francis.* Chicago: Franciscan Herald Press, 1972.

Head, Thomas, ed. *Medieval Hagiography: An Anthology.* New York and London: Garland: New York, 2000.

Henderson, Ernest F. ed. and trans. *Select Historical Documents of the Middle Ages.* London: George Bell & Sons, 1892.

Hollister, C. Warren, Joe W. Leedom, Marc A. Meyer, and David Spear, eds. *Medieval Europe: A Short Sourcebook.* New York: McGraw Hill, 1997.

Knox, Ronald. *The Holy Bible: Translated from the Latin Vulgate in the Light of the Hebrew & Greek.* New York: Sheed and Ward, 1956.

Latini, Brunetto. *L'ethica d'Aristotile ridotta in compendio et altre traduttioni e scritti di quei tempi con alcuni dotti avvertimenti intorno alla lingua.* Lyon: Jean de Tornes, 1598.

Little, A.G., ed. *Franciscan Papers, Lists, and Documents.* Manchester: Manchester University Press, 1943.

McGinn, Bernard, translator and editor. *Apocalyptic Spirituality: Treatises and Letters of Lactantius, Adso of Montier-en-Der, Joachim of Fiore, the Franciscan Spirituals, Savonarola.* Preface by Marjorie Reeves. Mahwah: Paulist Press, 1979.

Ockham, Gullelmi de. *Opera Politica.* 2 vols. Edited by R.F. Bennet & H. S. Offler. Manchester: Manchester University Press, 1963.

Ovid. *Metamorphoses.* 2 vols. Translated by Frank Justus Miller. Revised by G.P. Goold. Cambridge: Harvard University Press, 1984.

Patrologia Latina. Paris: J.P. Migne, 1865.

Peters, Edward ed. *Heresy and Authority in Medieval Europe: Documents in Translation.* Philadelphia: University of Pennsylvania Press, 1980.

—. *The First Crusade: The Chronicle of Fulcher of Chartres and Other Source Materials*. Philadelphia: University of Pennsylvania Press, 1971.

—. *Christian Society and the Crusades 1198-1229*. Philadelphia: University of Pennsylvania Press, 1971, reprint.

Petry, Ray C., ed. *A History of Christianity: Readings in the History of the Early and Medieval Church*. Englewood Cliffs: Prentice-Hall, Inc., 1962.

Phillips, Jonathan and Martin Hoch, eds. *The Second Crusade: Scope and Consequences*. Manchester: Manchester University Press, 2001.

Scott, Jonathan F., Albert Hyma, Arthur H. Noyes, eds. *Readings in Medieval History*. New York: Appleton-Century-Crofts, Inc., 1933.

Segre, Cesare, M. Marti, eds. *La Prosa del Duecento. La Letteratura Italiana: Storia e Testi* .Milano: Riccardo Ricciardi, 1959.

Shinners, John, ed. *Medieval Popular Religion 1000-1500: A Reader*. Toronto: Broadview Press, 1997.

Stone, Edward Noble, trans. *Three Old French Chronicles of the Crusades*. Seattle: University of Washington, 1939.

Tanner, Norman ed. *Decrees of the Ecumenical Councils*. 2 vols. Washington and London: Sheed and Ward and Georgetown University Press, 1990.

Thatcher, Oliver J., and Edgar H. McNeal, eds. *A Source Book for Mediaeval History: Selected Documents Illustrating the History of Europe in the Middle Ages*. New York: AMS, 1971, reprint.

Vicinelli, Augusto, ed. *Gli scritti di San Francesco d'Assisi e I Fioretti*. Verona: Arnoldo Mondadori, 1955.

Viscardi, A., B. & T. Nardi, G. Vidossi, F. Arese, eds. *Le Origini: Testi Latini. Italiani Provenzali, e Franco-Italiani. La Letteratura Italiana: Storia e Testi*. Milano: Riccardo Ricciardi, 1956.

Wakefield, Walter P. and Austin P. Evans. *Heresies of the High Middle Ages*. New York and London: Columbia University Press, 1969.

Secondary Sources

Abulafia, David, J. Riley Smith, D. Luscombe. *The New Cambridge Medieval History: Vols. IV (parts 1 &2), and Vol. V*. Cambridge University Press: Cambridge, 1999-2004.

Abulafia, David, J. Franklin, and M. Rubin, eds. *Church and City 1000-1500: Essays in Honour of Christopher Brooke*. Cambridge: Cambridge University Press, 1992.

Anderson, William. *Dante the Maker*. New York: Crossroad, 1982.

Aries, Philippe. *Western Attitudes toward Death from the Middle Ages to the Present.* Translated by Patricia Ranum. Baltimore: John Hopkins University Press, 1974.

Armour, Peter. *Dante's Griffin and the History of the World: A Study of the Earthly Paradise (Purgatorio, cantos XXIX-XXXIII).* Oxford: Clarendon Press, 1989.

Asad, Talal. *Genealogies of Religion: Discipline and Reasons of Power in Christianity and Islam.* Baltimore and London: John Hopkins University Press, 1993.

Asali, K.J., ed. *Jerusalem in History.* New York: Olive Branch Press, 1990.

Asbridge, Thomas. *The First Crusade: A New History.* Oxford: Oxford University Press, 2004.

Auerbach. Erich. *Mimesis: The Representation of Reality in Western Literature.* Introduced by Edward Said. Translated by Willard R.Trask. Princeton and Oxford: Princeton University Press, 2003.

Baker, Derek, ed. *Studies in Church History 14: Renaissance and Renewal in Christian History.* The Ecclesiastical History Society. Oxford: Basil Blackwell, 1977.

—. *Studies in Church History 9: Schism Heresy and Religious Protest.* Cambridge: Cambridge University Press, 1972.

Balthasar, Hans Urs von. *The Theology of Henri de Lubac: An Overview.* San Francisco: Ignatius Press, 1991.

—. *The Glory of the Lord. A Theological Aesthetics,* (5 vols.). Edited by John Riches and Joseph Fessio S.J. Multiple Translators. Edinburgh: T.T. Clark, 1982-1991.

Barasch., Mosche. *Giotto and the Language of Gesture.* Cambridge: Cambridge University Press, 1987.

Barber, Malcolm. *The Cathars: Dualist Heretics in Languedoc in the High Middle Ages.* Harlow: Pearson, 2000.

Barbero, Giuseppe. *La dottrina Eucaristica negli scritti di Papa Innocenzo III.* Roma: Edizioni Paoline, 1953.

Barolini, Teodolinda. *Dante's Poets: Textuality and Truth in the Comedy.* Princeton: Princeton University Press, 1986.

Bartolini, Agostino. *I Francescani nella Divina Commedia.* Roma: Pontificia Accademia Tiberina, 1890.

Bauch, Karl. "Das mittelateriche Grabbild Figurliche Grabmaler." *Jahrunderts in Europa* Berlin: 1976.

Belperon, Pierre. *La Croisade contre les Albigeios et l'union du Languedoc a la France, 1209-1249.* Paris: Plon, 1961.

Belting, Hans. *The Image and its Public in the Middle Ages: Form and Function of Early Paintings of the Passion.* Trans. by Mark Bartusis and Raymond Meyer. New Rochelle: Aristides D. Caratzas, 1981.

Benson, Robert L. and G. Constable, eds. *Renaissance and Renewal in the Twelfth Century.* Cambridge: Harvard University Press, 1982.

Bestul, Thomas H. *Texts of the Passion; Latin Devotional Literature and Medieval Society.* Philadelphia: University of Pennsylvania Press, 1996.

Biller, Peter and A.J. Minnis, eds. *Medieval Theology and the Natural Body.* York: York Medieval Press, 1997.

Biller, Peter and Barrie Dobson, eds. *The Medieval Church: Universities, Heresy, and the Religious Life: Essays in Honour of Gordon Leff.* Suffolk: The Boydell Press, 1999

Bishop, Morris. *St. Francis of Assisi.* Boston: Little, Brown, and Company, 1974.

Boas, Adrian J. *Jerusalem in the Time of the Crusades: Society, landscape, and art in the Holy City under Frankish rule.* London and New York: Routledge, 2001.

—. *Crusader Archaeology: The Material Culture of the Latin East.* London and New York: Routledge1999.

Bologne, Jean Claude. *Du Flambeau au Bucher: Magie et superstition au Moyen Age.* Paris: Plon, 1993.

Bossy, John. "The Mass as a Social Institution 1200-1700." *Past and Present*, no. 100, 1983, pp. 29-61.

Boyle, Leonard. *A Study of the Works attributed to William of Pagula, with special reference to the Oculus Sacerdotis and the Summa Summarum.* Thesis: Oxford University, Trinity, 1956.

Braeckmans, L. *Confession et Communion au Moyen Age et au Concile de Trent.* J. Gembloux: Duculot, S.A., 1971.

Bredero, Adriaan H. *Christendom and Christianity in the Middle Ages: The Relations between Religion Church and Society.* Translated by Reinder Bruinsma. Grand Rapids: Eerdmans, 1994.

Brentano, Robert. *Two Churches: England and Italy in the Thirteenth Century.* Berkeley: University of California Press, 1968.

Brett, Annabel S. *Liberty, Right, and Nature: Individual Rights in Later Scholastic Thought.* Cambridge: Cambridge University Press, 1997.

Brooke, Christopher and Rosalind. *Popular Religion in the Middle Ages, Western Europe 1000-1300.* London: Thames and Hudson, 1984.

Burns, J.H. ed. *The Cambridge History of Medieval Political Thought, c. 350-c.1450.* Cambridge: Cambridge University Press, 1988.

Burr, David. *Eucharistic Presence and Conversion in Late Thirteenth Century Franciscan Thought.* Vol. 74, part 3. Philadelphia: Transactions of the American Philosophical Society, 1984.

Bynum, Caroline Walker. "Did the Twelfth Century Discover the Individual?" *The Journal of Ecclesiastical History*, no. 31, 1980, pp. 1-17.

—. *Jesus as Mother: Studies in the Spirituality of the High Middle Ages.* Berkeley: University of California Press: Berkeley, 1982.

—. *The Resurrection of the Body in Western Christianity, 200-1336.* New York: Columbia University Press, 1995.

Callaey, P. Fredegand. "L'influence et la diffusion de l'Arbor Vitae d'Ubertin de Casale", *Revue d'Histoire Ecclesiastique* XVII, (1921), pp. 533-546.

Campagnole, Stanislao da, P. Tuscano. *San Francesco e il francescanesimo nella letteratura Italiana dal XIII al XV secolo. Atti del convegno nazionale (Assisi, 10-12 December, 1999).* Assisi: Accademia Properziano del Subiaso, 2001.

Campbell, Joseph. *The Masks of God: Creative Mythology.* New York: Viking Press, 1968.

Cannon, Joanna and B. Williamson, eds. *Art, Politics, and Civic Religion in Central Italy 1261-1352: Essays by Postgraduate Students at the Courtauld Institute.* London: Ashgate, 2000.

Carrithers, Michael, S. Collins, S. Lukes, eds. *The Category of the Person: Anthropology, Philosophy, History.* Cambridge: Cambridge University Press, 1985.

Chareyron, Nicole. *Pilgrims to Jerusalem in The Middle Ages.* Translated by Donald Wilson. New York: Columbia University Press, 2005.

Charland, M. ed. *Artes Praedicandi: Contribution a l'histoire de la rhetorique au Moyen Age.* Ottawa: Publications de l'Insitut d'etudes Medievales: Ottawa, 1934.

Christin, Olivier & Dario Gamboni, eds. *Crises de l'image religieuse.* Paris: Editions de la Maison des sciences de l'homme, 1999.

Cipollone, Giulio. *Cristianita-Islam Cattivitita e Liberazione in nome di Dio: Il tempo di Innocenzo III dopo il 1187.* Roma: Editrice Pontificia Universita Gregoriana, 1992.

Cirlot, J. E. *A Dictionary of Symbols.* Translated by Jack Sage. New York: Philosophical Library, 1962.

Colish, Marcia L. *Medieval Foundations of the Western Intellectual Tradition 400-1400.* New Haven and London: Yale University Press, 1997.

Copleston, Frederick. *History of Philosophy. Volume II Augustine to Scotus.* Westminster: The Newman Press, 1960.

Cross F.L., and E. A. Livingstone, eds. *The Oxford Dictionary of the Christian Church.* Oxford and New York: Oxford University Press, 1997.

Cuming, G.J. and D. Baker, eds. *Popular Belief and Practice.* Cambridge: Cambridge University Press, 1972.

Curtius, Ernst Robert. *European Literature and the Latin Middle Ages.* Translated by William Trask. Princeton: Princeton University Press, 1953.

Dameron, George W. *Episcopal Power and Florentine Society 1000-1320.* Cambridge: Harvard University Press, 1991.

Damiata, Marino. *Guglielmo d'Ockham: Poverta e potere evangelica e francescana nel secolo XIII e XIV.* Firenze: Studi Francescani, 1978.

Davis, Charles T. *Dante and the Idea of Rome.* Oxford: Oxford University Press, 1957.

Davis, Stephen, D. Kendall and G. O'Collins. *An Interdisciplinary Symposium on the Incarnation of the Son of God.* Oxford: Oxford University Press, 2002.

D'Avray, David Levesley. *The Transformation of the Medieval Sermon.* Thesis: Oxford University, Trinity, 1976.

De Benedictis, Matthew. *The Social Thought of Saint Bonaventure.* Westport: Greenwood Press, 1946.

Derbes, A., and M. Sandona, eds. *The Cambridge Companion to Giotto.* Cambridge: Cambridge University Press, 2004.

Charles Allen Dinsmore. *Aids to the Study of Dante.* Boston and New York: Houghton Mifflin, and Co., 1903.

Di Scipio, Giuseppe and Aldo Scaglione, eds.*The Divine Comedy and the Encyclopedia of Arts and Sciences.* Amsterdam and Philadelphia: John Benjamins Publishing Co., 1988.

Donnini, Ambrogio. "Appunti per una storia di Dante al movimento Gioachimita", *Annual Report of the Dante Society XLVII & XLVIII* (1930), pp. 49-69.

Dronke, Peter. *Dante and Medieval Latin Traditions.* Cambridge: Cambridge University Press, 1986.

Duby, Georges. *The Chivalrous Society.* Translated by Cynthia Postan. Berkeley and Los Angeles: University of California Press, 1977.

Dunbar, Helen Flanders. *Symbolism in Medieval Thought and its Consummation in the Divine Comedy.* New York: Russell & Russell, 1961. Reprint.

Dvorak, Max. *Idealism and Naturalism in Gothic Art.* Translated by Randolph J. Klawiter. Notre Dame: University of Notre Dame Press, 1967.

Edgerton, Samuel Y. *The Heritage of Giotto's Geometry: Art and Science on the Eve of the Scientific Revolution.* Ithaca and London: Cornell University Press, 1991.

Elliott, Dylan. "True Presence/ False Christ: The Antinomies of Embodiment in Medieval Spirituality." *Pontifical Institute of Mediaeval Studies* vol. 64, 2002, pp. 241-265.

Emerson, Jan Swango and Hugh Feiss, eds. *Imagining Heaven in the Middle Ages: A Book of Essays.* New York and London: Garland, 2000.

Emmerson, Richard K. and Bernard McGinn, editors. *The Apocalypse in the Middle Ages.* Ithaca: Cornell University Press, 1992.

Emery, Kent and J. P. Wawrykow, eds. *Christ Among the Medieval Dominicans: Representations of Christ in the Texts and Images of the Order of the Preachers.* Notre Dame: Notre Dame University Press, 1998.

Erlande-Brandenburg, Alain. *L'Art Gothique.* Paris: Mazenod, 1983.

Evans, G.R. *The Medieval Theologians: An Introduction to the Theology in the Medieval Period.* Oxford: Blackwell, 2001.

Fallani, Giovanni. *Dante e la cultura figurativa Medievale.* Roma: Minerva Italica, 1971.

Falvy, Zoltan. *Mediterranean Culture and Troubadour Music.* Budapest: Akademiai Kiado, 1986.

Fehlner, Peter D. *The Role of Charity in the Ecclesiology of St. Bonaventure.* Rome: Miscellanea Francescana, 1965.

Ferguson, George. *Signs and Symbols in Christian Art.* London: Oxford University Press, 1954.

Ferrier, Francis. *What is the Incarnation?* Translated by Edward Sillem. New York: Hawthorn Books, 1962.

Finaldi, Gabriele. *The Image of Christ.* London: Yale University Press, 2000.

Fisher, Lizette A. *The Mystic Vision in the Grail Legend and the Divine Comedy.* New York: Columbia University Press, 1917.

Flood, David ed. *Poverty in the Middle Ages. Franziskanische Forschungen.* Werl: Dietrich Coelde, 1975.

Foster, Kenelm. *The Two Dantes and Other Studies.* London: Darton, Longman, and Todd, 1977.

Freccero, John. *Dante: The Poetics of Conversion.* Cambridge: Harvard University Press, 1986.

Frugoni, Carla. *Francesco e l'invenzione delle stimmate: Una storia per parole e immagini fino a Bonaventura e Giotto.* Torino: Einaudi, 1993.
Fudge, Erica, R. Gilbert, S. Wiseman, eds. *At the Borders of the Human: Beasts, Bodies, and Natural Philosophy in the Early Modern Period.* London: Macmillan, 1999.
Gaffuri, Laura and Riccardo Quinto, eds. *Predicazione e Societa nel Medioevo: Riflessione etica, valori e modello di comportamento.* Padova: Centro Studi Antoniani, 2002.
Gardner, Edmund G. *The Arthurian Legend in Italian Literature.* London: J.M. Dent & Sons, 1930.
—. *Dante and the Mystics.* London: J.M. Dent & Sons, 1913.
Gauvard, C., A. de Libera and M. Zink, eds. *Dictionnaire du Moyen Age.* Paris: Presses Universitaires de France, 2002.
Geremek, Bronislaw. *Poverty: A History.* Translated by Agnieszka Kolakowska. Oxford: Blackwell, 1994.
Gervers, Michael, ed. *The Second Crusade and the Cistercians.* New York: St. Martin's Press: New York,
Gil, Moishe. *A History of Palestine, 634-1099.* Translated by Ethel Broido. Cambridge: Cambridge University Press, 1992.
Gilson, Etienne. *A Gilson Reader: Selections from the Writings of Etienne Gilson.* Edited by Anton C. Pegis. New York: Hanover House, 1957.
Gleason, Robert, ed. *A Theology Reader.* London: The Macmillan Company, 1966.
Gracia, Jorge J.E., ed. *Individuation in Scholasticism: The Later Middle Ages and the Counter Reformation, 1150-1650.* Albany: SUNY Press, 1994.
Gross, Kenneth. "Infernal Metamorphoses: An Interpretation of Dante's 'Counterpass.'" *MLN*, vol. 100, no. 1, Italian Issue (Jan. 1985), pp. 42-69.
Gurevich, Aaron. *The Origins of European Individualism.* Translated by Katherine Judelson. Oxford: Blackwell, 1995.
—. *Medieval Popular Culture: Problems of Belief and Perception.* Translated by Janos M. Bak and Paul Hollingsworth. Cambridge: Cambridge University Press, 1988.
Hamburger, Jeffrey. *Nuns as Artists: The Visual Culture of a Medieval Convent.* Los Angeles: University of California Press, 1997.
—. J.H. and Annie Marie Bouche, eds. *The Minds Eye: Art and Theological Argument in the Middle Ages.* Princeton: Princeton University Press, 2005.
Harper, John. *The Forms and Orders of the Western Liturgy from the Tenth to the Eighteenth Century.* Oxford: Clarendon Press, 1991.

Hastings, A., Mason, A., and Hugh Pyper, eds. *The Oxford Companion to Christian Thought: Intellectual, Spiritual, and Moral Horizons of Christianity.* New York: Oxford University Press, 2002.

Havely, Nick. *Dante and the Franciscans: Poverty and the Papacy in the Commedia.* Cambridge: Cambridge University Press, 2004.

Holmes, George. *Florence, Rome and the Origins of the Renaissance.* Oxford: Clarendon Press, 1986.

—. Ed. *The Oxford History of Medieval Europe.* Oxford: Oxford University Press, 1988.

Hopper, Vincent Foster. *Medieval Number Symbolism. Its Sources, Meaning, and Influence on thought and Expression.* New York: Dover, 1938.

Hourani, Albert. *A History of the Arab Peoples.* New York: Warner Books, 1991.

Hourihane, Colum, ed. *Object, Images, and the Word: Art in the Service of the Liturgy.* Princeton: Princeton University Press, 2003.

Housley, Norman. *The Italian Crusades: The Papal-Angevin Alliance and the Crusades against Christian Lay Powers, 1254-1343.* Oxford: Clarendon Press, 1982.

Hyde, J.K. *Society and Politics in Medieval Italy: The Evolution of the Civil Life, 1000-1350.* London: Macmillan, 1973.

Jaeger, C. Stephen. *The Origins of Courtliness: Civilizing Trends and the Formation of Courtly ideals 939-1210.* Philadelphia: University of Pennsylvania Press, 1985.

Jordan, William Chester. *Europe in the High Middle Ages.* New York: Viking-Penguin, 2001.

Jung, Carl Gustav. *Psychological Types or the Psychology of Individuation.* Translated by H. Godwin Baynes. New York: Pantheon Books, 1923.

—. *Psychological Reflections: An Anthology from the Writings of C. G. Jung.* Edited by Jolande Jacobi. New York: Pantheon, 1953.

Jungmann, Joseph A. *The Mass of the Roman Rite.* Translated by Francis A. Brunner. Westminster: Christian Classics, 1951.

—. *The Place of Christ in Liturgical Prayer.* Translated by A. Peeler. Collegeville: The Liturgical Prayer, 1989. Reprint.

Keen, Maurice. *Chivalry.* New Haven and London: Yale University Press, 1984.

Kessler, Herbert L. and Johanna Zacharias. *Rome 1300: On the Path of the Pilgrim.* New Haven and London: Yale University Press, 2000.

Khanh-Norbert, Nguyen van. *Le Christ dans le pensee de Saint Francois d'Assise d'apres ses ecrits.* Paris: Editions Franciscaines, 1989.

Knowles, David. *The Evolution of Medieval Thought.* Longman, Ltd: London, 1962.
—. *The Nature of Mysticism.* Hawthorn Books: New York, 1966.
Kretzmann, Norman, A. Kenny, J. Pinborg, eds. *The Cambridge History of Later Medieval Philosophy.* Cambridge University Press: Cambridge, 1982.
Kristeller, Paul Oskar. *Renaissance Thought And Its Sources.* New York: Columbia University Press, 1979.
Kuhnel, Bianca. *The Real and Ideal Jerusalem: Jewish, Christian, and Islamic Art. Studies in Honor of Bezalel Narkiss.* Jerusalem: Journal of the Center for Jewish Art, 1998.
Kutsko, John F. *Between Heaven and Earth: Divine Presence and Absence in the Book of Ezekiel.* Winona Lake: Eisenbrauns, 2000.
Ladner, Gerhart B. *Images and Ideas in the Middle Ages: Selected Studies in History and Art.* Roma: Edizioni di Storia e Letteratura, 1983.
—. *Ad Imaginem Dei: The Image of Man in Medieval Art.* Latrobe: Archabbey Press, 1965.
Lambert, Malcolm D. *Franciscan Poverty: The Doctrine of the Absolute Poverty of Christ and the Apostles in the Franciscan Order 1210-1323.* New York: The Franciscan Institute, 1998.
—. *Medieval Heresy: Popular Movements from the Gregorian Reform to the Reformation.* 3rd Edition. Oxford: Blackwell, 2002.
Lambertini, Roberto. *La Poverta Pensata: Evoluzione storica della definizione dell'identita minoritica da Bonaventura ad Ockham.* Modena: Mucchi, 2000.
Lansing, Carol. *Power and Purity: Cathar Heresy in Medieval Italy.* New York: Oxford University Press, 1998.
Lansing, Richard, ed. *The Dante Encyclopedia.* New York: Garland, 2000.
—. *Dante: The Critical Complex. 4. Dante and Theology. The Biblical Tradition and Christian Allegory.* New York: Routledge, 2003.
Larner, John. *Italy in the Age of Dante and Petrarch 1216-1380.* London and New York: Longman, 1980.
Leclerq, Jean. *Bernard of Clairvaux and the Cistercian Spirit.* Translated by Claire Lavoie. Kalamazoo: Cistercian Publications, 1976.
Leff, Gordon. *The Dissolution of the Medieval Outlook: An Essay on the Intellectual and Spiritual Change in the Fourteenth Century.* New York: New York University Press, 1976.
—. *Heresy in the Later Middle Ages: The Relation of Heterodoxy to Dissent c. 1250-1450.* 2 vols. Manchester: Manchester University Press, 1967.

—. *The Changing Pattern of Thought in the Earlier Fourteenth Century.* Bulletin of John Rylands Library, vol. 43, no.2. Manchester: John Rylands Library, 1961.

Le Goff, Jacques, ed. *Medieval Callings.* Translated by Lydia Cochrane. Chicago and London: The University of Chicago Press, 1990.

—. *The Medieval Imagination.* Translated by Arthur Goldhammer. Chicago and London: University of Chicago Press, 1988.

—. *The Birth of Purgatory.* Translated by Arthur Goldhammer. Chicago: University of Chicago Press, 1984.

—. *La civilization de l'Occident medieval.* Paris: Arthaud, 1964.

Le Roy Ladurie, Emmanuel. *Montaillou: The Promised Land of Error.* Translated by Barbara Bray. New York: George Braziller, 1978.

Lesnick, Daniel R. *Preaching in Medieval Florence: The Social World of Franciscan and Dominican Spirituality.* Athens and London: University of Georgia Press, 1989.

Leupin, Alexandre. *Fiction and Incarnation: Rhetoric, Theology and Literature in the Middle Ages.* Translated by David Laatsch. Minneapolis and London: University of Minnesota Press, 2003.

Levi, Anthony. *Renaissance and Reformation: The Intellectual Genesis.* New Haven and London: Yale University Press, 2002.

Lewis, Clive Staples. *The Allegory of Love: A Study in Medieval Tradition.* Oxford: Oxford University Press, 1938.

Lindahl, C., Lindow, J. and McNamara, J. eds. *Medieval Folklore: A Guide to Myths, Legends, Tales, Beliefs, and Customs.* Oxford: Oxford University Press, 2002.

Linehan, Peter and J. Nelson, eds. *The Medieval World.* London: Routledge, 2001.

Lines, David. "The Commentary Literature on Aristotle's Nichomachean Ethics in early Renaissance Italy: Preliminary Considerations." *Traditio: Studies in Ancient and Medieval History, Thought, and Religion.* Vol. 54 (1999), pp. 245-282.

Macy, Gary. "The Dogma of Transubstantiation in the Middle Ages." *Journal of Ecclesiastical History.* Vol. 45, no. 1, 1994.

Makinen, Virpi. *Property Rights in the Late Medieval Discussion on Franciscan Poverty.* Leuven: Peeters, 2001.

Male, Emile. *Religious Art from the Twelfth to the Eighteenth Century.* Princeton: Princeton University Press, 1982.

Manselli, Raoul. *L'eresia del male.* Napoli: Morano, 1963.

La religion populaire au Moyen Age: Problemes de methode et d'histoire. Montreal: Institut d'etudes Medievales Albert le Grand, 1975.

—. *San Francesco.* Roma: Bulzoni, 1980.

—. *Secolo XII: Religione popolare ed eresia.* Roma: Jouvence, 1983.
Manuel, Frank and Fritzie. *Utopian Thought in the Western World.* Cambridge: Belknap, 1979.
Marcombe, David. *Leper Knights: The Order of St. Lazarus of Jerusalem in England, c. 1150-1544.* Woodbridge: The Boydell Press, 2003.
Martin, Sean. *The Cathars: The Most Successful Heresy of the Middle Ages.* Avalon Press: New York, 2005.
Martindale, Andrew. "Patrons and Minders: The Introduction of the Secular into Sacred Spaces in the Late Middle Ages." *Studies in Church History*, vol. 28. Edited by Diana Wood. Blackwell: Oxford, 1992, pp. 143-178.
Mazzeo, Joseph Anthony. *Structure and Thought in the Paradiso.* Ithaca: Cornell University Press, 1958.
McDonnell, Kilian. *John Calvin, the Church, and the Eucharist.* Princeton: Princeton University Press, 1967.
Mein, Andrew. *Ezekiel and the Ethics of Exile.* Oxford: Oxford University Press, 2001.
Meiss, Millard, ed. *De Artibus Opuscula XL Essays in Honor of Erwin Panofsky.* 2vols. New York: New York University Press, 1961.
Mesnard, Pierre. *La Conception de l'Humilite dans l'Imitation de Jesus Christ.* In *L'Homme Devant Dieu: Melanges offerts au Pere Henri de Lubac. Vol. 2. Du Moyen Age au Siecle des Lumieres.* Paris: Aubier, 1964, pp. 199-222.
Metzger, Bruce and Michael Coogan,eds. *The Oxford Companion to the Bible.* New York: Oxford University Press, 1993.
Miles, Margaret. *The Word Made Flesh: A History of Christian Thought.* Oxford: Blackwell, 2005.
Miller, James ed. *Dante and the Unorthodox: The Aesthetics of Transgression.* Waterloo: Wilfrid Laurier Press, 2005.
Minnis, Alastair and Ian Johnson, eds. *The Cambridge History Of Literary Criticism: Volume 2-The Middle Ages.* Cambridge: Cambridge University Press, 2005.
Moleta, Vincent. *Guinizzelli in Dante.* Roma: Edizioni di Storia e Letteratura, 1980.
Molho Anthony and John Tedeschi, eds. *Renaissance: Studies in Honor of Hans Baron.* Firenze: Sansoni, 1971.
Mollat, Michel and Philippe Wolff. *The Popular Revolutions of the Late Middle Ages.* Translated by A. L. Lytton-Sells. London: George Allen & Unwin Ltd., 1973.
Monahan, W.B. *St. Thomas Aquinas on the Incarnation.* London: Trinity Press, 1946.

Montgomery, Marion. *The Reflective Journey toward Order: Essays on Dante, Wordsworth, Eliot, and Others*. Athens: University of Georgia Press, 1973.

Moore, R. I. *The Formation of a Persecuting Society: Power and Deviance in Western Europe 950-1250*. Oxford: Blackwell, 1987.

—. ed. *The Birth of Popular Heresy. Documents of Medieval History*. London: Edward Arnold, 1975.

Moorman, V.J. *A History of the Franciscan Order from it origins to the year 1517*. Oxford: Oxford University Press, 1968.

Morris, Colin. *The Discovery of the Individual 1050-1200*. Toronto: University of Toronto Press, 2004, reprint.

—. *The Papal Monarchy: The Western Church from 1050-1250*. Oxford: Clarendon Press, 1989.

Morrison, Karl. *"I Am You." The Hermeneutics of Empathy in Western Literature, Theology, and Art*. Princeton: Princeton University Press, 1988.

Morse, Ruth. *Truth and Convention in the Middle Ages: Rhetoric, Representation, and Reality*. Cambridge: Cambridge University Press, 1991.

Mundy, John H. *Europe in the High Middle Ages 1150-1309*. London: Longman Press, 1973.

Murphy, James J. *Rhetoric in the Middle Ages: A History of Rhetorical Theory from Saint Augustine to the Renaissance*. Berkeley: University of California Press, 1974.

Murphy, James J., ed. *Three Medieval Rhetorical Arts*. Berkeley: University of California Press, 1971.

Murray, Alexander. *Reason and Society in the Middle Ages*. Oxford: Clarendon Press, 1957.

Murray, Peter and Linda. *The Oxford Companion to Christian Art and Architecture*. Oxford and New York: Oxford University Press, 1996.

Murtaugh, Daniel. "Figurando il paradiso': The Signs that Render Dante's Heaven", in *PMLA*, vol. 90, No. 2 (March, 1975), pp. 277-284.

Neander, Augustus. *General History of the Christian Religion and Church*. 5 vols. Translated by Joseph Torrey. Sixth American Edition. Boston: Crocker & Brewster, 1856.

Niccoli, Ottavia. *Prophecy and People in Renaissance Italy*. Translated by Lydia G. Cochrane. Princeton: Princeton University Press, 1990.

Nolthenius, Helene. *Duecento: The Late Middle Ages in Italy*. New York: McGraw-Hill, 1968.

Oschema, Klaus. "Sacred or Profane? Reflections on Love and Friendship in the Middle Ages." *Love, Friendship, and Faith in Europe, 1300-*

1800. Edited by L. Gowing, M. Hunter, M. Rubin. London: Palgrave Macmillan, 2005.

The Oxford Dante Society. *Centenary Essays on Dante.* Oxford: Clarendon Press, 1965.

Palazzo, Eric. *Liturgie et societe au Moyen Age.* Paris: Aubier, 2000.

Paoli, Camillo. *Il Riformatore Veltro: Giochinismo e Francescanesimo nell'allegoria fondamentale della Divina Commedia.* Pisa: Giardini, 1971.

Paterson, Linda M. *Troubadours and Eloquence.* Oxford: Clarendon Press, 1975.

Pelikan, Jaroslav. *Limits of Thought and Power in Medieval Europe.* Ashgate; Variorum: Aldershot, 2001.

—. *Jesus Through the Centuries: His Place in the History of Culture.* New Haven: Yale University Press, 1999.

—. *Christianity and Classical Culture: The Metamorphosis of Natural Theology in the Christian Encounter with Hellenism.* New Haven and London: Yale University Press, 1993.

—. *The Christian Tradition. A History of the Development of Doctrine. Vol. 3. The Growth of Medieval Theology (600-1300).* Chicago: University of Chicago Press, 1978.

Phillips, J. and M. Hoch, eds. *The Second Crusade: Scope and Consequences.* Manchester: Manchester University Press, 1993.

Poppi, Antonio. *Studi sull'etica della prima scuola Francescana.* Padova: Centro Studi Antoniani, 1996.

Prawer, Joshua and Haggai Ben-Shammai, eds. *The History of Jerusalem: The Early Muslim Period, 638-1099.* New York and Jerusalem: New York University Press and Yad Izhak Ben-Zvi, 1996.

Prawer, Joshua. *The History of the Jews in the Latin Kingdom of Jerusalem.* Oxford: Clarendon Press, 1988.

—. *The Latin Kingdom of Jerusalem: European Colonialism in the Middle Ages.* London: Weidenfeld and Nicolson, 1972.

Price, Simon and Emily Kearns, eds. *The Oxford Dictionary of Classical Myth & Religion.* Oxford: Oxford University Press, 2003.

Quaglioni, D. "The Legal Definition of Citizenship in the Late Middle Ages" in *City States in Classical Antiquity and Medieval Italy.* Edited by Molho, Raaflaub, and Emlen. Stuttgart, 1991, pp. 155-167.

Raffa, Guy. *Divine Dialectic: Dante's Incarnational Poetry.* Toronto: University of Toronto Press, 2000.

Raitt, Thomas M. A *Theology of Exile: Judgment/ Deliverance in Jeremiah and Ezekiel.* Philadelphia: Fortress Press, 1977.

Reeves, Marjorie. *The Influence of Prophecy in the Later Middle Ages: A Study of Joachimism.* Oxford: Clarendon Press, 1969.

Reeves, Marjorie and Beatrice Hirsch-Reich. *The Figurae of Joachim of Fiore.* Oxford: Clarendon Press, 1972.

Reid, Jane Davidson. *The Oxford University Press Classical Mythology in the Arts, 1300-1990's.* 2 volumes. New York: Oxford University Press, 1993.

Riesenberg, Peter. "Citizenship at Law in Late Medieval Italy." *Viator V* (1974) pp, 333-346.

Riley-Smith, Jonathan. *The Feudal Nobility and the Kingdom of Jerusalem, 1174-1277.* London and Basingstoke: Macmillan, 1973.

—. *A History of the Crusades.* New Haven and London: Yale University Press, 1987.

—. *The First Crusaders, 1095-1131.* Cambridge: Cambridge University Press, 1997.

Roach, Andrew P. *The Devil's World: Heresy and Society 1100-1300.* Harlow: Pearson, 2005.

Robbins, Keith ed. *Studies in Church History: Vol. 17. Religion and Humanism.* Oxford: Blackwell, 1981.

Roberts, J.C. *The Influence of Aristotle on Late Medieval Ethics: A Study of the Treatise "De via Paradisi" by Remigio de Girolami O.P. (d. 1319).* Dissertation: Oxford University, Hilary, 1990.

Robertson, Jr., D.W. *Essays in Medieval Culture.* Princeton: Princeton University Press, 1980.

Rowbotham, John F. *The Troubadours and the Courts of Love.* London: Swan Sonnenschein, 1895.

Rowe, J.G. and W. H. Stockdale. *Florilegium Historiale: Essays Presented to Wallace Ferguson.* Toroto: University of Toronto Press, 1971.

Rubin, Miri. *Corpus Christi: The Eucharist in Late Medieval Culture.* Cambridge: Cambridge University Press, 1991.

Rubio, Juan Canto. *Giotto y la Secularizacion.* Madrid: Alicante, 1975.

Ruggiers, Paul G. *Florence in the Age of Dante.* Norman: University of Oklahoma Press, 1964.

Runciman, Steven. *A History of the Crusades.* 3vols. Cambridge: Cambridge University Press, 1952.

—. *The Medieval Manichee: A Study of the Christian Dualist Heresy.* Cambridge: Cambridge University Press, 1947.

Sabatier, Paul. *The Road to Assisi: The Essential Biography of St. Francis.* Edited by Jon M. Sweeney. Brewster: Paraclete Press, 2004.

Saffioti, Tito. *I Giullari in Italia: Lo spettacolo, il pubblico, i testi.* Milano: Xenia, 1990.
Schiller, Gertrud. *Ikonographie der christlichen Kunst.* Vol.1.Guterslo: Gutersloher Verlaghaus, 1966.
Schnapp, Jeffrey T. *The Transfiguration of History at the Center of Dante's Paradise.* Princeton: Princeton University Press, 1986.
Seay, Albert. *Music in the Medieval World.* Englewood Cliffs: Prentice Hall, 1965.
Seung, T.K. *The Fragile Leaves of the Sibyl: Dante's Master Plan.* Westminster: The Newman Press, 1962.
Sheedy, Charles. *The Eucharistic Controversy of the Eleventh Century Against the Background of Pre-Scholastic Theology.* New York: AMS Press, 1947.
Singleton, Charles. *Dante Studies 2: Journey to Beatrice.* Cambridge: Harvard University Press, 1958.
Snoek, G.J.C. *A Medieval Piety from Relics to the Eucharist: A Process of Mutual Interaction.* Leiden: E.J. Brill, 1995.
Spade, Paul Vincent, ed. *The Cambridge Companion to Ockham.* Cambridge: Cambridge University Press, 1999.
Steinberg, Leo. *The Sexuality of Christ in Renaissance Art and the Modern Oblivion.* Chicago: University of Chicago Press, 1983.
Steinmann. *La Prophete Ezechiel et las debuts de l'exil.* Paris: Cerf, 1953.
Stone, Darwell. *A History of the Doctrine of the Holy Eucharist.* London: Longmans, Green, and Co., 1909.
Stone, Gregory B. *The Death of the Troubadour: The Late Medieval Resistance to the Renaissance.* Philadelphia: University of Pennsylvania Press, 1994.
Swanson, R.N. *The Twelfth Century Renaissance.* Manchester: Manchester University Press, 1999.
—. ed. *The Holy Land, Holy Lands, and Christian History.* The Ecclesiastical History Society: Woodbridge: Boydell Press, 2000.
Taylor, Henry Osborn. *The Mediaeval Mind: The History of the Development of Thought and Emotion in the Middle Ages.* 2 vols. Cambridge: Harvard University Press, 1949.
Tierney, Brian. *Religion, Law, and the Growth of Constitutional Thought 1150-1650.* Cambridge: Cambridge University Press, 1982.
—. *Medieval Poor Law: A Sketch of Canonical Theory and Its Application in England.* Berkeley and Los Angeles: University of California Press, 1959.
Took, J.F. *L'Etterno Piacer: Aesthetic Ideas in Dante.* Clarendon Press: Oxford, 1984.

Trexler, Richard. *Religion and Social Context in Europe and America, 1200-1700.* Arizona State University: Tempe, 2002.
—. *Naked Before the Father: The Renunciation of Francis of Assisi. Humana Civiltas 9.* New York: Peter Lang, 1989.
Trinkaus, Charles. *In Our Image and Likeness: Humanity and Divinity in Italian Humanist Thought.* 2 vols. Notre Dame: University of Notre Dame Press, 1995.
—. "Renaissance Ideas and the Idea of the Renaissance." *The Journal of the History of Ideas* 51, 1990, pp. 667-684.
—. "Humanism, Religion, Society: Concepts and Motivations of Some Recent Studies." *Renaissance Quarterly* 29, 1976, pp. 676-713.
Tuck, Richard. *Natural rights theories: Their origin and development.* Cambridge: Cambridge University Press, 1979.
Ullmann, Walter. *The Individual and Society in the Middle Ages.* London: Methuen & Co., 1967.
—. *A Short History of the Papacy in the Middle Ages.* London: Methuen & Co., 1972.
—. *Medieval Foundations of Renaissance Humanism.* Itahca: Cornell University Press, 1977.
Verdon, Timothy and John Henderson. *Christianity and the Renaissance: Image and Religious Imagination in the Quattrocento.* Syracuse: Syracuse University Press, 1990.
Verger, Jacques. *Les Gens de Savoir en Europe a la fin du Moyen Age.* Paris: Presses Universitaires de France, 1997.
Vogel, Cyrille. *Medieval Liturgy: An Introduction to the Sources.* Revised and translated by G. Storey and Niels Krogh Rasmussen. Washington: Pastoral Press, 1986.
Volpe, Gioachino. *Movimenti religiosi e sette ereticali nella societa Medioevale Italiana.* Firenze: Olschiki, 1924.
Vossler, Karl. *Mediaeval Culture: An Introduction to Dante and His Times.* 2 vols. Translated by W. C. Lawton. New York: Frederick Ungar, 1929.
Waddell, Helen, ed. *Mediaeval Latin Lyrics.* London: Constable and Co., 1948.
Walsh, Katherine, D. Wood eds. *The Bible in the Medieval World: Essays in Honor of Beryl Smalley.* Oxford: Ecclesiastical History Society, 1985.
Ward, Graham. *Christ and Culture.* Oxford: Blackwell, 2005.
Waugh, Scott L. and Peter D. Diehl, eds. *Christendom and its discontents: Exclusion, persecution, and rebellion, 1000-1500.* Cambridge: Cambridge University Press, 1996.

Weber, Max. *The Interpretation of Social Reality.* J.E.T. Eldridge, ed. New York: Scribner, 1971.

Wegman, Hermann A. J. *Christian Worship In East and West: A Study Guide to Liturgical History.* Translated by Gordon Lathrop. Collegeville: The Liturgical Press, 1990.

Weingart, Richard E. *The Logic of Divine Love: A Critical Analysis of the Soteriology of Peter Abailard.* Oxford: Clarendon Press, 1970.

Wieruszowski, Helene. *Politics and Culture in Medieval Spain and Italy.* Roma: Edizioni di Storia e Letteratura, 1971.

Williams, Rowan, ed. *The Making of Orthodoxy: Essays in Honour of Henry Chadwick.* Cambridge: Cambridge University Press, 1989.

Wirth, Jean. *L'Image Medieval; Naissance et developpements (VIe-XVe siecle).* Paris: Meridiens Klincksieck, 1989.

Woodhouse, J.R., ed. *Dante and Governance.* Oxford: Clarendon Press: Oxford, 1997.

INDEX

Abelard, 13, 14, 15, 16
   Commentary of Paul's Epistle to the Romans, 14
Achilles, 111
Albigensian, 40, 75, 152
Ambrose, 41
Anselm, 14, 16, 124
   Cur Deus Homo, 14
Anthony of Padua, 65
Apollo, 129, 131
Aristotle, 15, 176, 180
   Politics, 15
Arnaut Daniel, 120, 122, 123, 126, 127, 128, 135
Atonement, 13, 14
Augustine, 7, 15, 72, 77, 96, 144, 152, 157, 162, 169, 178
   City of God, 7
Autun, 17, 105
Bernard of Clairvaux, 4, 16, 162, 175
Beziers. See Cathars
Bonagiunta da Lucca, 121, 122, 124
Bonaventure, 41, 43, 45, 51, 52, 54, 57, 59, 87, 89, 90, 91, 92, 93, 94, 95, 97, 98, 99, 100, 105, 106, 169, 171
   Apologia Pauperum, 92, 93, 94.

Cadi el-Fadel, 11
Caesarius of Heisterbach, 37, 78
   Dialogus Miraculorum, 37
Calvinism, 156, 158, 176
campanilismo, 76
Carl Gustav Jung, 160, 173
Casella, 121
Cathars, 31, 39, 53, 54, 69, 70, 75, 76, 77, 78, 79, 80, 81, 82, 83, 84, 85, 86, 109, 152, 153, 166, 176
   Bagnolo, 79

Concorezzo, 79
consolamentum, 80, 82
credentes, 77
Desenzano, 79, 82
katharos, 77
Orvieto, 79, 83, 84
Perfects, 53, 77, 78
Celestine III, 48
Chanson d'Antioche, 5, 6
Christ, 1, 2, 4, 5, 6, 7, 8, 10, 11, 13, 14, 15, 16, 17, 20, 23, 26, 27, 29, 30, 31, 32, 34, 35, 36, 37, 38, 39, 41, 42, 44, 46, 50, 51, 52, 53, 56, 57, 58, 59, 60, 61, 62, 65, 66, 73, 74, 75, 77, 81, 83, 84, 86, 87, 89, 93, 94, 95, 97, 98, 99, 100, 101, 104, 106, 107, 108, 110, 138, 142, 144, 145, 148, 149, 150, 151, 152, 153, 155, 156, 157, 170, 171, 173, 174, 177, 182, 183
   Body of Christ, 4
   Christus Pantokrator, 1
   Christus paupertas, 95 148
   Jesus, 5, 8, 12, 14, 17, 30, 41, 50, 52, 53, 58, 64, 66, 73, 106, 148, 152, 156, 159, 168, 177, 179
   Messiah, 12, 13, 148
   Rex mundi, 148
   True Image, 17
Christendom, 1, 5, 23, 24, 26, 28, 32, 37, 39, 47, 69, 70, 71, 72, 76, 79, 144, 145, 167, 184
Church, 2, 3, 7, 8, 12, 14, 15, 16, 21, 23, 24, 26, 27, 29, 30, 32, 33, 36, 39, 49, 50, 51, 52, 53, 54, 55, 62, 69, 70, 71, 72, 73, 74, 77, 79, 80, 85, 88, 90, 98, 144, 146, 148, 152, 153, 156, 158, 163, 164,

165, 166, 167, 169, 176, 178, 180
Circe, 115, 134, 135
Cistercian, 43, 47, 78, 162, 175
communion. See Eucharist
contrapasso, 113, 118, 127
cross, 2, 3, 5, 8, 11, 12, 13, 31, 49, 52, 56, 60, 149
crucifixion, 11, 12, 13, 14, 60, 153, 157
Crusade, concept of 2, 4, 6, 8, 10, 14, 20, 31, 40, 152, 164, 166, 172, 179
Crusaders, 1, 3, 5, 10, 18, 24, 180
Crusades, 3, 4, 5, 8, 9, 13, 16, 18, 19, 24, 36, 69, 148, 159, 162, 163, 164, 165, 167, 173, 180, 181
Dante Alighieri, 41, 44, 46, 48, 54, 57, 59, 88, 104, 106, 107, 109, 110, 111, 112, 113, 114, 115, 116, 117, 118, 119, 120, 121, 122, 123, 124, 125, 126, 127, 128, 129, 130, 131, 134, 135, 136, 137, 138, 139, 140, 141, 142, 143, 144, 149, 151, 154, 155, 162, 163, 165, 166, 169, 170, 171, 172, 174, 175, 177, 178, 179, 180, 181, 182, 183, 184
    Beatrice, 60, 110, 129, 131, 134, 135, 136, 142, 143, 180, 181
    Convivio, 121
    Divine Comedy, 88, 109, 110, 111 112, 120,129, 130, 134, 136, 139, 155, 162, 166, 170, 171
    Inferno, 110, 111, 112, 113, 114, 115, 118, 120, 127
    Paradiso, 46, 54, 57, 119, 121, 128, 129, 130, 131, 134, 135, 136, 137, 139, 142, 143, 144, 176
    Purgatorio, 107, 115, 118, 119, 120, 121, 122, 123, 124, 126, 127, 137, 139, 165
    terza rima, 104
Diomedes, 111, 113
dolce stil nova, 123, 125, 154
Dominic, 53, 63, 104, 162
Dominicans, 50, 63, 64, 65, 85, 104, 175
Donatello, 143
Duns Scotus, 32, 33, 43, 44
Elijah, 52
eschatology, 50, 73, 138, 139, 151, 153
Eucharist, 20, 23, 24, 27, 29, 30, 32, 33, 34, 37, 38, 81, 82, 105, 106, 150, 151, 168, 176, 181, 182
    Corpus Christi, 27, 33, 144, 181
    Real Presence, 23, 24, 29, 30, 32, 33, 37, 81
    transubstantiation, 20, 26, 28, 37, 50, 81, 86, 150
exemplum, 7, 14, 78, 115, 116, 117, 123
Ezekiel, 57, 109, 123, 138, 139, 140, 141, 142, 143, 174, 177, 180
Farinata, 118
Feudalism, 3
Fourth Lateran Council, 20, 24, 26, 27, 29, 31, 38, 47, 48, 49, 51, 57, 69, 86
    De fide catholica, 30
Francis of Assisi, 23, 26, 28, 39, 41, 42, 43, 44, 45, 46, 47, 48, 49, 50, 52, 53, 54, 55, 56, 57, 58, 59, 60, 61, 62, 63, 65, 71, 74, 85, 87, 88, 93, 95, 97, 98, 99, 101, 102, 103, 104, 105, 106, 108, 124, 144, 145, 146, 147, 151, 156, 157, 163, 167, 171, 173, 181, 182
    creche, 60
    stigmata, 56, 57, 58, 104
Franciscan, 8, 30, 32, 41, 42, 43, 44, 46, 47, 48, 50, 52, 53, 55, 57, 58, 60, 61, 62, 63, 64, 65, 66, 79, 80, 82, 85, 87, 88, 89, 90, 91, 92, 94, 95, 98, 99, 100, 101, 102, 103, 104, 105, 108, 126, 140, 144,

146, 154, 155, 163, 164, 168, 174, 175, 176, 178
Franciscans, 17, 32, 44, 46, 58, 59, 67, 75, 80, 85, 90, 92, 93, 99, 100, 104, 108, 109, 172
   Friars Minor, 64, 65, 67, 85, 87, 97, 100, 101, 104, 106
   Minorites, 94, 95, 98, 99
Franks, 3, 6, 12, 13, 17, 20
Frederick II, 32, 76
fuga mundi, 7, 9
Gerard of Borgo San Donnino, 49
Giotto di Bondone, 44, 58, 61, 87, 88, 89, 101, 102, 103, 104, 105, 106, 107, 108, 155, 166, 169, 170, 171, 181
   Life of Francis, 102
   Scrovegni Chapel, 102
Giovanni de Causibus de Sancto Geminiani, 65
Giullari, 63, 64, 181
Glaucus, 57, 129, 130, 131, 132, 134, 135, 141, 142, 143
Gregory the VIII, 1
Guido Cavalcanti, 119
Guido Guinizelli, 119, 120, 122, 123, 125, 163
haeresis. See heresy
Hattin, 12, 14, 18, 19, 25, 108, 149, 150
Heaven, 10, 12, 73, 116, 129, 135, 136, 137, 139, 142, 144, 145, 170, 174, 178
Hell, 77, 81, 113, 115, 117, 118, 136
heresy, 24, 26, 29, 31, 32, 39, 53, 63, 65, 67, 70, 71, 72, 73, 74, 75, 76, 81, 82, 84, 86, 92, 98, 110, 152, 153, 155
heretics, 31, 70, 71, 74, 75, 82, 84, 98
Holy Land, 4, 6, 17, 19, 20, 25, 31, 32, 47, 69, 74, 182
Homer, 120
homo viator, 6, 7, 108, 149, 156
Horace, 120

Hugh de Digne, 48
Hypostatic Union, 65
imago dei, 56, 61
imitatio Christi, 56
Incarnation, 15, 16, 17, 19, 20, 31, 32, 50, 52, 53, 56, 64, 66, 75, 81, 83, 86, 93, 99, 106, 111, 119, 130, 138, 142, 143, 144, 148, 149, 160, 169, 171, 175, 177
   Incarnational Age, 26, 27, 33, 34, 36, 47, 50, 51, 57, 58, 59, 60, 61, 65, 67, 70, 72, 74, 75, 79, 85, 87, 88, 89, 93, 95, 97, 98, 100, 101, 103, 104, 107, 108, 109, 111, 117, 122, 124, 126, 128, 130, 135, 136, 138, 139, 142, 143, 144, 154, 155, 156
Innocent III (Lotario dei Segni), 8, 19, 20, 23, 24, 25, 26, 27, 28, 34, 38, 47, 50, 69, 70, 74, 83, 84, 149, 150, 156
   De Contemptu Mundi, 28, 84
   De Miseria Humanae Conditionis, 28
   De Sacro Altaris Mysterio, 29, 30
Inquisition, 85
Islam, 11, 147, 165, 169
ius fori, 96
ius poli, 96
James Capelli, 80
   Summa contra haereticos, 80
Jerusalem, 1, 2, 3, 4, 5, 6, 8, 9, 10, 11, 12, 13, 15, 16, 17, 18, 19, 20, 24, 25, 32, 36, 108, 139, 149, 150, 165, 167, 168, 174, 176, 179, 180
   Church of the Holy Sepulcher, 3, 16
   Dome of the Rock, 13
   ordo peregrinationis, 18
   Temple, 141, 142, 143, 154
Jews, 11, 13, 19, 179
Joachim of Fiore, 46, 47, 53, 60, 99, 151, 164, 180

Exposition on the Apocalypse, 48
Ten Stringed Psaltery, 48
The Book of Concordance, 48
John of Lugio, 79
　Book of the Two Principles, 79
John of Pecham, 90
John the Baptist, 52
John XXII, 89, 91, 92, 94, 96, 99
　Quia vir reprobus, 89
kenosis, 52, 66, 103, 117, 129, 136, 144, 155
King Baldwin I, 3
Koran, 11, 12
Languedoc, 12, 39, 67, 69, 78, 152, 166
Latin Kingdom, 3, 9, 179
Leonardo da Vinci, 143
liturgy, 2, 18, 19, 21, 35, 62
Lorenzo de Medici, 158
Lucan, 120
magnaminitas, 118
Manichees, 77
Marsyas, 57, 129, 130, 131, 135, 141, 142, 143
Martin Luther, 157
Mass, 27, 28, 37, 38, 82, 105, 106, 154, 167, 173
Michelangelo, 143
Mohammed, 151
Mu'in ad-Din, 13
Nicholas III, 91
　Exiit qui seminat, 91
Outremer, 2, 9, 153
Ovid, 110, 120, 129, 130, 131, 132, 164
　Metamorphoses, 130, 131, 132, 133, 164, 172
Oxford, 25
Padre Pio, 57
Paris, 25
Peace of Westphalia, 158
Penance, 34, 50, 80, 82, 119, 127, 150
Pentecost, 50, 117
Peter Lombard, 49, 51

　Sentences, 49, 51.
Peter of Apulia, 48
Pico della Mirandola, 114
Pietro Parenzo, 83
pilgrimage, 6, 8, 10, 16, 17, 18, 36, 47, 157
poverty, 8, 39, 42, 43, 45, 46, 60, 61, 62, 74, 85, 88, 90, 91, 92, 93, 94, 95, 96, 97, 98, 100, 103, 146, 147, 155, 157
Purgatory, 80, 112, 115, 118, 122, 125, 126, 127, 175
Rainerius Sacconi, 80
　Summa de Catharis et Pauperibus de Lugduno, 80
Raphael, 143
Reformation, 16, 52, 61, 70, 74, 147, 155, 156, 157, 159, 172, 174, 175
Renaissance, 7, 11, 35, 42, 51, 56, 104, 110, 111, 114, 138, 143, 148, 155, 156, 157, 158, 159, 166, 167, 172, 174, 175, 176, 177, 178, 182, 183
renovatio, 9, 18
Rome, 10, 17, 140, 142, 160, 169, 171, 172, 173
Saladin, 1, 10, 12, 14, 20
Salimbene, 41, 48, 163
Savonarola, 53, 158, 164
sigillum Christie. See Francis: stigmata
speculum, 7, 36, 45, 56, 87, 101, 104, 135, 136, 138, 144, 151, 155
Statius, 112, 120
Thomas Aquinas, 32, 74, 177
Thomas of Celano, 41, 52, 56
　First Life of Francis of Assisi, 52, 56
Trinity, 26, 33, 49, 51, 63, 106, 167, 169, 177
True Cross, 11, 12, 149
Ubertino da Casale, 99
Ulysses, 111

Virgil, 111, 113, 116, 120, 121, 122, 123, 124, 131, 136
William Durandus, 37, 38
   Rationale Divinorum Officiorum, 37, 38, 163

William of Ockham, 43, 44, 87, 88, 89, 90, 91, 92, 95, 96, 97, 98, 100, 101, 108, 155, 164, 169, 174, 182
   Opus nonagintum dierum, 89, 92
Wolfram von Eschenbach, 154, 163